S0-CJE-050

Discussions of Jonathan Swift

SAVILE BOOK SHOP
3236 P ST., N. W.
WASHINGTON 7, D. C.

1·95

DISCUSSIONS OF LITERATURE

General Editor JOSEPH H. SUMMERS, Washington University

Edited by

The *Divine Comedy*	IRMA BRANDEIS, Bard College
The *Canterbury Tales*	CHARLES A. OWEN, JR., University of Connecticut
Hamlet	J. C. LEVENSON, University of Minnesota
Shakespeare's Problem Comedies	ROBERT ORNSTEIN, University of Illinois
John Donne	FRANK KERMODE, University of Manchester
Jonathan Swift	JOHN TRAUGOTT, University of California, Berkeley
Alexander Pope	RUFUS A. BLANSHARD, University of Connecticut
William Blake	JOHN E. GRANT, University of Connecticut
Jane Austen	WILLIAM HEATH, Amherst College
Charles Dickens	WILLIAM ROSS CLARK, University of Connecticut
George Eliot	RICHARD STANG, Washington University
Moby-Dick	MILTON R. STERN, University of Connecticut
The Novel	ROGER SALE, Amherst College
Poetry: Rhythm and Sound	GEORGE HEMPHILL, University of Connecticut

DISCUSSIONS

OF

JONATHAN SWIFT

Edited with an Introduction by

John Traugott

THE UNIVERSITY OF CALIFORNIA, BERKELEY

D. C. Heath and Company

BOSTON

Copyright © 1962 by D. C. Heath and Company
No part of the material covered by this copyright may be reproduced
for any purpose without written permission of the publisher.
Printed in the United States of America (6 K 1)

CONTENTS

Biography

    Samuel Johnson, The Life of Swift   1
    William Makepeace Thackeray, Swift   14
    W. B. C. Watkins, Absent Thee from Felicity   22

Rhetoric

    F. R. Leavis, The Irony of Swift   35
    A. E. Dyson, Swift: The Metamorphosis of Irony   44
    Martin Price, Swift's Symbolic Works   52

Historical Imagination

    William Butler Yeats, "Preface" to *The Words upon the Window-pane*   71
    George Orwell, Politics vs. Literature: An Examination of *Gulliver's Travels*   80
    Norman O. Brown, The Excremental Vision   92

Politics

    Arthur E. Case, Personal and Political Satire in *Gulliver's Travels*   105
    J. C. Beckett, Swift as an Ecclesiastical Statesman   121

INTRODUCTION

SAMUEL JOHNSON, happy to point a moral, and perhaps equally happy to utter a final judgment of Jonathan Swift, for whom he had little use, reduced the terrible Dean to an apt illustration of "the vanity of human wishes":

> From Marlborough's eyes the streams of dotage flow
> And Swift expires a driveller and a show.

Thus with invidious irony Johnson coupled the brilliant wit and his chosen enemy, the object of his hateful libel, the hero of Blenheim. Johnson's couplet is a signpost to the criticism of Swift ever since. He is a "show" —a moral show. Anyone who reads through the commentary of two hundred years cannot but be thrilled or dismayed, depending upon his critical principles, by the way in which the sensational aspects of Swift's personality and the virulence of his satire have made moralists of men who, with a less refractory subject, might have been critics. Swift's reply would be, of course, that "satire is a sort of glass, wherein beholders do generally discover everybody's face but their own."

And yet, though the puerilities of this criticism are manifest, the most judicious critics have evidently suffered the strain Swift imposes upon the common reader's moral sensibilities. Even a critic so fastidiously devoted to formal questions of art as F. R. Leavis will commence by considering the structure of Swift's irony and end, seemingly willy-nilly, by lamenting his moral perversity. Leavis, among the first to chart the withering mazes of Swift's irony, gives the devil his due—"the genius delights in its mastery, in its power to destroy, and negation is felt as self-assertion"—but concludes that the moral implication of this technique is "the self-defeat of life." Similarly George Orwell, who owes so much to Swift, insists upon the nihilistic bent of his character and is willing to use such epithets as "quisling" and "anarchist." "The self-defeat of life" is a rubric that does organize the moral suspicions of generations of readers of Swift, many of whom would still grant, as does Orwell, his awesome greatness.

So great a body of critical commentary stressing the unnerving moral implications of Swift's thought cannot be entirely wrong, if we assume Johnson's principle that the "common reader," spokesman of generations, gives us a reliable estimate of a writer's quality. Just as one of the first milestones in Swiftian criticism, the comments upon his life and art by his rather pompous friend Patrick Delany, points a new moral direction from the moralistic attack of his even more pompous friend, Lord Orrery; and just as Deane Swift leapt into the fray to interpret his cousin's suspect religion as the deepest-dyed orthodoxy and thereby gave us the first "Christian" interpretation of the "Voyage to the Houyhnhnms"; so in large part the criticism of our day has an obvious relation to the moral questions Swift poses for the common reader.

A considerable body of criticism now exists, mainly the work of American "background" scholars, which, in placing Swift in his age, has tended to deny his heterodoxy and indeed seems "designed," as one recent critic puts it, "to housebreak and domesticate this tiger of English literature."

We are to learn from these scholars that the Dean's exceptions to his age were not in fact eccentric, that he did not, as Thackeray would have it, "gnash in the darkness." They would reveal Swift's position—his position perhaps as opposed to his method—as not unreasonable, dyspeptic, or extremist. With a clearer idea of the religious, social, and political realities with which Swift dealt, we are to see him as attached to a religious and political orthodoxy, doing his best with the unpromising possibilities of his time. One apologist for Swift's religious orthodoxy has even argued that his notorious "filth" symbols are to be understood not as Swift's peculiar vision—"excremental vision" it is called in an essay following—but as part of a long Christian tradition of denigration of the flesh. Another apologist for what we may now call Swift's newfound normality, has argued that he was a man who understood the compromises of that age of trimmers and was himself a trimmer. One scholar has explored the economic theories of the age to discover that *A Modest Proposal* is underneath the horror essentially an ironic argument in support of the prevailing economic doctrine of mercantilism! (Another has argued the opposite.) We begin to see the *"saeva indignatio"* fading away as a posture and Jonathan Swift newly dressed a respectable Anglican, illustrating in a traditional way the ninth of the Thirty-nine Articles, on original sin; a reasonable statesman rather than a violent, hateful political partisan; a defender of the new commerce rather than a medieval mind hysterically afraid of "progress"; a topical satirist requiring a scholar's key, rather than a universal moralist. In short we are asked to reject the evidence of our senses for the facts of science.

An interesting speculative venture of the scientific revaluation of Swift has been a series of novel "Christianizing" interpretations of the Fourth Voyage of Gulliver, by which the verdict of the "common reader," perhaps best represented by Coleridge's comment that "in his horses he [Swift] gives the misanthropic ideal of man," has been reversed. The Houyhnhnms are to be seen as only another object of satire. Variously, they are rational man without grace, rather like the inhabitants of Dante's Limbo; the embodiment of Bolingbroke's sort of deism; and man good and dull, before the fortunate Fall. Such interpretations have sought to wash the heterodox blot from Swift's escutcheon. A recent welling-up in critical circles of sardonic commentary on this "backgrounding" reassures the common reader that he may continue to read Swift as a passionate, iconoclastic, and radical moralist—and yet a good Christian.

Perhaps the best we can do is to look upon criticism as an endless conversation, discovering ourselves, our age, and our fathers before us—as well as Swift. Over two decades ago, for example, Professor George Sherburn felt that it was time to call a halt to the "Swift-as-tiger" tradition. In an important essay, he admonished future writers to restrain their love of thrills. "When Swift becomes theatrical, let them remember to control their romantic souls and remain critical of the nature of his performance." It was and remains a just caution, but the need for its enunciation was very pressing at that particular date when the tiger had become entirely too thrilling. Professor Sherburn even took Professor Quintana to task for "attribution of melodramatic motives to Swift" in his then recent critical biography. But Quintana's work can now be seen as the herald of an era of scientific criticism! Such revolutions of critical taste are fatiguing but instructive.

Another incisive remark in Sherburn's essay, however, seems to have set the stage for an entirely new kind of critical study, representative of our own time—the analysis of Swift's rhetorical genius. "No book on Swift," Sherburn wrote, "has ever done justice to the infinite playfulness of Swift's mind; the trait is, nevertheless, fundamental to all his works and in all his behaviour. . . . It is Swift's rhetoric rather than his life that is thrilling." On the whole, the rhetorical studies of the past several decades have returned us to the special quality of Swift's habits of thought, and so, ultimately, by a less polemical, more responsible path, to his peculiar moral stance. The rhetorical studies republished in this volume, those of Leavis, Dyson, and Price, recognize the special suppleness of mind required of Swift's reader, a suppleness for which the intervening centuries with their ever-increasing solemnity have ill prepared us. These discussions may then limber the mind. Dyson speaks of Swift's irony as "not only a battle but a game: a civilized game, at that, since irony is by its very nature civilized, presupposing both intelligence and at least some type of moral awareness." Only Swift's own aristocratic circle seems to have had the playfulness of mind necessary to entertain Swiftian thoughts easily, and they address one another as "Yahoo" and "Houyhnhnm" in their letters. Lord Bathurst, a late-comer to the circle, shows his mettle by rebuking his wife for not serving up the forequarters of her baby, as Dr. Swift recommends. The joke commences to get a bit edgy even among the elite.

Another group of essays in this collection is biographical, and again the critical tradition shows that moral considerations loom imperatively in such studies. In the Whiggish nineteenth century Swift achieved his apotheosis as full fiend: a renegade Tory, a despiser of freedom and individualism, so thoroughly un-English as to be capable of thinking of ladies at stool! Who would not, like Thackeray, wish to "hoot" the moral outlawry of such a personality? Yet Thackeray, so strangely moved by the Dean, recognized perversities in Swift's personality which continue to be lively issues in biographical studies. True, Thackeray made of Swift's life a sentimental novel—we have two pitiful, pure, and mistreated virgins, Stella and Vanessa, and an imperious cad who is really underneath it all a tragically alienated wretch; yet, while one may suspect a certain Victorian prurience in this surrogate assault on pure maidens, the per-

ception of Swift's paradoxical personality leads Thackeray to interesting judgments. He sees, for example, a strange mixture of piety and skepticism which is not at all described in the term "Anglican." Swift, he says, did not "hiccup" Church and State in the simple-minded way of "poor Dick Steele and poor Harry Fielding."

So many opposing interpretations of Swift's character are really arguable because his soul did embrace misanthropy and love, playful wit and hateful passion, fantasy and realism, subversion and conservatism. Voltaire's keen comment that Swift was *Rabelais dans son bon sens,* and Coleridge's, that in Swift was the "soul of Rabelais inhabiting a dry place," both imply impossible contradictions. Another, more modern way of putting this dubious quality of Swift's personality is W. B. C. Watkins'. He grants to Swift, with evident sympathy, his right to a "perilous balance" between sanity and madness. Such a "balance" is seen as a virtue in the twentieth century, for Swift in his hatred of inspiration and demagoguery and "adjustment" seems now to have had our own age particularly in view. One can predict that Swift's "perilous balance" will be viewed sympathetically until the present political climate changes so as to relieve us of the urgency of a nay-sayer.

Finally, this collection includes five essays which present Swift in historical perspectives. Those by A. E. Case and J. C. Beckett place him in quotidian politics. In these essays we see the politician and churchman at the conventional crossroads of his society. These "trivia" can never lose their fascination in the study of a man who allegorized the most mundane events of his own and his friends' lives. Once they have taken on Swift's reality, the antique battles in Church and State revive.

The essays by Norman O. Brown, William Butler Yeats, and George Orwell, on the other hand, evaluate the symbolic significance of Swift's ideas in history. Noting that there is room in Dr. Swift's hospital for the psychologizing critics who have left his character without a shred of integrity, Brown reads what he calls Swift's "excremental vision" as a description of "the anal character of civilization," rather than as a case history for a textbook of abnormal psychology for apprentice voyeurs. "Civilization" itself, rather than Swift, may be the Bedlam "show."

Such, certainly, is the point of view of Yeats. "Was Swift mad? Or was it the intellect itself that was mad?", Yeats asks. His answer is in the form of a myth, the play *Words upon the Window-pane,* in which the mad Dean speaks through a twentieth-century medium, a respectable Dublin woman who is scandalized by the mere mention of the nasty madman. He is indeed mad, too much the seer to become a mere begetter of children. To eat them seemed more appropriate to the times. For Yeats, Swift is a symbol of the arrogant free intellect, the intellect invoked in the poem "Blood and the Moon," which bears painfully its vision of the coming tyranny of the mass mind. The essay is an appreciation of Swift's historical imagination. (Swift yearned to be an historian.) Yeats, like Lecky before him, sees in Swift's historical imagination the creation of "the political nationality of Ireland."

George Orwell also makes of Swift a symbol for political history, but condemns the very attitude Yeats values, Swift's anti-democratic intellectual arrogance. Orwell speaks as a socialist who has not yet imagined *1984.* In saying everything against Swift's politics that a "liberal" can say, he defines certain of Swift's crucial positions. Yet Orwell shares Swift's fascination with the modes of tyranny and the corruption of language and thereby of the soul; reluctantly, he pays Swift a most handsome tribute in placing *Gulliver's Travels* among the six books most necessary to preserve when the holocaust comes.

From whatever ground the common reader looks upon Swift, he will understand what the historian G. M. Trevelyan has remarked: "We feel in Swift's writings and in the story of his life, what we do not feel in Defoe or Addison or Pope, the sense of greatness more than human, neither divine nor diabolic but titanic; a nature as big as Dr. Johnson's, less lovable indeed but as powerful in mundane contacts, and a yet greater master of the written word. The prose style of Swift is the strongest contrast to that of Johnson—the latter so formal, rotund, sententious and long drawn out; Swift's so simple, concise, almost conversational, dangerously polite and ironically restrained, yet, for all its quiet simplicity, serving as the vehicle for passion as explosive and devastating as gunpowder in store."

A SELECTIVE BIBLIOGRAPHY FOR FURTHER READING

Boyle, John, Earl of Cork and Orrery, *Remarks on the Life and Writings of Jonathan Swift,* London, 1752.

Craik, Sir Henry, *The Life of Jonathan Swift,* London, 1894.

Davie, Donald, "Academicism and Swift," *Twentieth Century,* 154 (Sept. 1953), 217–224.

Davis, Herbert, *The Satire of Jonathan Swift,* New York, 1947.

———, *Stella: A Gentlewoman of the Eighteenth Century,* New York, 1942.

Delany, Patrick, *Observations upon Lord Orrery's Remarks on the Life and Writings of Dr. Jonathan Swift,* London, 1754.

Eddy, William, *"Gulliver's Travels": A Critical Study,* Princeton, 1923.

Ehrenpreis, Irwin, *The Personality of Jonathan Swift,* London, 1958.

Elliott, Robert C., *The Power of Satire: Magic, Ritual, and Art,* Princeton, 1960.

Ewald, William B., *The Masks of Jonathan Swift,* Cambridge, Mass., 1954.

Fink, Z. S., "Political Theory in *Gulliver's Travels,*" *ELH, A Journal of English Literary History,* 14 (1947), 151–161.

Firth, C. H., "The Political Significance of

Gulliver's Travels," *Proceedings of the British Academy*, 9 (1919–1920), 237–259; reprinted in *Essays, Historical and Literary*, Oxford, 1938.

Frye, Roland M., "Swift's Yahoo and the Christian Symbols for Sin," *Journal of the History of Ideas*, 15 (1954), 201–217.

Goodwin, A., "Wood's Halfpence," *English Historical Review*, 51 (Oct. 1936), 647–674.

Guthkelch, A. C., ed., "*The Battle of the Books*," *with Selections from the Literature of the Phalaris Controversy*, London, 1908.

Jackson, Robert Wyse, *Jonathan Swift, Dean and Pastor*, London, 1939.

Jefferson, D. W., "An Approach to Swift," in *Pelican Guide to English Literature*, vol. 4.

Johnson, Maurice, *The Sin of Wit: Swift as a Poet*, Syracuse, 1950.

Jones, A. F., *Ancients and Moderns: A Study of the Background of "The Battle of the Books"* (*Washington University Studies in Language and Literature*, no. 6), St. Louis, 1936.

Jourdan, G. V., "The Religion of Jonathan Swift," *Church Quarterly Review*, 126 (1938), 269–286.

Landa, Louis, "Swift, the Mysteries, and Deism," *University of Texas Studies in English, 1944*, 1945, pp. 239–256.

————, "*A Modest Proposal* and Populousness," *Modern Philology*, 40 (1942), 161–170.

————, *Swift and the Church of Ireland*, Oxford, 1954.

Lecky, W. E. H., "Swift," in *Leaders of Public Opinion in Ireland*, London, 1871.

Monk, Samuel, "The Pride of Lemuel Gulliver," *Sewanee Review*, 63 (1955), 48–71.

Newman, Bertram, *Jonathan Swift*, London, 1937.

Nicolson, Marjorie, and Nora Mohler, "The Scientific Background of Swift's Voyage to Laputa," *Annals of Science*, 2 (1937), 299–334.

————, "Swift's 'Flying Island' in the Voyage to Laputa," *Annals of Science*, 2 (1937), 405–430.

Pilkington, Letitia, *Memoirs, 1712–1750*, ed. J. Isaacs, London, 1928.

Pons, Emile, *Swift: Les années de jeunesse et le Conte du Tonneau*, Strasbourg, 1925.

Preu, James, "Jonathan Swift and the Common Man," *Florida State University Studies*, 11 (1953), 19–24.

Quintana, Ricardo, *The Mind and Art of Jonathan Swift*, London, 1936.

————, "Situational Satire: A Commentary on the Method of Swift," *University of Toronto Quarterly*, 17 (1948), 130–136.

Ross, John F., *Swift and Defoe: A Study in Relationship*, Berkeley, 1941.

————, "The Final Comedy of Lemuel Gulliver," in *Studies in the Comic* (*University of California Publications in English*, VIII, 2), Berkeley, 1941.

Sherburn, George, "Methods in Books about Swift," *Studies in Philology*, 35 (1938), 635–656.

Starkman, Miriam, *Swift's Satire on Learning in "A Tale of a Tub,"* Princeton, 1950.

Stephen, Leslie, *Jonathan Swift*, London, 1882.

Tuveson, Ernest, "Swift and the World-Makers," *Journal of the History of Ideas*, 11 (1950), 54–74.

————, "Swift: The Dean and Satirist," *University of Toronto Quarterly*, 22 (1953), 368–375.

Watt, Ian, "The Ironic Tradition in Augustan Prose from Swift to Johnson," in *Restoration and Augustan Prose*, William Andrews Clark Memorial Library, Los Angeles, 1956.

Wedel, T. O., "On the Philosophical Background of *Gulliver's Travels*," *Studies in Philology*, 23 (1926), 434–450.

Williams, Kathleen M., *Jonathan Swift and the Age of Compromise*, Lawrence, Kansas, 1958.

Wittkowsky, George, "Swift's *Modest Proposal*: The Biography of an Early Georgian Pamphlet," *Journal of the History of Ideas*, 4 (1943), 75–104.

JOHN TRAUGOTT

Discussions of Jonathan Swift

Jonathan Swift

Samuel Johnson

The Life of Swift

JONATHAN SWIFT was, according to an account said to be written by himself, the son of Jonathan Swift, an attorney, and was born at Dublin on St. Andrew's day, 1667: according to his own report, as delivered by Pope to Spence, he was born at Leicester, the son of a clergyman, who was minister of a parish in Herefordshire. During his life the place of his birth was undetermined. He was contented to be called an Irishman by the Irish; but would occasionally call himself an Englishman. The question may, without much regret, be left in the obscurity in which he delighted to involve it.

Whatever was his birth, his education was Irish. He was sent at the age of six to the school at Kilkenny, and in his fifteenth year (1682) was admitted into the University of Dublin.

In his academical studies he was either not diligent or not happy. It must disappoint every reader's expectation, that, when at the usual time he claimed the Bachelorship of Arts, he was found by the examiners too conspicuously deficient for regular admission, and obtained his degree at last by *special favour;* a term used in that university to denote want of merit.

Of this disgrace it may be easily supposed that he was much ashamed, and

shame had its proper effect in producing reformation. He resolved from that time to study eight hours a-day, and continued his industry for seven years, with what improvement is sufficiently known. This part of his story well deserves to be remembered; it may afford useful admonition and powerful encouragement to men, whose abilities have been made for a time useless by their passions or pleasures, and who, having lost one part of life in idleness, are tempted to throw away the remainder in despair. . . .

When he was about one-and-twenty (1688), being by the death of Godwin Swift his uncle, who had supported him, left without subsistence, he went to consult his mother, who then lived at Leicester, about the future course of his life, and by her direction solicited the advice and patronage of Sir William Temple, who had married one of Mrs. Swift's relations, and whose father Sir John Temple, Master of the Rolls in Ireland, had lived in great familiarity of friendship with Godwin Swift, by whom Jonathan had been to that time maintained. . . .

When Temple removed to Moor-park, he took Swift with him; and when he was consulted by the Earl of Portland about the expedience of complying with a bill then

From *Lives of the English Poets.* The present selection from "The Life of Swift" includes about two-thirds of Johnson's text. Where deletions have been made, they are of matters of fact rather than of opinion.

depending for making parliaments triennial, against which King William was strongly prejudiced, after having in vain tried to shew the Earl that the proposal involved nothing dangerous to royal power, he sent Swift for the same purpose to the King. Swift, who probably was proud of his employment, and went with all the confidence of a young man, found his arguments, and his art of displaying them, made totally ineffectual by the predetermination of the King; and used to mention this disappointment as his first antidote against vanity.

Before he left Ireland he contracted a disorder, as he thought, by eating too much fruit. The original of diseases is commonly obscure. Almost every boy eats as much fruit as he can get, without any great inconvenience. The disease of Swift was giddiness with deafness, which attacked him from time to time, began very early, pursued him through life, and at last sent him to the grave, deprived of reason.

Being much oppressed at Moor-park by this grievous malady, he was advised to try his native air, and went to Ireland; but, finding no benefit, returned to Sir William, at whose house he continued his studies, and is known to have read, among other books, *Cyprian* and *Irenaeus*. He thought exercise of great necessity, and used to run half a mile up and down a hill every two hours. . . .

While he lived with Temple, he used to pay his mother at Leicester an yearly visit. He travelled on foot, unless some violence of weather drove him into a wagon, and at night he would go to a penny lodging, where he purchased clean sheets for sixpence. This practice Lord Orrery imputes to his innate love of grossness and vulgarity: some may ascribe it to his desire of surveying human life through all its varieties; and others, perhaps with equal probability, to a passion which seems to have been deep fixed in his heart, the love of a shilling.

In time he began to think that his attendance at Moor-park deserved some other recompence than the pleasure, however mingled with improvement, of Temple's conversation; and grew so impatient, that (1694) he went away in discontent.

Temple, conscious of having given reason for complaint, is said to have made him Deputy Master of the Rolls in Ireland; which according to his kinsman's account, was an office which he knew him not able to discharge. Swift therefore resolved to enter into the Church, in which he had at first no higher hopes than of the chaplainship to the Factory at Lisbon; but being recommended to Lord Capel, he obtained the prebend of *Kilroot* in *Connor*, of about a hundred pounds a year.

But the infirmities of Temple made a companion like Swift so necessary, that he invited him back, with a promise to procure him English preferment, in exchange for the prebend which he desired him to resign. With this request Swift complied, having perhaps equally repented their separation, and they lived on together with mutual satisfaction; and, in the four years that passed between his return and Temple's death, it is probable that he wrote the *Tale of a Tub* and the *Battle of the Books*.

Swift began early to think, or to hope, that he was a poet, and wrote Pindarick Odes to Temple, to the King, and to the Athenian Society, a knot of obscure men, who published a periodical pamphlet of answers to questions, sent, or supposed to be sent, by Letters. I have been told that Dryden, having perused these verses, said, "Cousin Swift, you will never be a poet"; and that this denunciation was the motive of Swift's perpetual malevolence to Dryden.

In 1699 Temple died, and left a legacy with his manuscripts to Swift, for whom he had obtained, from King William, a promise of the first prebend that should be vacant at Westminster or Canterbury.

That this promise might not be forgotten, Swift dedicated to the King the posthumous works with which he was intrusted; but neither the dedication, nor tenderness for the man whom he once had treated with confidence and fondness, revived in King William the remembrance of his promise. Swift awhile attended the Court; but soon found his solicitations hopeless.

He was then invited by the Earl of Berkeley to accompany him into Ireland, as his private secretary; but after having done the business till their arrival at Dublin, he then found that one *Bush* had persuaded the Earl that a Clergyman was not a proper secretary, and had obtained the office for himself. In a man like Swift, such circumvention and inconstancy must have excited violent indignation.

But he had yet more to suffer. Lord Berkeley had the disposal of the deanery of Derry, and Swift expected to obtain it; but by the secretary's influence, supposed to have been secured by a bribe, it was bestowed on somebody else; and Swift was dismissed with the livings of *Laracor* and *Rathbeggin*, in the diocese of Meath, which together did not equal half the value of the deanery.

At Laracor he increased the parochial duty by reading prayers on Wednesdays and Fridays, and performed all the offices of his profession with great decency and exactness. . . .

Swift was not one of those minds which amaze the world with early pregnancy: his first work, except his few poetical Essays, was *The Dissentions in Athens and Rome*, published (1701) in his thirty-fourth year. After its appearance, paying a visit to some bishop, he heard mention made of the new pamphlet that Burnet had written, replete with political knowledge. When he seemed to doubt Burnet's right to the work, he was told by the bishop, that he was *a young man;* and, still persisting to doubt, that he was *a very positive young man.*

Three years afterward (1704) was published the *Tale of a Tub:* of this book charity may be persuaded to think that it might be written by a man of a peculiar character, without ill intention; but it is certainly of dangerous example. That Swift was its author, though it be universally believed, was never owned by himself, nor very well proved by any evidence; but no other claimant can be produced, and he did not deny it when Archbishop Sharpe and the Duchess of Somerset, by shewing it to the Queen, debarred him from a bishoprick. . . .

The digressions relating to Wotton and Bentley must be confessed to discover want of knowledge, or want of integrity; he did not understand the two controversies, or he willingly misrepresented them. But Wit can stand its ground against Truth only a little while. The honours due to learning have been justly distributed by the decision of posterity. . . .

For some time after Swift was probably employed in solitary study, gaining the qualifications requisite for future eminence. How often he visited England, and with what diligence he attended his parishes, I know not. It was not till about four years afterwards that he became a professed author, and then one year (1708) produced *The Sentiments of a Church-of-England Man;* the ridicule of Astrology, under the name of *Bickerstaff;* the *Argument against abolishing Christianity;* and the defence of the *Sacramental Test.*

The Sentiments of a Church-of-England Man is written with great coolness, moderation, ease, and perspicuity. The *Argument against abolishing Christianity* is a very happy and judicious irony. . . .

The reasonableness of a *Test* is not hard to be proved; but perhaps it must be allowed that the proper test has not been chosen. . . .

In the year following he wrote *A Project for the Advancement of Religion,* addressed to Lady Berkeley; by whose kindness it is not unlikely that he was advanced to his benefices. To this project, which is formed with great purity of intention, and displayed with spriteliness and elegance, it can only be objected, that, like many projects, it is, if not generally impracticable, yet evidently hopeless, as it supposes more zeal, concord, and perseverance, than a view of mankind gives reason for expecting. . . .

Soon after began the busy and important part of Swift's life. He was employed (1710) by the primate of Ireland to solicit the Queen for a remission of the First Fruits and Twentieth parts to the Irish Clergy. With this purpose he had recourse to Mr. Harley, to whom he was mentioned as a man neglected and oppressed by the last ministry, because he had refused to co-operate with some of their schemes. What he had refused, has never been told; what he had suffered was, I suppose, the exclusion from a bishoprick by the remonstrances of Sharpe, whom he describes as *the harmless tool of others' hate,* and whom he represents as afterwards *suing for pardon.*

Harley's designs and situation were such as made him glad of an auxiliary so well qualified for his service; he therefore soon admitted him to familiarity, whether ever to confidence some have made a doubt; but it would have been difficult to excite his zeal without persuading him that he was trusted, and not very easy to delude him by false persuasions.

He was certainly admitted to those meetings in which the first hints and original plan of action are supposed to have been formed; and was one of the sixteen Ministers, or agents of the Ministry, who met weekly at each other's houses, and were united by the name of *Brother.*

Being not immediately considered as an obdurate Tory, he conversed indiscriminately with all the wits, and was yet the friend of Steele; who, in the *Tatler,* which began in 1710, confesses the advantages of his conversation, and mentions something contributed by him to his paper. But he was now immerging into political controversy; for the same year produced the *Examiner,* of which Swift wrote thirty-three papers. In argument he may be allowed to have the advantage; for where a wide system of conduct, and the whole of

a publick character, is laid open to enquiry, the accuser having the choice of facts, must be very unskilful if he does not prevail; but with regard to wit, I am afraid none of Swift's papers will be found equal to those by which Addison opposed him.

Early in the next year he published a *Proposal for correcting, improving, and ascertaining the English Tongue,* in a Letter to the Earl of Oxford; written without much knowledge of the general nature of language, and without any accurate enquiry into the history of other tongues. The certainty and stability which, contrary to all experience, he thinks attainable, he proposes to secure by instituting an academy; the decrees of which every man would have been willing, and many would have been proud to disobey, and which, being renewed by successive elections, would in a short time have differed from itself.

He wrote in the same year a *Letter to the October Club,* a number of Tory Gentlemen sent from the country to Parliament, who formed themselves into a club, to the number of about a hundred, and met to animate the zeal and raise the expectations of each other. They thought, with great reason, that the Ministers were losing opportunities; that sufficient use was not made of the ardour of the nation; they called loudly for more changes, and stronger efforts; and demanded the punishment of part, and the dismission of the rest, of those whom they considered as publick robbers.

Their eagerness was not gratified by the Queen, or by Harley. The Queen was probably slow because she was afraid, and Harley was slow because he was doubtful; he was a Tory only by necessity, or for convenience; and when he had power in his hands, had no settled purpose for which he should employ it; forced to gratify to a certain degree the Tories who supported him, but unwilling to make his reconcilement to the Whigs utterly desperate, he corresponded at once with the two expectants of the Crown, and kept, as has been observed, the succession undetermined. Not knowing what to do, he did nothing; and, with the fate of a double-dealer, at last he lost his power, but kept his enemies.

Swift seems to have concurred in opinion with the *October Club;* but it was not in his power to quicken the tardiness of Harley, whom he stimulated as much as he could, but with little effect. He that knows not whither to go, is in no haste to move. Harley, who was perhaps not quick by nature, became yet more slow by irresolution; and was content to hear that dilatoriness lamented as natural, which he applauded in himself as politick.

Without the Tories, however, nothing could be done; and as they were not to be gratified, they must be appeased; and the conduct of the Minister, if it could not be vindicated, was to be plausibly excused.

Swift now attained the zenith of his political importance: he published (1712) the *Conduct of the Allies,* ten days before the Parliament assembled. The purpose was to persuade the nation to a peace; and never had any writer more success. The people, who had been amused with bonfires and triumphal processions, and looked with idolatry on the General and his friends, who, as they thought, had made England the arbitress of nations, were confounded between shame and rage, when they found that *mines had been exhausted, and millions destroyed,* to secure the Dutch or aggrandize the emperor, without any advantage to ourselves; that we had been bribing our neighbours to fight their own quarrel; and that amongst our enemies we might number our allies.

That is now no longer doubted, of which the nation was then first informed, that the war was unnecessarily protracted to fill the pockets of Marlborough; and that it would have been continued without end, if he could have continued his annual plunder. . . .

Yet, surely, whoever surveys this wonder-working pamphlet with cool perusal, will confess that its efficacy was supplied by the passions of its readers; that it operates by the mere weight of facts, with very little assistance from the hand that produced them. . . .

Swift, being now the declared favourite and supposed confidant of the Tory Ministry, was treated by all that depended on the Court with the respect which dependents know how to pay. He soon began to feel part of the misery of greatness; he that could say he knew him, considered himself as having fortune in his power. Commissions, solicitations, remonstrances, crowded about him; he was expected to do every man's business, to procure employment for one, and to retain it for another. In assisting those who addressed him, he represents himself as sufficiently diligent; and desires to have others believe, what he probably believed himself, that by his interposition many Whigs of merit, and among them Addison and Congreve, were continued in their places. But every man of known influence has so many petitions which he cannot grant, that he must necessarily offend more than he gratifies, because the preference given to one affords all the rest reason for complaint. *When I give away a place,* said Lewis XIV., *I make an hundred discontented, and one ungrateful.*

Much has been said of the equality and independence which he preserved in his conversation with the Ministers, of the frankness of his remonstrances, and the familiarity of his friendship. In accounts of this kind a few single incidents are set against the general tenour of behaviour. No man, however, can pay a more servile tribute to the Great, than by suffering his liberty in their presence to aggrandize him in his own esteem. Between different ranks of the community there is necessarily some distance: he who is called by his superior to pass the interval, may properly accept the invitation; but petulance and obtrusion are rarely produced by magnanimity; nor have often any nobler cause than the pride of importance, and the malice of inferiority. He who knows himself necessary may set, while that necessity lasts, a high value upon himself; as, in a lower condition, a servant eminently skilful may be saucy; but he is saucy only because he is servile. Swift appears to have preserved the kindness of the great when they wanted him no longer; and therefore it must be allowed, that the childish freedom, to which he seems enough inclined, was overpowered by his better qualities.

His disinterestedness has been likewise mentioned; a strain of heroism, which would have been in his condition romantick and superfluous. Ecclesiastical benefices, when they become vacant, must be given away; and the friends of Power may, if there be no inherent disqualification, reasonably expect them. Swift accepted (1713) the deanery of St. Patrick, the best preferment that his friends could venture to give him. That Ministry was in a great degree supported by the Clergy, who were not yet reconciled to the author of the *Tale of a Tub,* and would not without much discontent and indignation have borne to see him installed in an English Cathedral. . . .

In the midst of his power and his politicks, he kept a journal of his visits, his walks, his interviews with Ministers, and quarrels with his servant, and transmitted it to Mrs. Johnson and Mrs. Dingley, to whom he knew that whatever befel him was interesting, and no accounts could be too minute. Whether these diurnal trifles were properly exposed to eyes which had never received any pleasure from the presence of the Dean, may be reasonably doubted: they have, however, some odd attraction; the reader, finding frequent mention of names which he has been used to consider as important, goes on in hope of information; and, as there is nothing to fatigue attention, if he is disappointed he can hardly complain. It is easy to perceive, from every page, that though ambition pressed Swift into a life of bustle, the wish for a life of ease was always returning.

He went to take possession of his deanery, as soon as he had obtained it; but he was not suffered to stay in Ireland more than a fortnight before he was recalled to England, that he might reconcile Lord Oxford and Lord Bolingbroke, who began to look on one another with malevolence, which every day increased, and which Bolingbroke appeared to retain in his last years. . . .

But, by the disunion of his great friends, his importance and designs were now at an end; and seeing his services at last useless, he retired about June (1714) into Berkshire, where, in the house of a friend, he wrote what was then suppressed, but has since appeared under the title of *Free Thoughts on the present State of Affairs.*

While he was waiting in his retirement for events which time or chance might bring to pass, the death of the Queen broke down at once the whole system of Tory politicks; and nothing remained but to withdraw from the implacability of triumphant Whiggism, and shelter himself in unenvied obscurity. . . .

The Archbishop of Dublin gave him at first some disturbance in the exercise of his jurisdiction; but it was soon discovered, that between prudence and integrity he was seldom in the wrong; and that, when he was right, his spirit did not easily yield to opposition. . . .

Swift now, much against his will, commenced Irishman for life, and was to contrive how he might be best accommodated in a country where he considered himself as in a state of exile. It seems that his first recourse was to piety. The thoughts of death rushed upon him, at this time, with such incessant importunity, that they took possession of his mind, when he first waked, for many years together. . . .

Soon after (1716), in his forty-ninth year, he was privately married to Mrs. Johnson by Dr. Ashe, Bishop of Clogher, as Dr. Madden told me, in the garden. The marriage made no change in their mode of life; they lived in different houses, as before; nor did she ever lodge in the deanery but when Swift was seized with a fit of giddiness. "It would be difficult," says Lord Orrery, "to prove that they were ever afterwards together without a third person."

The Dean of St. Patrick's lived in a private manner, known and regarded only by his friends, till, about the year 1720, he, by a pamphlet, recommended to the Irish the use, and consequently the improvement, of their manufacture. For a man to use the productions of his own labour is surely a natural right, and to like best what he makes himself is a natural passion. But to excite this passion, and enforce this right, appeared so criminal to those who had an interest in the English trade, that the printer was imprisoned; and, as Hawkesworth justly observes, the attention of the publick being by this outrageous resentment turned upon the proposal, the author was by consequence made popular.

In 1723 died Mrs. Van Homrigh, a woman made unhappy by her admiration of wit, and ignominiously distinguished by the name of *Vanessa*, whose conduct has been already sufficiently discussed, and whose history is too well known to be minutely repeated. She was a young woman fond of literature, whom *Decanus* the *Dean*, called *Cadenus* by transposition of the letters, took pleasure in directing and instructing; till, from being proud of his praise, she grew fond of his person. Swift was then about forty-seven, at an age when vanity is strongly excited by the amorous attention of a young woman. If it be said that Swift should have checked a passion which he never meant to gratify, recourse must be had to that extenuation which he so much despised, *men are but men:* perhaps however he did not at first know his own mind, and, as he represents himself, was undetermined. For his admission of her courtship, and his indulgence of her hopes after his marriage to Stella, no other honest plea can be found, than that he delayed a disagreeable discovery from time to time, dreading the immediate bursts of distress, and watching for a favourable moment. She thought herself neglected, and

died of disappointment; having ordered by her will the poem to be published, in which Cadenus had proclaimed her excellence, and confessed his love. . . .

. . . it happened one day that some gentlemen dropt in to dinner, who were strangers to Stella's situation; and as the poem of *Cadenus and Vanessa* was then the general topic of conversation, one of them said, "Surely that Vanessa must be an extraordinary woman, that could inspire the Dean to write so finely upon her." Mrs. Johnson smiled, and answered, "that she thought that point not quite so clear; for it was well known the Dean could write finely upon a broomstick."

The great acquisition of esteem and influence was made by the *Drapier's Letters* in 1724. One Wood of Wolverhampton in Staffordshire, a man enterprising and rapacious, had, as is said, by a present to the Duchess of Munster, obtained a patent, empowering him to coin one hundred and eighty thousand pounds of halfpence and farthings for the kingdom of Ireland, in which there was a very inconvenient and embarrassing scarcity of copper coin; so that it was possible to run in debt upon the credit of a piece of money; for the cook or keeper of an alehouse could not refuse to supply a man that had silver in his hand, and the buyer would not leave his money without change.

The project was therefore plausible. The scarcity, which was already great, Wood took care to make greater, by agents who gathered up the old half-pence; and was about to turn his brass into gold, by pouring the treasures of his new mint upon Ireland, when Swift, finding that the metal was debased to an enormous degree, wrote Letters, under the name of *M. B.*, *Drapier*, to shew the folly of receiving, and the mischief that must ensue, by giving gold and silver for coin worth perhaps not a third part of its nominal value.

The nation was alarmed; the new coin was universally refused: but the governors of Ireland considered resistance to the

King's patent as highly criminal; and one Whitshed, then Chief Justice, who had tried the printer of the former pamphlet, and sent out the Jury nine times, till by clamour and menaces they were frighted into a special verdict, now presented the *Drapier*, but could not prevail on the Grand Jury to find the bill.

Lord Carteret and the Privy Council published a proclamation, offering three hundred pounds for discovering the author of the Fourth Letter. Swift had concealed himself from his printers, and trusted only his butler, who transcribed the paper. The man, immediately after the appearance of the proclamation, strolled from the house, and staid out all night, and part of the next day. There was reason enough to fear that he had betrayed his master for the reward; but he came home, and the Dean ordered him to put off his livery, and leave the house; "for," says he, "I know that my life is in your power, and I will not bear, out of fear, either your insolence or negligence." The man excused his fault with great submission, and begged that he might be confined in the house while it was in his power to endanger his master; but the Dean resolutely turned him out, without taking further notice of him, till the term of information had expired, and then received him again. Soon afterwards he ordered him and the rest of the servants into his presence, without telling his intentions, and bade them take notice that their fellow-servant was no longer Robert the butler; but that his integrity had made him Mr. Blakeney, verger of St. Patrick's; an officer whose income was between thirty and forty pounds a year: yet he still continued for some years to serve his old master as his butler.

Swift was known from this time by the appellation of *The Dean*. He was honoured by the populace, as the champion, patron, and instructor of Ireland; and gained such power as, considered both in its extent and duration, scarcely any man has ever enjoyed without greater wealth or higher station.

He was from this important year the oracle of the traders, and the idol of the rabble, and by consequence was feared and courted by all to whom the kindness of the traders or the populace was necessary. The *Drapier* was a sign; the *Drapier* was a health; and which way soever the eye or the ear was turned, some tokens were found of the nation's gratitude to the *Drapier*.

The benefit was indeed great; he had rescued Ireland from a very oppressive and predatory invasion; and the popularity which he had gained he was diligent to keep, by appearing forward and zealous on every occasion where the publick interest was supposed to be involved. Nor did he much scruple to boast his influence; for when, upon some attempts to regulate the coin, Archbishop Boulter, then one of the Justices, accused him of exasperating the people, he exculpated himself by saying, "If I had lifted up my finger, they would have torn you to pieces." . . .

This important year [1727] sent likewise into the world *Gulliver's Travels*, a production so new and strange, that it filled the reader with a mingled emotion of merriment and amazement. It was received with such avidity, that the price of the first edition was raised before the second could be made; it was read by the high and the low, the learned and illiterate. Criticism was for a while lost in wonder; no rules of judgement were applied to a book written in open defiance of truth and regularity. But when distinctions came to be made, the part which gave least pleasure was that which describes the *Flying Island*, and that which gave most disgust must be the history of the *Houyhnhnms*.

While Swift was enjoying the reputation of his new work, the news of the King's death arrived, and he kissed the hands of the new King and Queen three days after their accession. . . .

He seemed desirous enough of recommencing courtier, and endeavoured to gain the kindness of Mrs. Howard, remembering what Mrs. Masham had performed in former times; but his flatteries were, like those of the other wits, unsuccessful; the Lady either wanted power, or had no ambition of poetical immortality.

He was seized not long afterwards by a fit of giddiness, and again heard of the sickness and danger of Mrs. Johnson. He then left the house of Pope, as it seems, with very little ceremony, finding *that two sick friends cannot live together;* and did not write to him till he found himself at Chester.

He returned to a home of sorrow; poor Stella was sinking into the grave, and, after a languishing decay of about two months, died in her forty-fourth year, on January 28, 1728. How much he wished her life, his papers shew; nor can it be doubted that he dreaded the death of her whom he loved most, aggravated by the consciousness that himself had hastened it.

Beauty and the power of pleasing, the greatest external advantages that woman can desire or possess, were fatal to the unfortunate Stella. The man whom she had the misfortune to love was, as Delany observes, fond of singularity, and desirous to make a mode of happiness for himself, different from the general course of things and order of Providence. . . .

The rest of his life was spent in Ireland, in a country to which not even power almost despotick, nor flattery almost idolatrous, could reconcile him. He sometimes wished to visit England, but always found some reason of delay. He tells Pope, in the decline of life, that he hopes once more to see him; *but if not,* says he, *we must part, as all human beings have parted.*

After the death of Stella, his benevolence was contracted, and his severity exasperated; he drove his acquaintance from his table, and wondered why he was deserted. But he continued his attention to the publick, and wrote from time to time such directions, admonitions, or censures, as the exigency of affairs, in his opinion, made proper; and nothing fell from his pen in vain.

In a short poem on the Presbyterians, whom he always regarded with detestation, he bestowed one stricture on Bettesworth, a lawyer eminent for his insolence to the clergy, which, from very considerable reputation, brought him into immediate and universal contempt. Bettesworth, enraged at his disgrace and loss, went to Swift, and demanded whether he was the author of that poem? "Mr. Bettesworth," answered he, "I was in my youth acquainted with great lawyers, who, knowing my disposition to satire, advised me, that, if any scoundrel or blockhead whom I had lampooned should ask, *Are you the author of this paper?* I should tell him that I was not the author; and therefore, I tell you, Mr. Bettesworth, that I am not the author of these lines." . . .

His asperity continually increasing, condemned him to solitude; and his resentment of solitude sharpened his asperity. He was not, however, totally deserted: some men of learning, and some women of elegance, often visited him; and he wrote from time to time either verse or prose; of his verses he willingly gave copies, and is supposed to have felt no discontent when he saw them printed. His favourite maxim was *vive la bagatelle;* he thought trifles a necessary part of life, and perhaps found them necessary to himself. It seems impossible to him to be idle, and his disorders made it difficult or dangerous to be long seriously studious, or laboriously diligent. The love of ease is always gaining upon age, and he had one temptation to petty amusements peculiar to himself; whatever he did, he was sure to hear applauded; and such was his predominance over all that approached, that all their applauses were probably sincere. He that is much flattered, soon learns to flatter himself: we are commonly taught our duty by fear or shame, and how can they act upon the man who hears nothing but his own praises? . . .

He was always careful of his money, and was therefore no liberal entertainer; but was less frugal of his wine than of his meat. When his friends of either sex came to him, in expectation of a dinner, his custom was to give every one a shilling, that they might please themselves with their provision. At last his avarice grew too powerful for his kindness; he would refuse a bottle of wine, and in Ireland no man visits where he cannot drink.

Having thus excluded conversation, and desisted from study, he had neither business nor amusement; for having, by some ridiculous resolution or mad vow, determined never to wear spectacles, he could make little use of books in his later years: his ideas, therefore, being neither renovated by discourse, nor increased by reading, wore gradually away, and left his mind vacant to the vexations of the hour, till at last his anger was heightened into madness.

He however permitted one book to be published, which had been the production of former years; *Polite Conversation,* which appeared in 1738. The *Directions for Servants* was printed soon after his death. These two performances shew a mind incessantly attentive, and, when it was not employed upon great things, busy with minute occurrences. It is apparent that he must have had the habit of noting whatever he observed; for such a number of particulars could never have been assembled by the power of recollection.

He grew more violent; and his mental powers declined till (1741) it was found necessary that legal guardians should be appointed of his person and fortune. He now lost distinction. His madness was compounded of rage and fatuity. The last face that he knew was that of Mrs. Whiteway, and her he ceased to know in a little time. His meat was brought him cut into mouthfuls; but he would never touch it while the servant staid, and at last, after it had stood perhaps an hour, would eat it walking; for

he continued his old habit, and was on his feet ten hours a day.

Next year (1742) he had an inflammation in his left eye, which swelled it to the size of an egg, with boils in other parts; he was kept long waking with the pain, and was not easily restrained by five attendants from tearing out his eye.

The tumour at last subsided; and a short interval of reason ensuing, in which he knew his physician and his family, gave hopes of his recovery; but in a few days he sunk into lethargick stupidity, motionless, heeedless, and speechless. But it is said, that, after a year of total silence, when his housekeeper, on the 30th of November, told him that the usual bonfires and illuminations were preparing to celebrate his birthday, he answered, *It is all folly; they had better let it alone.*

It is remembered that he afterwards spoke now and then, or gave some intimation of a meaning; but at last sunk into perfect silence, which continued till about the end of October 1744, when, in his seventy-eighth year, he expired without a struggle.

When Swift is considered as an author, it is just to estimate his powers by their effects. In the reign of Queen Anne he turned the stream of popularity against the Whigs, and must be confessed to have dictated for a time the political opinions of the English nation. In the succeeding reign he delivered Ireland from plunder and oppression; and shewed that wit, confederated with truth, had such force as authority was unable to resist. He said truly of himself, that Ireland *was his debtor.* It was from the time when he first began to patronize the Irish, that they may date their riches and prosperity. He taught them first to know their own interest, their weight, and their strength, and gave them spirit to assert that equality with their fellow-subjects to which they have ever since been making vigorous advances, and to claim those rights which they have at last established. Nor can they be charged with ingratitude to their benefactor; for they reverenced him as a guardian, and obeyed him as a dictator.

In his works, he has given very different specimens both of sentiment and expression. His *Tale of a Tub* has little resemblance to his other pieces. It exhibits a vehemence and rapidity of mind, a copiousness of images, and vivacity of diction, such as he afterwards never possessed, or never exerted. It is of a mode so distinct and peculiar, that it must be considered by itself; what is true of that, is not true of any thing else which he has written.

In his other works is found an equable tenour of easy language, which rather trickles than flows. His delight was in simplicity. That he has in his works no metaphor, as has been said, is not true; but his few metaphors seem to be received rather by necessity than choice. He studied purity; and though perhaps all his strictures are not exact, yet it is not often that solecisms can be found; and whoever depends on his authority may generally conclude himself safe. His sentences are never too much dilated or contracted; and it will not be easy to find any embarrassment in the complication of his clauses, any inconsequence in his connections, or abruptness in his transitions.

His style was well suited to his thoughts, which are never subtilised by nice disquisitions, decorated by sparkling conceits, elevated by ambitious sentences, or variegated by far-sought learning. He pays no court to the passions; he excites neither surprise nor admiration; he always understands himself: and his reader always understands him: the peruser of Swift wants little previous knowledge: it will be sufficient that he is acquainted with common words and common things; he is neither required to mount elevations, nor to explore profundities; his passage is always on a level, along solid ground, without asperities, without obstruction. . . .

By his political education he was asso-ciated with the Whigs; but he deserted them when they deserted their principles, yet without running into the contrary extreme; he continued throughout his life to retain the disposition which he assigns to the *Church-of-England Man*, of thinking commonly with the Whigs of the State, and with the Tories of the Church.

He was a churchman rationally zealous; he desired the prosperity, and maintained the honour, of the Clergy; of the Dissenters he did not wish to infringe the toleration, but he opposed their encroachments.

To his duty as Dean he was very attentive. He managed the revenues of his church with exact oeconomy; and it is said by Delany, that more money was, under his direction, laid out in repairs than had ever been in the same time since its first erection. Of his choir he was eminently careful; and, though he neither loved nor understood musick, took care that all the singers were well qualified, admitting none without the testimony of skilful judges.

In his church he restored the practice of weekly communion, and distributed the sacramental elements in the most solemn and devout manner with his own hand. He came to church every morning, preached commonly in his turn, and attended the evening anthem, that it might not be negligently performed. . . .

The suspicions of his irreligion proceeded in a great measure from his dread of hypocrisy; instead of wishing to seem better, he delighted in seeming worse than he was. He went in London to early prayers, lest he should be seen at church; he read prayers to his servants every morning with such dexterous secrecy, that Dr. Delany was six months in his house before he knew it. He was not only careful to hide the good which he did, but willingly incurred the suspicion of evil which he did not. He forgot what himself had formerly asserted, that hypocrisy is less mischievous than open impiety. Dr. Delany, with all his zeal for his honour, has justly condemned this part of his character. . . .

In his oeconomy he practised a peculiar and offensive parsimony, without disguise or apology. The practice of saving being once necessary became habitual, and grew first ridiculous, and at last detestable. But his avarice, though it might exclude pleasure, was never suffered to encroach upon his virtue. He was frugal by inclination, but liberal by principle; and if the purpose to which he destined his little accumulations be remembered, with his distribution of occasional charity, it will perhaps appear that he only liked one mode of expence better than another, and saved merely that he might have something to give. He did not grow rich by injuring his successors, but left both Laracor and the Deanery more valuable than he found them.—With all this talk of his covetousness and generosity, it should be remembered that he was never rich. The revenue of his Deanery was not much more than seven hundred a year.

His beneficence was not graced with tenderness or civility; he relieved without pity, and assisted without kindness, so that those who were fed by him could hardly love him.

He made a rule to himself to give but one piece at a time, and therefore always stored his pocket with coins of different value.

Whatever he did, he seemed willing to do in a manner peculiar to himself, without sufficiently considering that singularity, as it implies a contempt of the general practice, is a kind of defiance which justly provokes the hostility of ridicule; he therefore who indulges peculiar habits is worse than others, if he be not better. . . .

He told stories with great felicity, and delighted in doing what he knew himself to do well. He was therefore captivated by the respective silence of a steady listener, and told the same tales too often.

He did not, however, claim the right of talking alone; for it was his rule, when he had spoken a minute, to give room by a pause for any other speaker. Of time, on all occasions, he was an exact computer, and knew the minutes required to every common operation.

It may be justly supposed that there was in his conversation, what appears so frequently in his Letters, an affectation of familiarity with the Great, an ambition of momentary equality sought and enjoyed by the neglect of those ceremonies which custom has established as the barriers between one order of society and another. This transgression of regularity was by himself and his admirers termed greatness of soul. But a great mind disdains to hold anything by courtesy, and therefore never usurps what a lawful claimant may take away. He that encroaches on another's dignity, puts himself in his power; he is either repelled with helpless indignity, or endured by clemency and condescension.

Of Swift's general habits of thinking, if his Letters can be supposed to afford any evidence, he was not a man to be either loved or envied. He seems to have wasted life in discontent, by the rage of neglected pride, and the languishment of unsatisfied desire. He is querulous and fastidious, arrogant and malignant; he scarcely speaks of himself but with indignant lamentations, or of others but with insolent superiority when he is gay, and with angry contempt when he is gloomy. From the Letters that pass between him and Pope it might be inferred that they, with Arbuthnot and Gay, had engrossed all the understanding and virtue of mankind, that their merits filled the world; or that there was no hope of more. They shew the age involved in darkness, and shade the picture with sullen emulation. . . .

The greatest difficulty that occurs, in analysing his character, is to discover by what depravity of intellect he took delight in revolving ideas, from which almost every other mind shrinks with disgust. The ideas of pleasure, even when criminal, may solicit the imagination; but what has disease, deformity, and filth, upon which the thoughts can be allured to dwell? Delany is willing to think that Swift's mind was not much tainted with this gross corruption before his long visit to Pope. He does not consider how he degrades his hero, by making him at fifty-nine the pupil of turpitude, and liable to the malignant influence of an ascendant mind. But the truth is, that Gulliver had described his *Yahoos* before the visit, and he that had formed those images had nothing filthy to learn.

I have here given the character of Swift as he exhibits himself to my perception; but now let another be heard, who knew him better; Dr. Delany, after long acquaintance, describes him to Lord Orrery in these terms:

"My Lord, when you consider Swift's singular, peculiar, and most variegated vein of wit, always rightly intended (although not always so rightly directed), delightful in many instances, and salutary, even where it is most offensive; when you consider his strict truth, his fortitude in resisting oppression and arbitrary power; his fidelity in friendship, his sincere love and zeal for religion, his uprightness in making right resolutions, and his steadiness in adhering to them; his care of his church, its choir, its oeconomy, and its income; his attention to all those that preached in his cathedral, in order to their amendment in pronunciation and style; as also his remarkable attention to the interest of his successors, preferably to his own present emoluments; invincible patriotism, even to a country which he did not love; his very various, well-devised, well-judged, and extensive charities, throughout his life,

and his whole fortune (to say nothing of his wife's) conveyed to the same Christian purposes at his death; charities from which he could enjoy no honour, advantage or satisfaction of any kind in this world. When you consider his ironical and humorous, as well as his serious schemes, for the promotion of true religion and virtue; his success in soliciting for the First Fruits and Twentieths, to the unspeakable benefit of the Established Church of Ireland; and his felicity (to rate it no higher) in giving occasion to the building of fifty new churches in London.

"All this considered, the character of his life will appear like that of his writings; they will both bear to be re-considered and re-examined with the utmost attention, and always discover new beauties and excellences upon every examination.

"They will bear to be considered as the sun, in which the brightness will hide the blemishes; and whenever petulant ignorance, pride, malice, malignity, or envy, interposes to cloud or sully his fame, I will take upon me to pronounce that the eclipse will not last long.

"To conclude—No man ever deserved better of any country than Swift did of his. A steady, persevering, inflexible friend; a wise, a watchful, and a faithful counsellor, under many severe trials and bitter persecutions, to the manifest hazard both of his liberty and fortune.

"He lived a blessing, he died a benefactor, and his name will ever live an honour to Ireland."

William Makepeace Thackeray

Swift

. . . Dr. Wilde of Dublin, who has written a most interesting volume on the closing years of Swift's life, calls Johnson "the most malignant of his biographers": it is not easy for an English critic to please Irishmen—perhaps to try and please them. And yet Johnson truly admires Swift: Johnson does not quarrel with Swift's change of politics, or doubt his sincerity of religion: about the famous Stella and Vanessa controversy the Doctor does not bear very hardly on Swift. But he could not give the Dean that honest hand of his; the stout old man puts it into his breast, and moves off from him.

Would we have liked to live with him? That is a question which, in dealing with these people's works, and thinking of their lives and peculiarities, every reader of biographies must put to himself. Would you have liked to be a friend of the great Dean? I should like to have been Shakspeare's shoeblack—just to have lived in his house, just to have worshipped him—to have run on his errands, and seen that sweet serene face. I should like, as a young man, to have lived on Fielding's staircase in the Temple, and after helping him up to bed perhaps, and opening his door with his latch-key, to have shaken hands with him in the morning, and heard him talk and crack jokes over his breakfast and his mug of small beer. Who would not give something to pass a night at the club with Johnson, and Goldsmith, and James Boswell, Esq., of Auchinleck? The charm of Addison's companionship and conversation has passed to us by fond tradition—but Swift? If you had been

his inferior in parts (and that, with a great respect for all persons present, I fear is only very likely), his equal in mere social station, he would have bullied, scorned, and insulted you; if, undeterred by his great reputation, you had met him like a man, he would have quailed before you, and not had the pluck to reply, and gone home, and years after written a foul epigram about you—watched for you in a sewer, and come out to assail you with a coward's blow and a dirty bludgeon. If you had been a lord with a blue riband, who flattered his vanity, or could help his ambition, he would have been the most delightful company in the world. He would have been so manly, so sarcastic, so bright, odd, and original, that you might think he had no object in view but the indulgence of his humour, and that he was the most reckless, simple creature in the world. How he would have torn your enemies to pieces for you! and made fun of the Opposition! His servility was so boisterous that it looked like independence; he would have done your errands, but with the air of patronizing you, and after fighting your battles masked in the street or the press, would have kept on his hat before your wife and daughters in the drawing-room, content to take that sort of pay for his tremendous services as a bravo.

He says as much himself in one of his letters to Bolingbroke:—"All my endeavours to distinguish myself were only for want of a great title and fortune, that I might be used like a lord by those who have an opinion of my parts; whether right or

From *The English Humourists of the Eighteenth Century*. The present selection from the lecture on Swift includes about two-thirds of Thackeray's text, although his footnotes have been omitted. Selection has been made to preserve continuity and opinion.

wrong is no great matter. And so the reputation of wit and great learning does the office of a blue riband or a coach and six."

Could there be a greater candour? It is an outlaw, who says, "These are my brains; with these I'll win titles and compete with fortune. These are my bullets; these I'll turn into gold"; and he hears the sound of coaches and six, takes the road like Macheath, and makes society stand and deliver. They are all on their knees before him. Down go my lord bishop's apron, and his Grace's blue riband, and my lady's brocade petticoat in the mud. He eases the one of a living, the other of a patent place, the third of a little snug post about the Court, and gives them over to followers of his own. The great prize has not come yet. The coach with the mitre and crosier in it, which he intends to have for *his* share, has been delayed on the way from St. James's; and he waits and waits until nightfall, when his runners come and tell him that the coach has taken a different road, and escaped him. So he fires his pistols into the air with a curse, and rides away into his own country.

Swift's seems to me to be as good a name to point a moral or adorn a tale of ambition, as any hero's that ever lived and failed. But we must remember that the morality was lax—that other gentlemen besides himself took the road in his day— that public society was in a strange disordered condition, and the State was ravaged by other condottieri. The Boyne was being fought and won, and lost—the bells rung in William's victory, in the very same tone with which they would have pealed for James's. Men were loose upon politics, and had to shift for themselves. They, as well as old beliefs and institutions, had lost their moorings and gone adrift in the storm. As in the South Sea Bubble almost every body gambled; as in the Railway mania— not many centuries ago—almost every one took his unlucky share; a man of that time, of the vast talents and ambition of

Swift, could scarce do otherwise than grasp at his prize, and make his spring at his opportunity. . . .

As fierce a beak and talon as ever struck —as strong a wing as ever beat, belonged to Swift. I am glad, for one, that fate wrested the prey out of his claws, and cut his wings and chained him. One can gaze, and not without awe and pity, at the lonely eagle chained behind the bars.

That Swift was born at No. 7, Hoey's-court, Dublin, on the 30th November, 1667, is a certain fact, of which nobody will deny the sister island the honour and glory; but, it seems to me, he was no more an Irishman than a man born of English parents at Calcutta is a Hindoo. Goldsmith was an Irishman, and always an Irishman: Steele was an Irishman, and always an Irishman: Swift's heart was English and in England, his habits English, his logic eminently English; his statement is elaborately simple; he shuns tropes and metaphors, and uses his ideas and words with a wise thrift and economy, as he used his money: with which he could be generous and splendid upon great occasions, but which he husbanded when there was no need to spend it. He never indulges in needless extravagance of rhetoric, lavish epithets, profuse imagery. He lays his opinion before you with a grave simplicity and a perfect neatness. Dreading ridicule too, as a man of his humour— above all an Englishman of his humour— certainly would, he is afraid to use the poetical power which he really possessed; one often fancies in reading him that he dares not be eloquent when he might; that he does not speak above his voice, as it were, and the tone of society.

His initiation into politics, his knowledge of business, his knowledge of polite life, his acquaintance with literature even, which he could not have pursued very sedulously during that reckless career at Dublin, Swift got under the roof of Sir William Temple. He was fond of telling in after life what quantities of books he devoured there, and how King William taught him to cut asparagus in the Dutch fashion. It was at Shene and at Moor Park, with a salary of twenty pounds and a dinner at the upper servants' table, that this great and lonely Swift passed a ten years' apprenticeship—wore a cassock that was only not a livery—bent down a knee as proud as Lucifer's to supplicate my lady's good graces, or run on his honour's errands. It was here, as he was writing at Temple's table, or following his patron's walk, that he saw and heard the men who had governed the great world—measured himself with them, looking up from his silent corner, gauged their brains, weighed their wits, turned them, and tried them, and marked them. Ah! what platitudes he must have heard! what feeble jokes! what pompous commonplaces! what small men they must have seemed under these enormous periwigs, to the swarthy, uncouth, silent Irish secretary. I wonder whether it ever struck Temple that that Irishman was his master? I suppose that dismal conviction did not present itself under the ambrosial wig, or Temple could never have lived with Swift. Swift sickened, rebelled, left the service—ate humble pie and came back again; and so for ten years went on, gathering learning, swallowing scorn, and submitting with a stealthy rage to his fortune. . . .

Cannot one fancy the uncouth young servitor, with downcast eyes, books and papers in hand, following at his Honour's heels in the garden walk; or taking his Honour's orders as he stands by the great chair, where Sir William has the gout, and his feet all blistered with moxa? When Sir William has the gout or scolds it must be hard work at the second table; the Irish secretary owned as much afterwards: and when he came to dinner, how he must have lashed and growled and torn the household with his gibes and scorn! What would the steward say about the pride of them Irish schollards—and this one had got no great credit even at his Irish college, if the truth were known—and what a contempt his Excellency's own gentleman must have had

for Parson Teague from Dublin. (The valets and chaplains were always at war. It is hard to say which Swift thought the more contemptible.) . . .

Perhaps, for the Irish secretary, his Excellency's condescension was even more cruel than his frowns. Sir William *would* perpetually quote Latin and the ancient classics *à propos* of his gardens and his Dutch statues and *plates bandes,* and talk about Epicurus and Diogenes Laertius, Julius Caesar, Semiramis, and the gardens of the Hesperides, Maecenas, Strabo describing Jericho, and the Assyrian kings. *A propos* of beans, he would mention Pythagoras's precept to abstain from beans, and that this precept probably meant that wise men should abstain from public affairs. *He* is a placid Epicurean; *he* is a Pythagorean philosopher; *he* is a wise man—that is the deduction. Does not Swift think so? One can imagine the downcast eyes lifted up for a moment, and the flash of scorn which they emit. Swift's eyes were as azure as the heavens; Pope says nobly (as everything Pope said and thought of his friend was good and noble), "His eyes are as azure as the heavens, and have a charming archness in them."

Twenty years afterwards Bishop Kennet, describing the same man, says, "Dr. Swift came into the coffeehouse and had a bow from everybody but me. When I came to the antechamber [at court] to wait before prayers, Dr. Swift was the principal man of talk and business. He was soliciting the Earl of Arran to speak to his brother, the Duke of Ormond, to get a place for a clergyman. He was promising Mr. Thorold to undertake, with my Lord Treasurer, that he should obtain a salary of 200 l. per annum as member of the English Church at Rotterdam. He stopped F. Gwynne, Esq., going in to the Queen with the red bag, and told him aloud, he had something to say to him from my Lord Treasurer. He took out his gold watch, and telling the time of day, complained that it was very late. A gentleman said he was too fast.

'How can I help it,' says the doctor, 'if the courtiers give me a watch that won't go right?' Then he instructed a young nobleman, that the best poet in England was Mr. Pope (a Papist), who had begun a translation of Homer into English, for which he would have them all subscribe; 'For,' says he, 'he shall not begin to print till I have a thousand guineas for him.' Lord Treasurer, after leaving the Queen, came through the room, beckoning Dr. Swift to follow him, —both went off just before prayers." There's a little malice in the Bishop's "just before prayers."

This picture of the great Dean seems a true one, and is harsh, though not altogether unpleasant. He was doing good, and to deserving men too, in the midst of these intrigues and triumphs. His journals and a thousand anecdotes of him relate his kind acts and rough manners. His hand was constantly stretched out to relieve an honest man—he was cautious about his money, but ready.—If you were in a strait would you like such a benefactor? I think I would rather have had a potato and a friendly word from Goldsmith than have been beholden to the Dean for a guinea and a dinner. He insulted a man as he served him, made women cry, guests look foolish, bullied unlucky friends, and flung his benefactions into poor men's faces. No; the Dean was no Irishman—no Irishman ever gave but with a kind word and a kind heart.

It is told, as if it were to Swift's credit, that the Dean of St. Patrick's performed his family devotions every morning regularly, but with such secrecy, that the guests in his house were never in the least aware of the ceremony. There was no need surely why a church dignitary should assemble his family privily in a crypt, and as if he was afraid of heathen persecution. But I think the world was right, and the bishops who advised Queen Anne, when they counselled her not to appoint the author of the *Tale of a Tub* to a bishopric, gave perfectly good advice. The man who wrote the arguments and illustrations in that wild book, could not but be aware what must be the sequel of the propositions which he laid down. . . .

I am not here, of course, to speak of any man's religious views, except in so far as they influence his literary character, his life, his humour. The most notorious sinners of all those fellow-mortals whom it is our business to discuss—Harry Fielding and Dick Steele, were especially loud, and I believe really fervent, in their expressions of belief; they belaboured freethinkers, and stoned imaginary atheists on all sorts of occasions, going out of their way to bawl their own creed, and persecute their neighbour's, and if they sinned and stumbled, as they constantly did with debt, with drink, with all sorts of bad behaviour, they got up on their knees, and cried "Peccavi" with a most sonorous orthodoxy. Yes; poor Harry Fielding and poor Dick Steele were trusty and undoubting Church of England men; they abhorred Popery, Atheism, and wooden shoes, and idolatries in general; and hiccupped Church and State with fervour.

But Swift? *His* mind had had a different schooling, and possessed a very different logical power. *He* was not bred up in a tipsy guardroom, and did not learn to reason in a Covent Garden tavern. He could conduct an argument from beginning to end. He could see forward with a fatal clearness. In his old age, looking at the *Tale of a Tub*, when he said, "Good God, what a genius I had when I wrote that book!" I think he was admiring not the genius, but the consequences to which the genius had brought him—a vast genius, a magnificent genius, a genius wonderfully bright, and dazzling, strong,—to seize, to know, to see, to flash upon falsehood and scorch it into perdition, to penetrate into the hidden motives, and expose the black thoughts of men,—an awful, an evil spirit.

Ah, man! you, educated in Epicurean Temple's library, you whose friends were Pope and St. John—what made you to swear to fatal vows, and bind yourself to a life-long hypocrisy before the Heaven which you adored with such real wonder, humility, and reverence? For Swift was a reverent, was a pious spirit—for Swift could love and could pray. Through the storms and tempests of his furious mind, the stars of religion and love break out in the blue, shining serenely, though hidden by the driving clouds and the maddened hurricane of his life.

It is my belief that he suffered frightfully from the consciousness of his own scepticism, and that he had bent his pride so far down as to put his apostasy out to hire. The paper left behind him, called "Thoughts on Religion," is merely a set of excuses for not professing disbelief. He says of his sermons that he preached pamphlets: they have scarce a Christian characteristic; they might be preached from the steps of a synagogue, or the floor of a mosque, or the box of a coffee-house almost. There is little or no cant—he is too great and too proud for that; and, in so far as the badness of his sermons goes, he is honest. But having put that cassock on, it poisoned him: he was strangled in his bands. He goes through life, tearing, like a man possessed with a devil. . . .

Against men in office, he having been overthrown; against men in England, he having lost his chance of preferment there, the furious exile never fails to rage and curse. Is it fair to call the famous *Drapier's Letters* patriotism? They are master-pieces of dreadful humour and invective: they are reasoned logically enough too, but the proposition is as monstrous and fabulous as the Lilliputian island. It is not that the grievance is so great, but there is his enemy —the assault is wonderful for its activity and terrible rage. It is Samson, with a bone in his hand, rushing on his enemies and felling them: one admires not the cause so much as the strength, the anger, the fury of the champion. As is the case with madmen, certain subjects provoke him, and awaken his fits of wrath. Marriage is one

of these; in a hundred passages in his writings he rages against it; rages against children; an object of constant satire, even more contemptible in his eyes than a lord's chaplain, is a poor curate with a large family. The idea of this luckless paternity never fails to bring down from him gibes and foul language. Could Dick Steele, or Goldsmith, or Fielding, in his most reckless moment of satire, have written anything like the Dean's famous "modest proposal" for eating children? Not one of these but melts at the thoughts of childhood, fondles and caresses it. Mr. Dean has no such softness, and enters the nursery with the tread and gaiety of an ogre. . . .

Amiable humourist! laughing castigator of morals! There was a process well known and practised in the Dean's gay days: when a lout entered the coffee-house, the wags proceeded to what they called "roasting" him. This is roasting a subject with a vengeance. The Dean had a native genius for it. As the *Almanach des Gourmands* says, *On naît rôtisseur.*

And it was not merely by the sarcastic method that Swift exposed the unreasonableness of loving and having children. In Gulliver, the folly of love and marriage is urged by graver arguments and advice. In the famous Lilliputian kingdom, Swift speaks with approval of the practice of instantly removing children from their parents and educating them by the State; and amongst his favourite horses, a pair of foals are stated to be the very utmost a well-regulated equine couple would permit themselves. In fact, our great satirist was of opinion that conjugal love was unadvisable, and illustrated the theory by his own practice and example—God help him— which made him about the most wretched being in God's world.

The grave and logical conduct of an absurd proposition, as exemplified in the cannibal proposal just mentioned, is our author's constant method through all his works of humour. Given a country of people six inches or sixty feet high, and by the mere process of the logic, a thousand wonderful absurdities are evolved, at so many stages of the calculation. Turning to the first minister who waited behind him with a white staff near as tall as the mainmast of the *Royal Sovereign,* the king of Brobdingnag observes how contemptible a thing human grandeur is, as represented by such a contemptible little creature as Gulliver. "The Emperor of Lilliput's features are strong and masculine (what a surprising humour there is in this description!)—the Emperor's features," Gulliver says, "are strong and masculine, with an Austrian lip, an arched nose, his complexion olive, his countenance erect, his body and limbs well-proportioned, and his deportment majestic. He is taller *by the breadth of my nail* than any of his court, which alone is enough to strike an awe into beholders."

What a surprising humour there is in these descriptions! How noble the satire is here! how just and honest! How perfect the image! Mr. Macaulay has quoted the charming lines of the poet, where the king of the pigmies is measured by the same standard. We have all read in Milton of the spear that was like "the mast of some tall admiral," but these images are surely likely to come to the comic poet originally. The subject is before him. He is turning it in a thousand ways. He is full of it. The figure suggests itself naturally to him, and comes out of his subject, as in that wonderful passage, when Gulliver's box having been dropped by the eagle into the sea, and Gulliver having been received into the ship's cabin, he calls upon the crew to bring the box into the cabin, and put it on the table, the cabin being only a quarter the size of the box. It is the *veracity* of the blunder which is so admirable. Had a man come from such a country as Brobdingnag he would have blundered so.

But the best stroke of humour, if there be a best in that abounding book, is that where Gulliver, in the unpronounceable country, describes his parting from his master the horse. "I took," he says, "a sec-

ond leave of my master, but as I was going to prostrate myself to kiss his hoof, he did me the honour to raise it gently to my mouth. I am not ignorant how much I have been censured for mentioning this last particular. Detractors are pleased to think it improbable that so illustrious a person should descend to give so great a mark of distinction to a creature so inferior as I. Neither am I ignorant how apt some travellers are to boast of extraordinary favours they have received. But if these censurers were better acquainted with the noble and courteous disposition of the Houyhnhnms they would soon change their opinion."

The surprise here, the audacity of circumstantial evidence, the astounding gravity of the speaker, who is not ignorant how much he has been censured, the nature of the favour conferred, and the respectful exultation at the receipt of it, are surely complete; it is truth topsy-turvy, entirely logical and absurd.

As for the humour and conduct of this famous fable, I suppose there is no person who reads but must admire; as for the moral, I think it horrible, shameful, unmanly, blasphemous; and giant and great as this Dean is, I say we should hoot him. Some of this audience mayn't have read the last part of Gulliver, and to such I would recall the advice of the venerable Mr. Punch to persons about to marry, and say "Don't." When Gulliver first lands among the Yahoos, the naked howling wretches clamber up trees and assault him, and he describes himself as "almost stifled with the filth which fell about him." The reader of the fourth part of *Gulliver's Travels* is like the hero himself in this instance. It is Yahoo language; a monster gibbering shrieks, and gnashing imprecations against mankind—tearing down all shreds of modesty, past all sense of manliness and shame; filthy in word, filthy in thought, furious, raging, obscene.

And dreadful it is to think that Swift knew the tendency of his creed—the fatal rocks towards which his logic desperately drifted. That last part of Gulliver is only a consequence of what has gone before; and the worthlessness of all mankind, the pettiness, cruelty, pride, imbecility, the general vanity, the foolish pretension, the mock greatness, the pompous dullness, the mean aims, the base successes—all these were present to him; it was with the din of these curses of the world, blasphemies against Heaven, shrieking in his ears, that he began to write his dreadful allegory—of which the meaning is that man is utterly wicked, desperate, and imbecile, and his passions are so monstrous, and his boasted powers so mean, that he is and deserves to be the slave of brutes, and ignorance is better than his vaunted reason. What had this man done? what secret remorse was rankling at his heart? what fever was boiling in him, that he should see all the world bloodshot? We view the world with our own eyes, each of us; and we make from within us the world we see. A weary heart gets no gladness out of sunshine; a selfish man is sceptical about friendship, as a man with no ear doesn't care for music. A frightful self-consciousness it must have been, which looked on mankind so darkly through those keen eyes of Swift.

A remarkable story is told by Scott, of Delany, who interrupted Archbishop King and Swift in a conversation which left the prelate in tears, and from which Swift rushed away with marks of strong terror and agitation in his countenance, upon which the archbishop said to Delany, "You have just met the most unhappy man on earth; but on the subject of his wretchedness you must never ask a question."

The most unhappy man on earth;— Miserrimus—what a character of him! And at this time all the great wits of England had been at his feet. All Ireland had shouted after him, and worshipped as a liberator, a saviour, the greatest Irish patriot and citizen. Dean Drapier Bickerstaff Gulliver —the most famous statesmen, and the greatest poets of his day, had applauded

him, and done him homage; and at this time writing over to Bolingbroke, from Ireland, he says, "It is time for me to have done with the world, and so I would if I could get into a better before I was called into the best, *and not to die here in a rage, like a poisoned rat in a hole.*"

We have spoken about the men, and Swift's behaviour to them; and now it behoves us not to forget that there are certain other persons in the creation who had rather intimate relations with the great Dean. Two women whom he loved and injured are known by every reader of books so familiarly that if we had seen them, or if they had been relatives of our own, we scarcely could have known them better. Who hasn't in his mind an image of Stella? Who does not love her? Fair and tender creature: pure and affectionate heart! Boots it to you, now that you have been at rest for a hundred and twenty years, not divided in death from the cold heart which caused yours, whilst it beat, such faithful pangs of love and grief—boots it to you now, that the whole world loves and deplores you? Scarce any man, I believe, ever thought of that grave, that did not cast a flower of pity on it, and write over it a sweet epitaph. Gentle lady, so lovely, so loving, so unhappy! you have had countless champions; millions of manly hearts mourning for you. From generation to generation we take up the fond tradition of your beauty; we watch and follow your tragedy, your bright morning love and purity, your constancy, your grief, your sweet martyrdom. We know your legend by heart. You are one of the saints of English story. . . .

It has been my business, professionally of course, to go through a deal of sentimental reading in my time, and to acquaint myself with love-making, as it has been described in various languages, and at various ages of the world; and I know of nothing more manly, more tender, more exquisitely touching, than some of these brief notes, written in what Swift calls "his little language" in his journal to Stella. . . . The dear eyes shine clearly upon him then—the good angel of his life is with him and blessing him. Ah, it was a hard fate that wrung from them so many tears, and stabbed pitilessly that pure and tender bosom. A hard fate: but would she have changed it? I have heard a woman say that she would have taken Swift's cruelty to have had his tenderness. He had a sort of worship for her whilst he wounded her. . . .

The love of Cadenus and Vanessa you may peruse in Cadenus's own poem on the subject, and in poor Vanessa's vehement expostulatory verses and letters to him; she adores him, implores him, admires him, thinks him something god-like, and only prays to be admitted to lie at his feet. As they are bringing him home from church, those divine feet of Dr. Swift's are found pretty often in Vanessa's parlour. He likes to be admired and adored. He finds Miss Vanhomrigh to be a woman of great taste and spirit, and beauty and wit, and a fortune too. He sees her every day; he does not tell Stella about the business: until the impetuous Vanessa becomes too fond of him, until the doctor is quite frightened by the young woman's ardour, and confounded by her warmth. He wanted to marry neither of them—that I believe was the truth; but if he had not married Stella, Vanessa would have had him in spite of himself. When he went back to Ireland, his Ariadne, not content to remain in her isle, pursued the fugitive Dean. In vain he protested, he vowed, he soothed, and bullied; the news of the Dean's marriage with Stella at last came to her, and it killed her—she died of that passion.

And when she died, and Stella heard that Swift had written beautifully regarding her, "That doesn't surprise me," said Mrs. Stella, "for we all know the Dean could write beautifully about a broomstick." A woman—a true woman! Would you have had one of them forgive the other?

In a note in his biography, Scott says that his friend Dr. Tuke, of Dublin, has a lock of Stella's hair, enclosed in a paper by Swift, on which are written in the Dean's hand, the words: "Only a woman's hair." An instance, says Scott, of the Dean's desire to veil his feelings under the mask of cynical indifference.

See the various notions of critics! Do those words indicate indifference or an attempt to hide feeling? Did you ever hear or read four words more pathetic? Only a woman's hair: only love, only fidelity, only purity, innocence, beauty; only the tenderest heart in the world stricken and wounded, and passed away now out of reach of pangs of hope deferred, love insulted, and pitiless desertion:—only that lock of hair left; and memory and remorse, for the guilty, lonely wretch, shuddering over the grave of his victim.

And yet to have had so much love, he must have given some. Treasures of wit and wisdom, and tenderness, too, must that man have had locked up in the caverns of his gloomy heart, and shown fitfully to one or two whom he took in there. But it was not good to visit that place. People did not remain there long, and suffered for having been there. He shrank away from all affections sooner or later. Stella and Vanessa both died near him, and away from him. He had not heart enough to see them die. He broke from his fastest friend, Sheridan; he slunk away from his fondest admirer, Pope. His laugh jars on one's ear after seven score years. He was always alone— alone and gnashing in the darkness, except when Stella's sweet smile came and shone upon him. When that went, silence and utter night closed over him. An immense genius: an awful downfall and ruin. So great a man he seems to me that thinking of him is like thinking of an empire falling. We have other great names to mention— none I think, however, so great or so gloomy.

W. B. C. Watkins

Absent Thee from Felicity

THE felicity of the complacent Englishman sitting down in pleasant anticipation to a hearty British breakfast Swift punctures by laying beside his plate, instead of the Tory paper, a *Modest Proposal.* I am taking his own definition from the *Tale of a Tub:* "the sublime and refined point of felicity, called the possession of being well-deceived; the serene peaceful state of being a fool among knaves." In this sense, the line from *Hamlet.* "Absent thee from felicity awhile," may be called the essential purpose of all Swift's satire.

I chose this title, however, not to play on the sense of a word, but to indicate a close resemblance. If asked to consider Swift in the light of Shakespeare, many would probably think at once of the bitterly satirical play *Troilus and Cressida* or the invective and misanthropy of *Timon of Athens.* Swift has much more in common with Hamlet than with Thersites or Timon; in many respects his problem is identically the problem of Hamlet, though he had no Ghost to give him injunctions, no uncle-father to kill.

Swift's melancholia is the melancholia of Hamlet, and its root is very much the same—a dichotomy of personality expressing itself in an abnormal sensitivity to the disparity between the world as it should be and the world as one sees it. This theme is not limited in Shakespeare's plays to *Hamlet;* it recurs so frequently that, without falling into dangerous speculation about Shakespeare the man, we can certainly in all safety say that it is a theme which interested him profoundly and over a period of years. "Hyperion to a satyr" is clearly a principal motive of *Hamlet.* The same disparity is implicit in the bitter contrast in *Lear:*

> Thou art a lady:
> If only to go warm were gorgeous . . .

and

> Thou art the thing itself; unaccommodated man is no more but such a poor, bare, forked animal as thou art.

It is again implicit in the *Tempest:*

> Miranda: O brave new world
>   That has such people in't!
> Prospero: 'Tis new to thee.

Its most perfect and complete expression, however, is to be found in Hamlet's speech of ironic and tragic disillusion:

> What a piece of work is a man! how noble in reason! how infinite in faculties! in form and moving how express and admirable! in action how like an angel! in apprehension how like a god! the beauty of the world, the paragon of animals! And yet to me what is this quintessence of dust?

He has lost faith in the Renaissance conception of the individual of noble potentialities. Idealization breaks down under criticism.

It may be objected that while in *Hamlet* this disintegration of the ideal is clear enough, in Swift the idealization itself is not strikingly apparent. This objection I shall attempt to answer later, at this point merely recalling Swift's extraordinary idealization of two men, Harley and St. John. His passionate loyalty to these two and his devotion even after the débâcle

Reprinted from *Perilous Balance: The Tragic Genius of Swift, Johnson, and Sterne,* Princeton, 1939, Chapter I, by permission of the Princeton University Press. Notes have been omitted without notice.

represent a tragedy of friendship too deep
for tears.

When we turn to the other side of the
picture, no one, certainly, can deny the
identity of such sentiments as these from
Hamlet:

> What should such fellows as I do, crawling be-
> tween earth and heaven? . . . Use every man
> after his desert, and who should scape whipping?

and Swift's

> I cannot but conclude the bulk of your natives
> to be the most pernicious race of little odious
> vermin that nature ever suffered to crawl upon
> the surface of the earth.

Disillusioned idealism is, of course, the
state of mind which usually generates the
satiric spirit. Mr. Willey puts the case succinctly: "The temper which views all things
in their theory rather than in their historical setting must also see little, as it gazes
upon human institutions, but failure and
futility, and as it contemplates human actions, little but departures from the rational norm." This "temper" of Mr. Willey's at times goes beyond satire and produces tragedy, especially if the "rational
norm" is passionately idealized; specifically, it produces the tragedy of Hamlet and
Swift. I do not refer merely to the tragedy
of Swift's life, but to definite satirical
works of his which are tragic in tone and
import.

Since satire by its very nature is akin to
comedy, we should expect to find our parallel to Swift in that type of comedy which
is so highly charged, so deeply moving and
serious that it approaches tragedy. About
this serious comedy Mr. Dobrée writes:
"The greatest comedy seems inevitably to
deal with the disillusion of mankind. . . .
It comes when the positive attitude has
failed, when doubt is creeping in to under-
mine values, and men are turning for comfort to the very ruggedness of life, and
laughing in the face of it all." Mr. Eliot
has maintained that the *Jew of Malta*, and
Mr. Shaw that *Coriolanus* are comedies in

this sense. Other instances which have
been cited are *Volpone*, the *Plain Dealer*,
and *Measure for Measure*. Undoubtedly
Swift's satire has a certain relationship to
these plays; but it is *relationship*, not identity—the relationship, say, of *Hamlet* to
Measure for Measure. Swift's true affinity
is with the type of complex tragedy of
which Shakespeare is the greatest exponent.

Writing before the days when strict decorum dominated, Shakespeare admitted
into his great tragedies not only broad
comedy but other discordant elements in-
conceivable in the tragedies of Corneille,
Racine, or even Dryden. The introduction
of the realistic strain of Enobarbus into
Antony and Cleopatra, with his running
cynical comment on the great love affair,
is an instance. *Hamlet* is the supreme
example of this complexity of treatment,
which involves shifting of focus, both in
dramatic milieu and in characterization.

The world of comedy is usually one of
everyday, normal reality; the world of
heroic tragedy is *imaginatively* real but
heightened. Shakespeare includes both. He
intensifies the horror of his tragedy by
glimpses into the world of everyday—that
is, the world of comedy. In the third scene
of the first act of *Hamlet* the very normality
of the warm affection and banter of the
Ophelia-Polonius-Laertes relationship acquires a certain horror from its context,
its violent contrast with the enveloping
gloom. On the Elizabethan stage it is only
a split second between Ophelia's dutiful,
"I shall obey, my lord," and Hamlet's
opening speech of the next scene, "The air
bites shrewdly; it is very cold," reassert-
ing the tragic atmosphere. Swift likewise
combines the everyday world with the abnormal one of his imagination:

> When I thought of my family, my friends, my
> countrymen [all perfectly wholesome, everyday
> people] . . . I considered them as they really
> were, *Yahoos* in shape and disposition. . . .
> As soon as I entered the house, my wife took
> me in her arms, and kissed me [again the most
> natural scene in the world]; at which, having not

been used to the touch of that odious animal for so many years, I fell in a swoon for almost an hour.

The final effect in both instances is the same: the tragedy becomes more horrible as it is thus made to appear not the exceptional but the normal. Just as the normal household of Polonius is sucked into the tragic world of death, so Swift eventually completely identifies Gulliver's English home with a Yahoo burrow.

Comedy is concerned primarily with man's limitations, tragedy with his potentialities. Shakespeare in *Hamlet* and Swift in *Gulliver's Travels* insist on man's limitations, yet in the very vehemence of denial show an acute awareness of his potentialities. In *Hamlet* the coarse, the brutal elements in the hero's character are at times definitely stressed; the complexity of his mind, his critical self-consciousness are the very substance of the play.

Mr. Aldous Huxley remarks that "the same situation may often be either tragic or comic, according as it is seen through the eyes of those who suffer or those who look on. (Shift the point of vision a little and Macbeth could be paraphrased as a roaring farce.)" In *Hamlet* Shakespeare forestalls Mr. Huxley. The "point of vision" is intentionally shifted by the main character, who frequently sees himself and all that concerns him critically, unsympathetically, objectively. Hamlet is not only intensely aware of his own faults; he is even aware that the hugger-mugger funeral of his father and hasty marriage of his mother are comical:

> Thrift, thrift, Horatio! The funeral bak'd meats
> Did coldly furnish forth the marriage tables.

Though there is this shift in focus, the "objectivity" is Hamlet's objectification; we never really lose his point of view. The very genuine, if macabre and ironic, comic element is entirely *subsumed* to the tragic, and merely intensifies, instead of distracts from our sympathy with Hamlet's suffering.

That similar complications arise in the development of satire has long been recognized. The phrase "tragical satire" as opposed to "comical" is used by Dryden to mark the distinction between Juvenal and Horace. Dryden also insists that "the end or scope of satire is to purge the passions," accepting this element of Heinsius' definition as being peculiarly applicable to the satires of Juvenal and Persius. He feels rightly the appropriateness of the Aristotelian terminology because of the distinct similarity between some types of satire and tragedy.

Except for mild, good-natured satire like Addison's, which Dryden would have called "raillery," the satirist lashes his fellows from the vantage point of at least implied superiority. With Voltaire, for instance, possibly excepting parts of *Candide*, there is little personal involvement; his cynicism is on the surface, largely exasperation with intellects less acute and supple than his own. But Swift, like Hamlet, is very much personally involved; he lashes first himself. The comparative objectivity and dispassionateness of the *First Voyage* disappear as we progress through *Gulliver's Travels*. When this self-laceration has no suspicion of professional pose, no suspicion of superiority; when it becomes intense and terrible suffering—then the satire which it produces becomes in a real sense tragedy, and, like Elizabethan tragedy, its only solution is death.

II

By the time of Queen Anne, tragedy as a dramatic form had been dissipated in heroic unrealities, and later in vain efforts by writers who felt its lost vitality as a form to revivify it and to seek new directions for the tragic impulse. Such tragedies as Dryden's *All for Love*, Congreve's *Mourning Bride*, Otway's *Venice Preserved* are in their way poetic and fine but anemic and moribund. Realistic tragedy was a possible refuge; but plays like the *London Merchant* are no real substitute for Elizabethan tragedy in power and scope. The nearest equivalent in the Augustan Age to expression of the most profound sense of tragedy, expressed by the Elizabethans in drama, is not to be found in the work of the dramatists, but at times in Pope, primarily in Swift, though neither ever wrote tragedy in dramatic form. Apart from the disintegration of tragedy as a form, of the men of his age Swift alone had the emotional and imaginative power of the great Elizabethans, and he wrote prose like a poet. This explains the arresting and moving quality of his prose, its extraordinary intensity.

Swift's own definition of style is familiar: "Proper words in proper places." Perhaps Coleridge in *Table Talk* had this in mind when he makes his distinction: "Prose = words in their best order; poetry the best words in the best order." Swift's characteristically laconic statement, however, does not do full justice to his prose style, nor does Coleridge's definition— even if we apply the second half to Swift, "the best words in the best order." Without attempting a complex analysis of Swift's style, I wish to emphasize a few elements, primarily his use of language, which contribute to the tragic effect of his best satire.

Swift is deservedly famous for his clarity, a clarity of style that at times, like Arnold's, conceals a muddiness of thought. But the most remarkable thing about his prose is that he uses words like a poet; and like a poet he achieves at his best an astounding compression and intensity of feeling, partly owing to his creative use, the poet's power to make old familiar words say new things or to revitalize them so that they acquire freshness of meaning. His language is never faded or dead; nor does he, like some writers of so-called "poetic" prose, ever resort to tumidity or elaborately calculated rhythms. His style, usually unadorned and colloquial but with occasional admixture of richer elements, is comparable in effect to some of Donne's poetry or to Shakespeare's. For example:

O, there has been much throwing about of brains.

Now boast thee, death, in thy possession lies
A lass unparallel'd.

When she (poor hen), fond of no second brood
Has cluck'd thee to the wars.

I wonder by my troth, what thou, and I
Did, till we lov'd? were we not wean'd till then?

Compare (in respect merely to verbal choice and vitality) these with Swift:

Whoever has an ambition to be heard in a crowd, must press, and squeeze, and thrust, and climb, with indefatigable pains, till he has exalted himself to a certain degree of altitude above them.

Last week I saw a woman flayed, and you will hardly believe how much it altered her person for the worse.

In this last instance, of course, the dramatic shock of the fact understated is largely responsible for the effect, but both quotations show Swift's genius for making simple, homely words tingle with imaginative power and intensity of feeling. Like Shakespeare and Donne, he knew the effectiveness of mingling unusual and simple words —*indefatigable, exalted, altitude,* for instance, in sharp contrast to *squeeze* and *thrust.*

More important, like those two earlier poets, he uses almost invariably highly figurative language and has an astonishing way of bringing out the latent figurative element in the most ordinary words. His meaning is conveyed to us largely by means of images which imprint themselves on our mind's eye with dramatic vividness. This explains the sense of life and movement in the first of the two sentences quoted above. An even better instance is to be found in *Abolishing Christianity:*

. . . the chaffering with dissenters . . . is but like opening a few wickets, and leaving them at jar, by which no more than one can get in at a time, and that, not without stooping, and sideling, and squeezing his body,

Swift is here concerned with his opposition to the repeal of the Test Act and to any compromise with the dissenters.

Chaffer shows his instinctive choice of the figurative word; it has not even yet lost its Old English meaning of actually going to market, with all the implications of gesture and haggling which bargaining entails. Likewise, *wicket* means not simply a small door, but a small door *inside a larger gate*, the opening of which would be necessary really to allow entrance to the pressing throng. When one adds the vivid descriptive words, *stooping, sideling, squeezing*, the sense of pressure is increased by the feeling of actual physical effort. Thus the inner meaning of the sentence is dramatized into a scene and brought sharply home to us, as is the poet's wont, by intensely vivid concrete images of men leaning over a large gate, gesticulating and driving a hard bargain with the throng outside, only a few of whom are allowed with much awkwardness and concentrated effort to squeeze through the little wicket. On the emotional level, Swift's feeling about the repeal of the Test Act is conveyed in the absurdity of the whole scene—proceeding from the action itself, and from the connotation of undignified and ridiculous behavior in such words as *chaffer, sidle,* and *squeeze.* The rich compression and complexity of this sentence would require for complete understanding as full an analysis as a poem.

Of all Shakespeare's characters, we feel most quickly Hamlet's force and personality, because of his supreme power of language. His opening aside is immediately arresting and his next few speeches complete the impression:

King: But now, my cousin Hamlet, and my son—
Hamlet: (Aside) *A little more than kin, and less than kind!*
King: How is it that the clouds still hang on you?
Hamlet: *Not so, my lord. I am too much i' th' sun.*
Queen: Good Hamlet, cast thy nighted colour off,

And let thine eye look like a friend on Denmark.
Do not for ever with thy vailed lids
Seek for thy noble father in the dust.
Thou know'st 'tis common. All that lives must die,
Passing through nature to eternity.
Hamlet: *Ay, madam, it is common.*
Queen: If it be,
Why seems it so particular with thee?
Hamlet: *Seems, madam? Nay, it is. I know not "seems."*

So, in the space of thirteen lines, only four his own speaking, Hamlet's personality has seized our imagination. Swift at his best has this same electric quality, this same immediacy of imaginative appeal. Take the brilliant opening of the *Modest Proposal,* or the opening of *Abolishing Christianity:*

I am very sensible what a weakness and presumption it is, to reason against the general humour and disposition of the world. I remember it was with great justice, and a due regard to the freedom both of the public and the press, forbidden upon several penalties to write, or discourse, or lay wagers against the Union, even before it was confirmed by parliament, because that was looked upon as a design, to oppose the current of the people, which, besides the folly of it, *is a manifest breach of the fundamental law that makes this majority of opinion the voice of God.*

In two sentences he has our attention in a vice, riveted fast by the imaginative impact of the final phrase. A passage like this has something of the breathtaking quality which one finds in Hamlet's opening speeches, or in such opening lines of Donne's as:

Busie old foole, unruly Sunne,
Why dost thou thus,
Through windowes, and through curtaines call on us?

For Godsake hold your tongue, and let me love.

This skill in handling emotion without letting it slip the leash and in achieving without strain concentrated imaginative power is admirably controlled, whence proceeds the extraordinary fusion of emotion, imagination, and intellect in Swift's best work. Let us take first an example in a vein of light, satiric comedy, which shows the ease and control, this sense of real poetry to be found in his prose. I have chosen the familiar episode of the spider and the bee, one of the two superlative fables in English literature. Few passages show more clearly the imaginative quality, the ease and flexibility of Swift's style, moulding itself perfectly to the shifting play of his mind. The mock-heroic is achieved with none of the sense of strain that occasionally mars even the *Rape of the Lock*. It is perfectly echoed in the shift from homely, colloquial words to more grandiose expression. Furthermore, in this fable Swift achieves a rapid imaginative change in scale from grandeur and distance to nearby littleness which surpasses Rossetti's attempt at much the same effect in the expansion and contraction of space in his *Blessed Damozel*. Swift begins by focusing on the corner of a window:

Things were at this crisis, when a material accident fell out. For, upon the highest corner of a large window, there dwelt a certain spider, swollen up to the first magnitude by the destruction of infinite numbers of flies—*now, with this stylistic transition in vocabulary ("magnitude," "infinite," and later, "avenue," "palisado," "constable," "port," "sally"), observe the shift in scale, carrying us completely into another world, though of course we do not forget the spider, and so the result is something of a double exposure*—whose spoils lay scattered before the gates of his palace, like human bones before the cave of some giant. The avenues to his castle were guarded with turnpike and palisadoes, all after the modern way of fortification. After you had passed several courts you came to the centre, wherein you might behold the constable himself in his own lodgings, which had windows fronting to each avenue, and ports to sally out, upon all occasions of prey or defence.—*Now the shift back to the window corner*—In this mansion he had for some time dwelt in peace and plenty, without danger to his person by swallows from above, or to his palace, by brooms from below; when it

was the pleasure of fortune to conduct thither a wandering bee, to whose curiosity a broken pane in the glass had discovered itself, and in he went; —*a phrase that comes in its eloquent context with a sharp and descriptive dramatic thrust*— where, expatiating a while—*the intentional echo of Milton reverting to the mock-heroic*—he at last happened to alight upon one of the outward walls of the spider's citadel; which, yielding to the unequal weight, sunk down to the very foundation. Thrice he endeavoured to force his passage, and thrice the centre shook. The spider within, feeling the terrible convulsion, supposed at first that nature was approaching her final dissolution; or else, that Beelzebub, with all his legions, was come to revenge the death of many thousands of his subjects, whom his enemy had slain and devoured.

Swift continues in this key for a few more sentences; then suddenly we are plunged into Restoration Comedy:

"A plague split you," said he, "for a giddy son of a whore! Is it you, with a vengeance, that have made this litter here? Could not you look before you, and be d——d? Do you think I have nothing else to do (in the devil's name) but to mend and repair after your arse?"—"Good words, friend," said the bee (having now pruned himself, and being disposed to droll), "I'll give you my hand and word to come near your kennel—*it was "palace" before*—no more; I was never in such a confounded pickle since I was born."

Within the space of one paragraph, with consummate skill Swift has fused into mock-heroic comedy the heroic feudal castle of giants, a domestic incident, insect encounter and fable, Miltonic echoes, and the dialogue of Etherege and Congreve; and the fusion of all these disparate elements is perfect. This imaginative complexity, achieved with such ease, shows his control over language.

The most brilliant single sentence in all Swift's satires is in the *Modest Proposal* where he digresses for a paragraph on the aged and diseased of Ireland:

But I am not in the least pain upon that matter, because it is very well known, that they are every day dying, and rotting, by cold, and famine, and filth, and vermin, as fast as can be reasonably expected.

". . . dying, and rotting, by cold, and famine, and filth, and vermin." Each adjective and noun has packed into it the intensity of emotion and imagination of Claudio's speech in *Measure for Measure*:

> Ay, but to die, and go we know not where;
> To lie in cold obstruction and to rot. . . .

This is what I mean by Swift's using words like a poet, creatively, vitalizing them in some inexplicable way. The word in the above sentence which is the masterstroke is the perfect thrust, cutting several ways, of *reasonably* in the final phrase—"as fast as can be reasonably expected." That one word in its context epitomizes and pillories the attitude Swift is exposing. Could compression go further? Pope, who is the only Augustan to rival Swift in imagination and skill in use of language, achieves a less brilliant but somewhat comparable power in his *Characters of Women*, in a line consisting of four adjectives and a conjunction:

> Alive, ridiculous, and dead, forgot.

It is not in his mastery of language alone that Swift writes prose like a poet. His persistent use of imagery is often strongly reminiscent of Shakespeare's, which has been so exhaustively studied recently by Miss Spurgeon, Mr. Knight, and others. We have already seen how he evokes the maximum imagistic element in even the most ordinary words; he goes further—he uses repetitive imagery symbolically. Like Shakespeare, he must have been unusually sensitive to smell. To take one simple instance, recall how persistently in conveying imaginatively an aristocratic scorn of the mob, particularly in the Roman plays, Shakespeare resorts to smell:

> Nor, showing (as the manner is) his wounds
> To th' people, beg their stinking breaths.

> . . . the mutable, rank-scented meiny. . . .

> . . . In their thick breaths,
> Rank of gross diet, shall we be enclouded,
> And forc'd to drink their vapour.

Swift uses the same device frequently:

> To this end I have some time since, with a world of pains and art, dissected the carcase of human nature, and read many useful lectures upon the several parts, both containing and contained: till at last it smelt so strong I could preserve it no longer.

> Accost the hole of another kennel, first stopping your nose, you will behold a surly, gloomy, nasty, slovenly mortal, raking in his own dung, and dabbling in his urine.

In the first of these instances, by the smell of putrefaction in a corpse he wishes to convey, as a poet would convey, his opinion of the rottenness of human nature; in the second the bad smell is intended to express his opinion of the Royal College of Physicians. Swift uses this device again in the *Second Voyage of Gulliver*, where he speaks in such repulsive terms of the breasts of the Brobdingnagian nurse and the offensive smell of the Maids of Honour; but most extensively and successfully, as we shall see later, in the *Fourth Voyage*.

The result of this poetic use of imagery in Shakespeare and Swift is an intensity of loathing. Both transfer outraged spiritual and ethical values into retching physical terms. At times the transference is too successful and we experience only the physical nausea; but when the balance is kept the result is strikingly and immediately effective.

It is this essentially poetic treatment of Swift's—his marvellous word sense, his ability at compression both of meaning and emotion, his resort to imagery used symbolically as well as concretely—which explains to a large extent the depth and power of his best satire, and which carries him into tragedy when he attempts to convey, as Shakespeare does in *Hamlet,* a profound and tragic disillusionment with himself and with all life.

III

Let us examine more closely the essential nature of this tragic disillusionment. We may best approach it through *Hamlet*, but always bearing Swift in mind.

Why is Hamlet so much occupied with the bestial? Already supersensitive to the animal nature of man, he does not have time to recover from the rude shock of his father's mortality before his mother's incest is a stench in his nostrils. In *Measure for Measure* Shakespeare chooses sex as the common denominator, bringing high and low—Isabellas, Angelos, Claudios, Pompeys, Lucios, and Overdones—to one focal point, thus simplifying a complex problem. So in *Hamlet* sex becomes the symbol of man's decay and corruption. Unfortunately, to Swift also sex, particularly woman, despite his deep love and friendship for individual women, is a symbol of man's bestiality. He victimizes woman by his own secret overidealization of her. His cruelty to Varina, Stella, Vanessa is the cruelty of Hamlet to Gertrude and Ophelia. Donne can at times revile his mistress in rank terms and still love her. Swift becomes obsessed by the morbidly physical, as we see in the *Progress of Beauty, Cassinus and Peter,* the *Lady's Dressing Room,* and in *Gulliver's Travels,* to such an extent that he cannot readjust the balance. We need not inquire into the secret experiences of his own life, but the result is plain. The chasm between spirit and flesh he cannot bridge, for flesh has become for him unclean.

The extent of this extreme disillusion, this revulsion from anything physical while still being morbidly attracted by it is largely owing to his having, like Hamlet, a "wit diseased." Hamlet transfers his hatred of his mother's sin to Ophelia, and, with his unhappy faculty of generalization, to all womankind. Each is betrayed by the very intensity of his own imagination, especially where anything physical is concerned. When Isabella, in the superb prison scene with her brother, her mind consumed

by Angelo's infamous proposal, bursts out:

> Dost thou think, Claudio?
> If I would yield him my virginity,
> Thou mightst be freed.
> . . . . . . This night's the time
> That I should do what I abhor to name . . .

we feel that the passionate intensity behind her words is partly owing to her imagination's having been at work picturing the darkness of that very night, the whispered secrecy, the little wicket gate opening upon physical violation. The shrinking of an overfastidious nature becomes torment when the scene between Hamlet and Gertrude reveals the images in which her deed is constantly present to his mind. Probably Swift could not always keep Celia from his thoughts while he was with Stella or Vanessa.

By the very nature of his mental obsession Hamlet becomes gradually sullied. He is perfectly aware of it, yet helpless to resist the slow corroding acid eating into his own purity and idealism. Thus the scene between him and Ophelia, which begins almost in the key of Lear's

> Thou art a soul in bliss; but I am bound
> Upon a wheel of fire . . .

changes key for Hamlet, because even the soul in bliss shows the taint of his bad dreams; the Ophelia of "Nymph, in thy orisons be all my sins remember'd" is only a passing hallucination. Ophelia's tender speech when she returns his gifts cuts him two ways, with the remembrance of those irrevocably past moments of untroubled love and with the unbearable suspicion of her hypocrisy. "Ha, ha! Are you honest?" His pun on *honest* symbolizes the duality and sends him off into the bitter cynicism of "I am myself indifferent honest . . . better my mother had not borne me. . ." to the final hysteria of "no moe marriages."

For Hamlet the tragedy, to a large extent, is this very inability, despite perfect awareness, to resist the surrender to his innate brutality, coarseness, and sense of ugliness—the complements to his noble qualities. Spiritually, he is in some ways a cornered animal. The result is bitter self-reproach, self-satire, agony of soul, with consequent lashing out in self-defense at all about him—Claudius, Gertrude, Polonius, Ophelia, Rosencrantz, Guildenstern, Osric—turning on them and on himself the tragic light of truth, which no man can bear because its intensity shrivels him to nothingness or worse. And the satirical reason, in the light of this revelation, negates not only man's finest dreams, but life itself. "A terrible thing is intelligence," says Unamuno; "it tends to death as memory tends to stability."

The process is much the same with Swift. He is intensely conscious of the bestial *and* the spiritual; totally unable to achieve unity, he becomes, like Hamlet, victim of his own aspiration and satirical reason, convulsed, as we see most clearly in the *Fourth Voyage of Gulliver*, by the shirt of Nessus. I say "satirical reason" because intellect is at once the motivating force and principal weapon of satire. Intellect is a two-edged sword.

Swift never wrote so feelingly or imaginatively of "this intellectual being," "those thoughts that wander through eternity" "still climbing after knowledge infinite" as did Marlowe, Shakespeare, Milton, because the vision of man "how noble in reason, how infinite in faculty" was fading for the Augustans as well as for Hamlet. Still, to Dryden, Pope, and Swift reason was not merely a necessity; it was an ideal. We today who are inclined to be out of sympathy with them too frequently dismiss this preoccupation as a cold rationalism, arid, rigid, abstract; therefore, among other liabilities, the deadly enemy of poetry. Yet, the more we study these men and seek to understand them, the more we are struck by the frequent irrationality of their so-called rationalism. Many of these "rationalists" were seemingly blind to their own illogic. Pope's refuge in Warburton's de-

fense of his *Essay on Man* is typical. Swift's beautiful displays of illogical logic are other examples. Johnson, of them all, though not the most brilliant, was the most truly rational.

To most of them reason was a not clearly defined, not perhaps fully understood, but passionately believed in ideal. It was in a sense the last refuge for the nobility of man in a world of closing horizons, a world becoming thoroughly small and dry. Consider the progression from Marlowe to Milton to Dryden to Swift and Pope. We can see the change from the Renaissance conception in these lines from *Religio Laici*:

Dim, as the borrow'd beams of Moon and Stars
To lonely, weary, wandring Travelers
Is Reason to the Soul: And as on high
Those rowling Fires discover but the Sky
Not light us here; So Reason's glimmering Ray
Was lent, not to assure our doubtfull way,
But guide us upward to a better day.

Think of these lines in the light of Marlowe and Milton, for whom intellect springs upward like a pyramid of fire. This is, of course, an extreme instance; Dryden elsewhere and Pope almost invariably speak of the efficacy of Reason with more confidence. Again, Dryden's humorous lines in *Mac Flecknoe*:

Some Beams of Wit on other souls may fall,
Strike through and make a lucid intervall;
But Shadwell's genuine night admits no ray,
His rising Fogs prevail upon the Day

have an undercurrent of serious implication, which becomes clearly apparent in the closing lines of that greater poem suggested by *Mac Flecknoe:*

Lo! thy dread Empire, CHAOS! is restored;
Light dies before thy uncreating word;
Thy hand, great Anarch! lets the curtain fall,
And universal Darkness buries All.

It is not in a spirit of satirical burlesque that Pope here reverses Milton's light that

at the voice
Of God, as with a Mantle didst invest
The rising world of waters dark and deep,
Won from the void and formless infinite.

He is reversing the process of creation in a spirit of real tragedy, for to Pope, much more than to Dryden, the eclipse of Reason by Dulness is tragic. At this point his mock-heroic becomes truly heroic, and the allusion is not parody but is in the same emotional and imaginative key as Milton.

Even Johnson shows this demand for an ideal world of "reasonable beings." But Johnson recognizes clearly the nature of the world around him and finally, reluctantly, accepts it fully, even in theory. Though he also suffers from melancholia, he has too sane a head and too much will power to be completely a Hamlet. Throttling his protest, he abandons his ideal for the pessimistic reality of *Rasselas*.

Swift certainly shares this idealistic, deeply emotional devotion to Reason. In the words of a later Irishman, W. B. Yeats, "Every writer, even every small writer, who has belonged to the great tradition, has had his dream of an impossibly noble life, and the greater he is the more does it seem to plunge him into some beautiful or bitter reverie." We are liable to lose sight of the beauty of Swift's reverie in its passionate bitterness.

The exact nature of his conception of Reason is difficult to determine. Mr. Quintana considers that 1) revealed religion and 2) *man's apprehension of God through reason* are the two bases of Swift's religion, insofar as it was intellectually defined by him. But Swift's conception of Reason is twofold. Without understanding that clearly, we are faced with the dilemma of a man who is at once a worshiper of Reason and an antirationalist.

Among the ideal Houyhnhnms Reason is not a point problematical as with us, where men can argue with plausibility on both sides of the question; but strikes you with immediate conviction; as it must needs do where it is not mingled, obscured, or discoloured by passion and interest.

In this sense, it would seem that Reason is itself actually a *revelation*—"strikes you with immediate conviction"—completely independent of intellectual argument or logic. Perhaps it would be safer to say that Reason is the faculty in man which enables God to reveal religion to him. In Swift's conception, then, this highest, purest aspect of Reason is really intuition; it is above and distinct from what we should ordinarily regard as intellectual processes. It is only reason in its lower manifestation, "discoloured by passion and interest," which resorts to argument for its own sake or private purpose. Reason as an intuitive faculty Swift worships; it alone "is sufficient to govern a rational creature," he says in his *Fourth Voyage*. His anti-intellectualism is his attack on the lower, impure manifestation, the "discursive reason." Man, unlike the Houyhnhnms, is not a "rational" (intuitive) creature, only *rationis capax*—potentially intuitive, but in actual practice capable merely of rationalizing his self-interest, his very vices. The dichotomy of spirit and flesh is thus reflected for Swift in pure and impure reason, the latter completely dominated by the flesh, the former a faculty of the soul.

Despite Mr. Leslie's contention, Swift had a soul. Possibly Mr. Eliot is right in calling it "an impure soul"; but it was a soul which must have vibrated in sympathy with Dryden's poetic tribute to Reason, with Pope's portrayal of disintegration, even more so with Hamlet's beautiful and ironical reduction to the quintessence of dust. For the clearest evidence of this, let us turn to the *Fourth Voyage of Gulliver*, which is Swift's *Hamlet*, though conceived and written perhaps more in the spirit of *King Lear*.

IV

The *Fourth Voyage* is an uncomfortable thing to study and to explain. It is, in a sense, an artistic failure, but a magnificent one. Is it, after all is said, possible to perceive a perfect artistic success in the grander work, *King Lear?* However that may be, readers invariably turn back with relief to the more assured, more finished, but far less profound and powerful *First Voyage.*

Mr. Quintana's critical remarks on *Gulliver's Travels* are excellent, though I do not agree with all of them or with his final interpretation. Mr. Quintana, however, is an exception; it is Mr. Eddy who crystallizes general academic opinion. After his analytic summary he remarks, "someone has blundered and I fear me it is Swift." Why? Primarily: there is little common sense here or even much appearance of it; the Houyhnhnms are merely grotesque; there are inconsistencies; there is extreme coarseness and brutality; finally, the indictment is too sweeping and scathing for credence.

There is certainly much truth in these criticisms, but they are the result of judging the *Fourth Voyage* exclusively in the light of the other three. The *Fourth Voyage* is actually quite different in scope, in intent, in tone. We can understand it better by taking a completely different approach. No doubt Swift planned and set out to write this voyage in the spirit of the rest, but he broke the shackles of his scheme. The result is unevenness of tone and a certain number of inconsistencies. For instance, according to his original scheme, Gulliver was probably meant to portray average man, who was to be thrown in relief against the two opposite extremes, reasoning beings and sheer animal nature. The Yahoos were to represent mankind only in his animal aspects, in a state of degradation. As Swift proceeded, however, he tended more and more to identify absolutely mankind and the Yahoos. What else can be inferred from the female Yahoo's falling violently in love with Gulliver and attacking him while he is bathing? What else is meant by such a passage as this:

When I thought of my family, my friends, my countrymen, or human race in general, I con-

sidered them as they really were, *Yahoos* in shape and disposition, perhaps a little more civilized, and qualified with the gift of speech, but making no other use of reason, than to improve and multiply those vices, whereof their brethren in this country had only the share that nature allotted them. When I happened to behold the reflection of my own form in a lake or fountain, I turned away my face in horror and detestation of myself. . . .

When Mr. Quintana insists that this complete identification was not Swift's intention, he is probably right to the extent that Swift did not *originally* plan for the voyage to turn out quite this way. But when Mr. Quintana dismisses the complete identification as merely a failure in artistry, I cannot agree. The important thing is that, whether against or with his will, Swift completely identifies man with Yahoo, and the identification has the power of tragic conviction. Possibly Shakespeare in *Lear* originally intended the tragedy of a grand old mythical king. As it is, the actual story and situations of that plot crack beneath the strain of the profound tragic feeling which it expresses. This is also true, to a less conspicuous extent, of *Hamlet.*

Bearing this in mind, let us examine more specifically the objections to the *Fourth Voyage* summarized by Mr. Eddy. First, its unreasonableness. Swift's usual satirical method is that of a devastating logic, but in a curious way. He more frequently gives an appearance of logic than actual logic—even logic on the basis of a preposterous major premise. Fundamentally, his reasoning is emotional, however cleverly he may mask it as superb common sense. Digressions are really an essential part of him, because his mind is the sort that kindles to an idea, then plays about it in flashes of lightning, like Donne with his metaphysical conceits. In the *Fourth Voyage,* unlike the first, he is not being rationally satirical most of the time, because here he is treating not incidental problems of human life, but the very core of his belief— the dichotomy, beast and reason in man.

His intense worship of reason combines here with the terrible disillusion of reason to produce a powerful emotional conviction in which common sense has no place.

The Yahoos are a disgusting incarnation of bestiality. They are Hamlet's "beast that wants discourse of reason." In the repeated imagery of excrement and filth Swift is not indulging in mere sensationalism; he is employing a poetic device used, among others, by Shakespeare, Spenser, Donne, and Milton. Are his Yahoos really more revolting than the portrayal of Error or the unmasking of Duessa? Is he less justifiable than Donne in such lines as

> Ranke sweaty froth thy Mistresse's brow defiles,
> Like spermatique issue of ripe menstruous boiles?

Are Swift's intentions less commendable than Shakespeare's in having Hamlet describe Gertrude and Claudius

> In the rank sweat of an enseamed bed,
> Stew'd in corruption, honeying and making love
> Over the nasty sty?

They are not, if we consider what despair and loathing of outraged sensitivity caused them.

The Houyhnhnms are not so successful an imaginative creation as the Yahoos, one must admit. A symbol of ideal perfection is more difficult, and Swift became entangled in the method of realistic narrative which he had used so brilliantly with the Lilliputians and Brobdingnagians. His marvellous skill in invention fails to make the horses convincing; they become at times ridiculous in a way which Swift could hardly have intended. But the satirical conception of prostrating man to kiss the hoof of the horse has its points.

It is this partial failure with the Houyhnhnms which blinds us to the magnificently conceived and executed finale to the *Fourth Voyage*, which portrays Gulliver as inconsolable at leaving the Houyhnhnms:

> When all was ready, and the day came for my departure, I took leave of my master and lady, and the whole family, my eyes flowing with tears, and my heart quite sunk with grief. . . .

> My design was, if possible, to discover some small island uninhabited, yet sufficient by my labour to furnish me with the necessaries of life, which I would have thought a greater happiness than to be first minister in the politest court of Europe; so horrible was the idea I conceived of returning to live in the society and under the government of *Yahoos*. For in such solitude as I desired, I could at least enjoy my own thoughts, and reflect with delight on the virtues of those inimitable Houyhnhnms, without any opportunity of degenerating into the vices and corruptions of my own species.

Finally, after sundry adventures with natives, Gulliver is picked up by a Portuguese ship:

> . . . I remained silent and sullen; I was ready to faint at the very smell of him and his men. . . . I would not undress myself, but lay on the bed-clothes, and in half an hour stole out, when I thought the crew was at dinner, and getting to the side of the ship was going to leap into the sea, and swim for my life, rather than continue among *Yahoos*. . . .

> As soon as I entered the house, my wife took me in her arms, and kissed me; at which, having not been used to the touch of that odious animal for so many years, I fell in a swoon for almost an hour . . . during the first year, I could not endure my wife or children in my presence, the very smell of them was intolerable. . . .

Gulliver, unable to bear the *smell* of human beings, seeks sanctuary in the ammoniac smells of the stables, with their nostalgic reminiscence of Houyhnhnmland. This last touch, like many in his treatment of the ideal horses, is consciously humorous, but humor of the serious import and macabre tone of Hamlet's

> Thrift, thrift, Horatio!

> Well said, old mole! Canst work i' th' earth so fast?

> A certain convocation of politic worms are e'en at him.

It is the bitter humor of the oversensitive, self-conscious man who can laugh at his own suffering, at his being such an unconscionable time in dying.

If we take this imagery of smells figuratively, it expresses perfectly the heart-breaking despair of a man who has had a vision of perfection from which he awaked to sordid reality. Gulliver's forced exile from Houyhnhnmland represents just that. The ideal makes the real unbearable. The separation of reason and body is, admittedly, too extreme; the relegation of man to the state of Yahoo, which that final identification of man with Yahoo certainly means, is too sweeping. But *Lear* is a sweeping condemnation of "the poor forked animal"; *Hamlet* demands why such fellows should be allowed to crawl between earth and heaven. This *Fourth Voyage of Gulliver* is not the most perfect but is the most profoundly moving thing Swift wrote. His satire passes over into tragedy.

v

Since his whole state of mind is one of negation, our acceptance of Hamlet's death is perhaps the most satisfying reconciliation with the tragic conclusion in all Shakespeare. Death is to Hamlet a release from suffering and self-torture, from a world in which happiness is no longer possible.

"I hate life," wrote Swift after the death of Lady Ashburnham, "when I think it exposed to such accidents; and to see so many thousand wretches burdening the earth, while such as her die, makes me think God did never intend life for a blessing." From the *Journal to Stella* we learn that he had early formed the practice of reading from *Job* the passage that begins, "Let the day perish wherein I was born, and the night in which it was said, There is a man child conceived." Many years later, in May 1733, he wrote to Pope: "When I was of your age, I thought every day of death, but now every minute." Such hatred of life was not with him the pose of the professional satirist or empty cynic. "Goodnight," he is reported to have said in his later years when taking leave of friends, "I hope I shall never see you again."

Swift's life was a long disease, with its disappointments, its self-torture, its morbid recriminations. No flights of angels hymned to his rest the solitary, terrible figure rotting in his chair like a post-Shakespearean conception of tragedy, muttering again and again, "I am what I am! I am what I am" —the extinction of reason, so long, so passionately believed in, in a travesty of Descartes. But one October afternoon Swift was no longer absent from felicity.

F. R. Leavis

The Irony of Swift

SWIFT is a great English writer. For opening with this truism I have a reason: I wish to discuss Swift's writings—to examine what they are; and they are (as the extant commentary bears witness) of such a kind that it is peculiarly difficult to discuss them without shifting the focus of discussion to the kind of man that Swift was. What is most interesting in them does not so clearly belong to the realm of things made and detached that literary criticism, which has certainly not the less its duties towards Swift, can easily avoid turning— unawares, and that is, degenerating—into something else. In the attempt to say what makes these writings so remarkable, reference to the man who wrote is indeed necessary; but there are distinctions. For instance, one may (it appears), having offered to discuss the nature and import of Swift's satire, find oneself countering imputations of misanthropy with the argument that Swift earned the love of Pope, Arbuthnot, Gay, several other men and two women: this should not be found necessary by the literary critic. But the irrelevancies of Thackeray and of his castigator, the late Charles Whibley—irrelevancies not merely from the point of view of literary criticism —are too gross to need placarding; more insidious deviations are possible.

The reason for the opening truism is also the reason for the choice of title. To direct the attention upon Swift's irony gives, I think, the best chance of dealing adequately, without deviation or confusion, with what is essential in his work. But it involves also (to anticipate an objection) a slight to the classical status of Gulliver's Travels, a book which, though it may represent Swift's most impressive achievement in the way of complete creation—the thing achieved and detached—does not give the best opportunities for examining his irony. And Gulliver's Travels, one readily agrees, hasn't its classical status for nothing. But neither is it for nothing that, suitably abbreviated, it has become a classic for children. What for the adult reader constitutes its peculiar force—what puts it in so different a class from Robinson Crusoe—resides for the most part in the fourth book (to a less extent in the third). The adult may re-read the first two parts, as he may Robinson Crusoe, with great interest, but his interest, apart from being more critically conscious, will not be of a different order from the child's. He will, of course, be aware of an ingenuity of political satire in Lilliput, but the political satire is, unless for historians, not very much alive to-day. And even the more general satire characteristic of the second book will not strike him as very subtle. His main satisfaction, a great deal enhanced, no doubt, by the ironic seasoning, will be that which Swift, the student of the Mariner's Magazine and of travellers' relations, aimed to supply in the bare precision and the matter-of-fact realness of his narrative.

But what in Swift is most important, the disturbing characteristic of his genius, is a peculiar emotional intensity; that which, in Gulliver, confronts us in the Struldbrugs and the Yahoos. It is what we find ourselves contemplating when elsewhere we examine his irony. To lay the stress upon an emotional intensity should be matter of commonplace: actually, in routine usage, the accepted word for Swift is "intellec-

Reprinted from *Determinations*, London, 1934, by permission of the publisher, Chatto and Windus, Ltd.

tual." We are told, for instance, that his is pre-eminently "intellectual satire" (though we are not told what satire is). For this formula the best reason some commentators can allege is the elaboration of analogies—their "exact and elaborate propriety" [1]—in *Gulliver*. But a muddled perception can hardly be expected to give a clear account of itself; the stress on Swift's "intellect" (Mr Herbert Read alludes to his "mighty intelligence") [2] registers, it would appear, a confused sense, not only of the mental exercise involved in his irony, but of the habitually critical attitude he maintains towards the world, and of the negative emotions he specializes in.

From "critical" to "negative" in this last sentence is, it will be observed, a shift of stress. There are writings of Swift where "critical" is the more obvious word (and where "intellectual" may seem correspondingly apt)—notably, the pamphlets or pamphleteering essays in which the irony is instrumental, directed and limited to a given end. The *Argument Against Abolishing Christianity* and the *Modest Proposal,* for instance, are discussible in the terms in which satire is commonly discussed: as the criticism of vice, folly, or other aberration, by some kind of reference to positive standards. But even here, even in the *Argument,* where Swift's ironic intensity undeniably directs itself to the defence of something that he is intensely concerned to defend, the effect is essentially negative. The positive itself appears only negatively—a kind of skeletal presence, rigid enough, but without life or body; a necessary pre-condition, as it were, of directed negation. The intensity is purely destructive.

The point may be enforced by the obvious contrast with Gibbon—except that between Swift's irony and Gibbon's the contrast is so complete that any one point is difficult to isolate. Gibbon's irony, in the fifteenth chapter, may be aimed against, instead of for, Christianity, but contrasted

[1] Churton Collins.
[2] *English Prose Style.*

with Swift's it is an assertion of faith. The decorously insistent pattern of Gibbonian prose insinuates a solidarity with the reader (the implied solidarity in Swift is itself ironical—a means to betrayal), establishes an understanding and habituates to certain assumptions. The reader, it is implied, is an eighteenth-century gentleman ("rational," "candid," "polite," "elegant," "humane"); eighteen hundred years ago he would have been a pagan gentleman, living by these same standards (those of absolute civilization); by these standards (present everywhere in the stylized prose and adroitly emphasized at key-points in such phrases as "the polite Augustus," "the elegant mythology of the Greeks") the Jews and early Christians are seen to have been ignorant fanatics, uncouth and probably dirty. Gibbon as a historian of Christianity had, we know, limitations; but the positive standards by reference to which his irony works represent something impressively realized in eighteenth-century civilization; impressively "there" too in the grandiose, assured and ordered elegance of history. (When, on the other hand, Lytton Strachey, with a Gibbonian period or phrase or word, a "remarkable," "oddly," or "curious," assures us that he feels an amused superiority to these Victorian puppets, he succeeds only in conveying his personal conviction that he feels amused and superior.)

Gibbon's irony, then, habituates and reassures, ministering to a kind of judicial certitude or complacency. Swift's is essentially a matter of surprise and negation; its function is to defeat habit, to intimidate and to demoralize. What he assumes in the *Argument* is not so much a common acceptance of Christianity as that the reader will be ashamed to have to recognize how fundamentally unchristian his actual assumptions, motives and attitudes are. And in general the implication is that it would shame people if they were made to recognize themselves unequivocally. If one had to justify this irony according to the conventional notion of satire, then its satiric efficacy would be to make comfortable non-recognition, the unconsciousness of habit, impossible.

A method of surprise does not admit of description in an easy formula. Surprise is a perpetually varied accompaniment of the grave, dispassionate, matter-of-fact tone in which Swift delivers his intensities. The dissociation of emotional intensity from its usual accompaniments inhibits the automatic defence-reaction:

He is a Presbyterian in politics, and an atheist in religion; but he chooses at present to whore with a Papist.

What bailiff would venture to arrest Mr Steele, now he has the honour to be your representative? and what bailiff ever scrupled it before?

—Or inhibits, let us say, the normal response; since "defence" suggests that it is the "victim" whose surprise we should be contemplating, whereas it is our own, whether Swift's butt is Wharton or the atheist or mankind in general. "But satire, being levelled at all, is never resented for an offence by any, since every individual makes bold to understand it of others, and very wisely removes his particular part of the burden upon the shoulders of the World, which are broad enough and able to bear it." [3] There is, of course, no contradiction here; a complete statement would be complex. But, actually, the discussion of satire in terms of offence and castigation, victim and castigator, is unprofitable, though the idea of these has to be taken into account. What we are concerned with (the reminder is especially opportune) is an arrangement of words on the page and their effects—the emotions, attitudes and ideas that they organize.

Our reaction, as Swift says, is not that of the butt or victim; nevertheless, it necessarily entails some measure of sympathetic self-projection. We more often, probably, feel the effect of the words as an intensity in the castigator than as an effect upon a victim: the dissociation of animus from the

[3] *A Tale of a Tub:* the Preface.

usual signs defines for our contemplation a peculiarly intense contempt or disgust. When, as sometimes we have to do, we talk in terms of effect on the victim, then "surprise" becomes an obviously apt word; he is to be betrayed, again and again, into an incipient acquiescence:

Sixthly, This would be a great Inducement to Marriage, which all wise Nations have either encouraged by Rewards, or enforced by Laws and Penalties. It would increase the Care and Tenderness of Mothers towards their Children, when they were sure of a Settlement for Life, to the poor Babes, provided in some Sort by the Publick, to their annual Profit instead of Expence; we should soon see an honest Emulation among the married Women, *which of them could bring the fattest Child to the Market.* Men would become as *fond* of their Wives, during the Time of their Pregnancy, as they are now of their *Mares* in Foal, their *Cows* in Calf, or *Sows* when they are ready to farrow, nor offer to beat or kick them (as is too *frequent* a Practice) for fear of a Miscarriage.

The implication is: "This, as you so obligingly demonstrate, is the only kind of argument that appeals to you; here are your actual faith and morals. How, on consideration, do you like the smell of them?"

But when in reading the *Modest Proposal* we are most engaged, it is an effect directly upon ourselves that we are most disturbingly aware of. The dispassionate, matter-of-fact tone induces a feeling and a motion of assent, while the burden, at the same time, compels the feelings appropriate to rejection, and in the contrast—the tension—a remarkably disturbing energy is generated. A sense of an extraordinary energy is the general effect of Swift's irony. The intensive means just indicated are reinforced extensively in the continuous and unpredictable movement of the attack, which turns this way and that, comes now from one quarter and now from another, inexhaustibly surprising—making again an odd contrast with the sustained and level gravity of the tone. If Swift does for a moment appear to settle down to a formula it is only in order to betray; to induce a trust in the solid ground before opening the pitfall.

"His *Tale of a Tub* has little resemblance to his other pieces. It exhibits a vehemence and rapidity of mind, a copiousness of images, a vivacity of diction, such as he afterwards never possessed, or never exerted. It is of a mode so distinct and peculiar, that it must be considered by itself; what is true of that, is not true of anything else he has written."—What Johnson is really testifying to here is the degree in which the *Tale of a Tub* is characteristic and presents the qualities of Swift's genius in concentrated form. "That he has in his works no metaphors, as has been said, is not true," says Johnson a sentence or two later, "but his few metaphors seem to be received rather by necessity than choice." This last judgment may at any rate serve to enforce Johnson's earlier observation that in the *Tale of a Tub* Swift's powers function with unusual freedom. For the "copiousness of images" that Johnson constates is, as the phrase indicates, not a matter of choice but of essential genius. And, as a matter of fact, in this "copiousness of images" the characteristics that we noted in discussing Swift's pamphleteering irony have their supreme expression.

It is as if the gift applied in *Gulliver* to a very limiting task—directed and confined by a scheme uniting a certain consistency in analogical elaboration with verisimilitude—were here enjoying free play. For the bent expressing itself in this "copiousness" is clearly fundamental. It shows itself in the spontaneous metaphorical energy of Swift's prose—in the image, action or blow that, leaping out of the prosaic manner, continually surprises and disconcerts the reader: "such a man, truly wise, creams off Nature, leaving the sour and the dregs for philosophy and reason to lap up." It appears with as convincing a spontaneity in the sardonic vivacity of comic vision that characterizes the narrative, the presentment of action and actor. If, then, the continual elaborate play of analogy is a matter of

cultivated habit, it is a matter also, of cultivated natural bent, a congenial development. It is a development that would seem to bear a relation to the Metaphysical fashion in verse (Swift was born in 1667). The spirit of it is that of a fierce and insolent game, but a game to which Swift devotes himself with a creative intensity.

And whereas the mind of man, when he gives the spur and bridle to his thoughts, does never stop, but naturally sallies out into both extremes of high and low, of good and evil, his first flight of fancy commonly transports him to ideas of what is most perfect, finished, and exalted, till, having soared out of his own reach and sight, not well perceiving how near the frontiers of height and depth border upon each other, with the same course and wing he falls down plump into the lowest bottom of things, like one who travels the east into the west, or like a straight line drawn by its own length into a circle. Whether a tincture of malice in our natures makes us fond of furnishing every bright idea with its reverse, or whether reason, reflecting upon the sum of things, can, like the sun, serve only to enlighten one half of the globe, leaving the other half by necessity under shade and darkness, or whether fancy, flying up to the imagination of what is highest and best, becomes over-short, and spent, and weary, and suddenly falls, like a dead bird of paradise, to the ground. . . .

—One may (without difficulty) resist the temptation to make the point by saying that this is poetry; one is still tempted to say that the use to which so exuberant an energy is put is a poet's. "Exuberant" seems, no doubt, a paradoxical word to apply to an energy used as Swift uses his; but the case is essentially one for paradoxical descriptions.

In his use of negative materials—negative emotions and attitudes—there is something that it is difficult not to call creative, though the aim always is destructive. Not all the materials, of course, are negative: the "bird of paradise" in the passage above is alive as well as dead. Effects of this kind, often much more intense, are characteristic of the *Tale of a Tub*, where surprise and contrast operate in modes that there is some point in calling poetic. "The most heterogeneous ideas are yoked by violence together"—and in the juxtaposition intensity is generated.

"Paracelsus brought a squadron of stink-pot-flingers from the snowy mountains of Rhaetia"—this (which comes actually from the *Battle of the Books*) does not represent what I have in mind; it is at once too simple and too little charged with animus. Swift's intensities are intensities of rejection and negation; his poetic juxtapositions are, characteristically, destructive in intention, and when they most seem creative of energy are most successful in spoiling, reducing, and destroying. Sustained "copiousness," continually varying, and concentrating surprise in sudden local foci, cannot be represented in short extracts; it must suffice here to say that this kind of thing may be found at a glance on almost any page:

> Meantime it is my earnest request that so useful an undertaking may be entered upon (if their Majesties please) with all convenient speed, because I have a strong inclination before I leave the world to taste a blessing which we mysterious writers can seldom reach till we have got into our graves, whether it is that fame, being a fruit grafted on the body, can hardly grow and much less ripen till the stock is in the earth, or whether she be a bird of prey, and is lured among the rest to pursue after the scent of a carcass, or whether she conceives her trumpet sounds best and farthest when she stands on a tomb, by the advantage of a rising ground and the echo of a hollow vault.

It is, of course, possible to adduce Swift's authority for finding that his negations carry with them a complementary positive —an implicit assertion. But (*pace* Charles Whibley) the only thing in the nature of a positive that most readers will find convincingly present is self-assertion—*superbia*. Swift's way of demonstrating his superiority is to destroy, but he takes a positive delight in his power. And that the reader's sense of the negativeness of the *Tale of a Tub* is really qualified comes out

when we refer to the Yahoos and the Struldbrugs for a test. The ironic detachment is of such a kind as to reassure us that this savage exhibition is mainly a game, played because it is the insolent pleasure of the author: "demonstration of superiority" is as good a formula as any for its prevailing spirit. Nevertheless, about a superiority that asserts itself in this way there is something disturbingly odd, and again and again in the *Tale of a Tub* we come on intensities that shift the stress decisively and remind us how different from Voltaire Swift is, even in his most complacent detachment.

I propose to examine in illustration a passage from the *Digression Concerning the Original, the Use, and Improvement of Madness in a Commonwealth* (*i.e.* Section IX). It will have, in the nature of the case, to be a long one, but since it exemplifies at the same time all Swift's essential characteristics, its length will perhaps be tolerated. I shall break up the passage for convenience of comment, but, except for the omission of nine or ten lines in the second instalment, quotation will be continuous:

> For the brain in its natural position and state of serenity disposeth its owner to pass his life in the common forms, without any thought of subduing multitudes to his own power, his reasons, or his visions, and the more he shapes his understanding by the pattern of human learning, the less he is inclined to form parties after his particular notions, because that instructs him in his private infirmities, as well as in the stubborn ignorance of the people. But when a man's fancy gets astride on his reason, when imagination is at cuffs with the senses, and common understanding as well as common sense is kicked out of doors, the first proselyte he makes is himself; and when that is once compassed, the difficulty is not so great in bringing over others, a strong delusion always operating from without as vigorously as from within. For cant and vision are to the ear and the eye the same that tickling is to the touch. Those entertainments and pleasures we most value in life are such as dupe and play the wag with the senses. For if we take an examination of what is generally understood by happiness, as it

has respect either to the understanding or to the senses, we shall find all its properties and adjuncts will herd under this short definition, that it is a perpetual possession of being well deceived.

Swift's ant-like energy—the business-like air, obsessed intentness and unpredictable movement—have already had an effect. We are not, at the end of this instalment, as sure that we know just what his irony is doing as we were at the opening. Satiric criticism of sectarian "enthusiasm" by reference to the "common forms"—the Augustan standards—is something that, in Swift, we can take as very seriously meant. But in the incessant patter of the argument we have (helped by such things as, at the end, the suggestion of animus in that oddly concrete "herd") a sense that direction and tone are changing. Nevertheless, the change of tone for which the next passage is most remarkable comes as a disconcerting surprise:

And first, with relation to the mind or understanding, it is manifest what mighty advantages fiction has over truth, and the reason is just at our elbow; because imagination can build nobler scenes and produce more wonderful revolutions than fortune or Nature will be at the expense to furnish. . . . Again, if we take this definition of happiness and examine it with reference to the senses, it will be acknowledged wonderfully adapt. How sad and insipid do all objects accost us that are not conveyed in the vehicle of delusion! How shrunk is everything as it appears in the glass of Nature, so that if it were not for the assistance of artificial mediums, false lights, refracted angles, varnish, and tinsel, there would be a mighty level in the felicity and enjoyments of mortal men. If this were seriously considered by the world, as I have a certain reason to suspect it hardly will, men would no longer reckon among their high points of wisdom the art of exposing weak sides and publishing infirmities—an employment, in my opinion, neither better nor worse than that of unmasking, which, I think, has never been allowed fair usage, either in the world or the playhouse.

The suggestion of changing direction does not, in the first part of this passage, bring with it anything unsettling: from ridicule of "enthusiasm" to ridicule of human capacity for self-deception is an easy transition. The reader, as a matter of fact, begins to settle down to the habit, the steady drift of this irony, and is completely unprepared for the sudden change of tone and reversal of attitude in the two sentences beginning: "How sad and insipid do all objects," etc. Exactly what the change means or is, it is difficult to be certain (and that is of the essence of the effect). But the tone has certainly a personal intensity and the ironic detachment seems suddenly to disappear. It is as if one found Swift in the place—at the point of view—where one expected to find his butt. But the ambiguously mocking sentence with which the paragraph ends reinforces the uncertainty.

The next paragraph keeps the reader for some time in uneasy doubt. The irony has clearly shifted its plane, but in which direction is the attack going to develop? Which, to be safe, must one dissociate oneself from, "credulity" or "curiosity"?

In the proportion that credulity is a more peaceful possession of the mind than curiosity, so far preferable is that wisdom which converses about the surface to that pretended philosophy which enters into the depths of things and then comes gravely back with informations and discoveries, that in the inside they are good for nothing. The two senses to which all objects first address themselves are the sight and the touch; these never examine further than the colour, the shape, the size, and whatever other qualities dwell or are drawn by art upon the outward of bodies; and then comes reason officiously, with tools for cutting, and opening, and mangling, and piercing, offering to demonstrate that they are not of the same consistence quite through. Now I take all this to be the last degree of perverting Nature, one of whose eternal laws is to put her best furniture forward. And therefore, in order to save the charges of all such expensive anatomy for the time to come, I do here think fit to inform the reader that in such conclusions as these reason is certainly in the right; and that in most corporeal beings which have fallen under my cognisance the outside hath been infinitely preferable to the in, whereof I have been further convinced from some late experiments. Last week

I saw a woman flayed, and you will hardly believe how much it altered her person for the worse.

The peculiar intensity of that last sentence is, in its own way, so decisive that it has for the reader the effect of resolving uncertainty in general. The disturbing force of the sentence is a notable instance of a kind already touched on: repulsion is intensified by the momentary co-presence, induced by the tone, of incipient and incompatible feelings (or motions) of acceptance. And that Swift feels the strongest animus against "curiosity" is now beyond all doubt. The natural corollary would seem to be that "credulity," standing ironically for the "common forms"—the sane, socially sustained, common-sense illusions—is the positive that the reader must associate himself with and rest on for safety. The next half-page steadily and (to all appearances) unequivocally confirms this assumption:

Yesterday I ordered the carcass of a beau to be stripped in my presence, when we were all amazed to find so many unsuspected faults under one suit of clothes. Then I laid open his brain, his heart, and his spleen, but I plainly perceived at every operation that the farther we proceeded, we found the defects increase upon us in number and bulk; from all of which I justly formed this conclusion to myself, that whatever philosopher or projector can find out an art to sodder and patch up the flaws and imperfections of Nature, will deserve much better of mankind and teach us a much more useful science than that, so much in present esteem, of widening and exposing them (like him who held anatomy to be the ultimate end of physic). And he whose fortunes and dispositions have placed him in a convenient station to enjoy the fruits of this noble art, he that can with Epicurus content his ideas with the films and images that fly off upon his senses from the superficies of things, such a man, truly wise, creams off Nature, leaving the sour and the dregs for philosophy and reason to lap up.

Assumption has become habit, and has been so nourished that few readers note

anything equivocal to trouble them in that last sentence: the concrete force of "creams off," "sour," "dregs" and "lap up" seems unmistakably to identify Swift with an intense animus against "philosophy and reason" (understood implicitly to stand for "curiosity" the anatomist). The reader's place, of course, is with Swift.

The trap is sprung in the last sentence of the paragraph:

This is the sublime and refined point of felicity called the possession of being well-deceived, the serene peaceful state of being a fool among knaves.

What is left? The next paragraph begins significantly: "But to return to madness." This irony may be critical, but "critical" turns out, in no very long run, to be indistinguishable from "negative." The positives disappear. Even when, as in the Houyhnhnms, they seem to be more substantially present, they disappear under our "curiosity." The Houyhnhnms, of course, stand for Reason, Truth and Nature, the Augustan positives, and it was in deadly earnest that Swift appealed to these; but how little at best they were anything solidly realized comparison with Pope brings out. Swift did his best for the Houyhnhnms, and they may have all the reason, but the Yahoos have all the life. Gulliver's master "thought Nature and reason were sufficient guides for a reasonable animal," but nature and reason as Gulliver exhibits them are curiously negative, and the reasonable animals appear to have nothing in them to guide. "They have no fondness for their colts or foals, but the care they take in educating them proceeds entirely from the dictates of reason." This freedom from irrational feelings and impulses simplifies other matters too: "their language doth not abound in variety of words, because their wants and passions are fewer than among us." And so conversation, in this model society, is simplified: "nothing passed but what was useful, expressed in the fewest and most significant words. . . ." "Courtship, love, presents, jointures, settlements, have no place in their thoughts, or terms whereby to express them in their language. The young couple meet and are joined, merely because it is the determination of their parents and friends: it is what they see done every day, and they look upon it as one of the necessary actions of a reasonable being." The injunction of "temperance, industry, exercise, and cleanliness . . . the lessons enjoined to the young ones of both sexes," seems unnecessary; except possibly for exercise, the usefulness of which would not, perhaps, be immediately apparent to the reasonable young.

The clean skin of the Houyhnhnms, in short, is stretched over a void; instincts, emotions and life, which complicate the problem of cleanliness and decency, are left for the Yahoos with the dirt and the indecorum. Reason, Truth and Nature serve instead; the Houyhnhnms (who scorn metaphysics) find them adequate. Swift too scorned metaphysics, and never found anything better to contend for than a skin, a surface, an outward show. An outward show is, explicitly, all he contends for in the quite unironical *Project for the Advancement of Religion*, and the difference between the reality of religion and the show is, for the author of the *Tale of a Tub*, hardly substantial. Of Jack we are told, "nor could all the world persuade him, as the common phrase is, to eat his victuals like a Christian." It is characteristic of Swift that he should put in these terms, showing a complete incapacity even to guess what religious feeling might be, a genuine conviction that Jack should be made to kneel when receiving the Sacrament.

Of the intensity of this conviction there can be no doubt. The Church of England was the established "common form," and, moreover, was Swift's church: his insane egotism reinforced the savagery with which he fought to maintain this cover over the void, this decent surface. But what the savagery of the passage from the *Digression* shows mainly is Swift's sense of insecurity and of the undisguisable flimsiness of any surface that offered.

The case, of course, is more complex. In the passage examined the "surface" becomes, at the most savage moment, a human skin. Swift's negative horror, at its most disturbing, becomes one with his disgust-obsession: he cannot bear to be reminded that under the skin there is blood, mess and entrails; and the skin itself, as we know from *Gulliver*, must not be seen from too close. Hypertrophy of the sense of uncleanness, of the instinct of repulsion, is not uncommon; nor is its association with what accompanies it in Swift. What is uncommon is Swift's genius, and the paradoxical vitality with which this self-defeat of life—life turned against itself—is manifested. In the *Tale of a Tub* the defeat is also a triumph; the genius delights in its mastery, in its power to destroy, and negation is felt as self-assertion. It is only when time has confirmed Swift in disappointment and brought him to more intimate contemplation of physical decay that we get the Yahoos and the Struldbrugs.

Here, well on this side of pathology, literary criticism stops. To attempt encroachments would be absurd, and, even if one were qualified, unprofitable. No doubt psychopathology and medicine have an interesting commentary to offer, but their help is not necessary. Swift's genius belongs to literature, and its appreciation to literary criticism.

We have, then, in his writings probably the most remarkable expression of negative feelings and attitudes that literature can offer—the spectacle of creative powers (the paradoxical description seems right) exhibited consistently in negation and rejection. His verse demands an essay to itself, but fits in readily with what has been said. "In poetry," he reports of the Houyhnhnms, "they must be allowed to excel all other mortals; wherein the justness of their similes and the minuteness as well as exactness of their descriptions are, indeed, inimitable. Their verses abound very much in both of these. . . ." The actuality of presentment for which Swift is notable, in prose as well as verse, seems always to owe its convincing "justness" to, at his least actively malicious, a coldly intense scrutiny, a potentially hostile attention. "To his domesticks," says Johnson, "he was naturally rough; and a man of rigorous temper, with that vigilance of minute attention which his works discover, must have been a master that few could bear." *Instructions to Servants* and the *Polite Conversation* enforce obviously the critical bearing and felicity of Johnson's remark.

A great writer—yes; that account still imposes itself as fitting, though his greatness is no matter of moral grandeur or human centrality; our sense of it is merely a sense of great force. And this force, as we feel it, is conditioned by frustration and constriction; the channels of life have been blocked and perverted. That we should be so often invited to regard him as a moralist and an idealist would seem to be mainly a witness to the power of vanity, and the part that vanity can play in literary appreciation: *saeva indignatio* is an indulgence that solicits us all, and the use of literature by readers and critics for the projection of nobly suffering selves is familiar. No doubt, too, it is pleasant to believe that unusual capacity for egotistic animus means unusual distinction of intellect; but, as we have seen, there is no reason to lay stress on intellect in Swift. His work does indeed exhibit an extraordinary play of mind; but it is not great intellectual force that is exhibited in his indifference to the problems raised—in, for instance, the *Voyage to the Houyhnhnms*—by his use of the concept, or the word, "Nature." It is not merely that he had an Augustan contempt for metaphysics; he shared the shallowest complacencies of Augustan common sense: his irony might destroy these, but there is no conscious criticism.

He was, in various ways, curiously unaware—the reverse of clairvoyant. He is distinguished by the intensity of his feelings, not by insight into them, and he certainly does not impress us as a mind in possession of its experience.

We shall not find Swift remarkable for intelligence if we think of Blake.

A. E. Dyson

Swift: The Metamorphosis of Irony

IN an age of few or shifting values irony becomes, very often, a tone of urbane amusement; assuming the right to be amused, but offering no very precise positives behind the right. It can degenerate into a mere gesture of superiority, superficially polished and civilized, but too morally irresponsible to be really so. *Eminent Victorians* is an example of such irony which springs to mind. Lytton Strachey uses the tone of Gibbon in order to deflate the Victorians, but divorces the tone from any firm moral viewpoint, and so makes of it a negative and somewhat vicious instrument.

Irony can, also, become a mode of escape, as we have good cause to know in the twentieth century. To laugh at the terrors of life is in some sense to evade them. To laugh at oneself is to become less vulnerable to the scorn or indifference of others. An ironic attitude is, as we should all now agree, complex and unpredictable: fluctuating with mood and situation, and too subtle in its possibilities for any simple definition in terms of moral purpose or a "test of truth" to be generally applicable.

This is not, however, a state of affairs as new, or unusual, as we might be tempted to think. Even in that great age of moral irony, the eighteenth century, the technique is far from being simple. Irony is, in its very nature, the most ambivalent of modes, constantly changing colour and texture, and occasionally suffering a sea-change into something decidedly rich and strange. In the work of Swift, who will concern us here, we find, at characteristic moments, that the irony takes a leap. It escapes from its supposed or apparent purpose, and does some-

thing not only entirely different from what it set out to do, but even diametrically opposite. Nor is this just a matter of lost artistic control or structural weakness. At the moments I have in mind the irony is at its most complex and memorable. It seems, in undergoing its metamorphosis, to bring us nearer to Swift's inner vision of man and the universe. It ceases to be a functional technique serving a moral purpose, and becomes the embodiment of an attitude to life. And just as Alice was forced, on consideration, to accept the metamorphosis of the Duchess's baby into a pig as an improvement ("it would have made a dreadfully ugly child: but it makes rather a handsome pig, I think"), so the readers of Swift will have to agree that the final impact of his irony, however disturbing, is more real, and therefore more worth while, than its continuation as simple moral satire would have been.

But this is to anticipate. We must begin by reminding ourselves that Swift *is* a satirist: and that satire, fiercer than comedy in its moral intentions, measures human conduct not against a norm but against an ideal. The intention is reformative. The satirist holds up for his readers to see a distorted image, and the reader is to be shocked into a realization that the image is his own. Exaggeration of the most extreme kind is central to the shock tactics. The reader must see himself as a monster, in order to learn how far he is from being a saint.

The Augustan age, as Professor Willey has most interestingly shown, was especially adapted to satiric writing. An age which does not really believe in sin, and which

Reprinted from *Essays and Studies*, new series, vol. XI, 1958, pp. 53–67, by permission of the author. Several footnotes have been omitted without notice.

imagines that its most rational and enlightened ideals have been actualized as a norm, is bound to be aware also, at times, of a radical gulf between theory and practice.

... if you worship "Nature and Reason," you will be the more afflicted by human unreason; and perhaps only the effort to see man as the world's glory will reveal how far he is really its jest and riddle.[1]

Economic and acquisitive motives were coming more and more into the open as mainsprings of individual and social action; Hobbes's sombre account of human nature in terms of competition and conflict was altogether too plausible on the practical level for the comfort of gentlemen philosophers who rejected it, as a theory, out of hand. The turning of Science, Britannia and The Moderns into idols was bound, in any case, to produce sooner or later some iconoclasm of the Swiftian kind. Satire thrives on moral extremes: and at this period, with Hobbes at hand to provide a view of man which was at once alarmingly possible and entirely opposite to the prevailing one, satire was bound to be very much at home.

It should follow from this, and to some extent really does, that Swift was a moralist, concerned, as he himself puts it, to "wonderfully mend the world," in accordance with the world's most ideal picture of itself. *Gulliver's Travels* is far more complex and elusive, however, than this intention would suggest. It is, indeed, a baffling work: I have been re-reading a number of excellent and stimulating commentaries on Book IV, and find that there are disagreements upon even the most fundamental points of interpretation. Clearly, we cannot arrive at Swift's "true" meaning merely by reversing what he actually says. The illusion that he is establishing important positives with fine, intellectual precision breaks down when we try to state what these positives *are*.

On the surface, at least, the irony does

[1] Basil Willey, *Eighteenth Century Background,* Chapter VI.

work in ways that can be precisely defined. Swift has a number of techniques which he is skilled in using either singly, or in powerful combination. At one moment he will make outrageously inhuman proposals, with a show of great reasonableness, and an affected certainty that we shall find them acceptable; at another, he will make soundly moral or Christian proposals, which are confidently held up for scorn. Again, we find him offering, with apparent sympathy and pride, an account of our actual doings, but in the presence of a virtuous outsider whose horrified reactions are sufficient index of their true worth. Swift can, notoriously, shift from one technique to another with huge dexterity; setting his readers a problem in mental and moral gymnastics if they are to evade all of his traps. In Book III, for example, the Professors at Balnibarbi are presented as progressive scientists, of a kind whom the Augustan reader would instinctively be prepared to admire. We quickly find that they are devoid of all common sense; and that unless we are to approve of such extravagant projects as "softening marble for pincushions" we have to dissociate ourselves from them entirely. But when we do this, Swift is still ready for us. "In the school of political projectors," says Gulliver, "I was but ill entertained; the Professors appearing in my judgement wholly out of their senses" (a pleasant reassurance, this, that we have done well to come to a similar conclusion some time before). The crowning absurdity is that these "unhappy people were proposing schemes for persuading monarchs to choose favourites upon the score of their wisdom, capacity and virtue . . . of rewarding merit, great abilities and eminent services . . ." and so on. Dissociated from the Professors, we find ourselves, once more, in Swift's snare.

The technique is, of course, one of betrayal. A state of tension, not to say war, exists between Swift and his readers. The very tone in which he writes is turned into a weapon. It is the tone of polite conversation, friendly, and apparently dealing in commonplaces. Naturally our assent is captured, since the polite style, the guarantee of gentlemanly equality, is the last one in which we expect to be attacked or betrayed. But the propositions to which we find ourselves agreeing are in varying degrees monstrous, warped or absurd. The result is the distinctively satiric challenge: why, we have to ask, are we so easily trapped into thinking so? And is this, perhaps, the way we really do think, despite our normal professions to the contrary?

The technique of betrayal is made all the more insidious by Swift's masterly use of misdirection. No conjuror is more adept at making us look the wrong way. His use of the polite style for betrayal is matched by his use of the traveller's tale. The apparently factual and straightforward narrative with which *Gulliver's Travels* opens (the style of *Robinson Crusoe*) precludes suspicion. We readily accept Gulliver as a representative Englishman fallen into the hands of an absurd crew of midgets, and only gradually realize that the midgets, in fact, are ourselves, and Gulliver, in this instance, the outside observer. The same technique is used, I shall argue, in Book IV: though there, the misdirection is even more subtle, and the way to extricate ourselves from a disastrous committal to Gulliver's point of view far more difficult to discover.

So much, then, for the purpose of the irony, and its normal methods. It is, we notice, accomplished, full of surprises, and admirably adapted to the task of shocking the reader for his moral good. For a great part of the time, moreover, it functions as it is intended to. When Swift is satirizing bad lawyers, bad doctors, bad politicians and *id genus omne*, he is driven by a genuine humanity, and by a conviction that people ought not to act in this way, and need not act so. His tone of savage indignation is justified by the content, and relates directly to normal ideals of justice, honesty, kindness.

On looking closely, however, we find that his irony is by no means directed only against things which can be morally changed. Sometimes it is deflected, and turned upon states of mind which might, or might not, be alterable. Consider, for example, the Laputians. These people never, we are told, enjoy a moment's peace of mind, "and their disturbances proceed from causes which very little affect the rest of mortals." They are preoccupied with fears of cosmic disasters, and apprehensions that the world will come to an end. The ironic treatment pre-supposes that Swift is analysing a moral flaw, but it seems doubtful whether such fears can be regarded wholly as a matter of culpable weakness, and even more doubtful whether ridicule could hope to effect a cure. The problem exists in a hinterland between the moral and the psychological, between sin and sickness. The Laputians are temperamentally prone to worry: and worry is not usually regarded, except by the most austerely stoical, as simply a moral weakness.

This dubious usage points the way to the real metamorphosis, which occurs when the irony is deflected again, and turned against states of mind, or existence, which cannot be changed at all. The irony intended to "wonderfully mend the world" transmutes itself into a savage exploration of the world's essential unmendability. It is turned against certain limitations, or defects (as Swift sees them), in the human predicament that are, by the nature of things, inevitable. When this happens, Swift seems to generate his fiercest intensity. The restless energy behind the style becomes a masochistic probing of wounds. The experience of reading him is peculiarly disturbing at such moments; and it is then that his tone of savage indignation deepens into that *disgust* which Mr. T. S. Eliot has called his distinctive characteristic.

In the first two books of *Gulliver* alterations of perspective usually precipitate this type of irony. The Lilliputians are ridiculous not only because they are immoral, but because they are small. The life of their court is as meaningless as it is unpleasant: their intrigues and battles a game, which Gulliver can manipulate like a child playing with toys, and as easily grow tired of. Gulliver himself becomes ridiculous when he is placed beside the Brobdingnagians; whose contempt for him, once again, is not wholly, or even primarily, a moral matter. The King, after hearing Gulliver prattling about his "beloved England," comments "how contemptible a thing was human grandeur, which could be mimicked by such diminutive insects," and continues

Yet I dare engage, these creatures have their titles and distinctions of honour; they contrive little nests and burrows, that they call houses and cities; they make a figure in dress and equipage; they love, they fight, they dispute, they cheat, they betray.

The force, here, is in "mimicked," "diminutive insects," "creatures," "little." The smallness of Gulliver and his kind makes anything they do equally contemptible, their loves as much as their battles, their construction of houses and cities as much as their destructiveness. The survey is Olympian; and the human setting, seen from this height, becomes, irrespective of moral evaluation, a tale of little meaning though the words are strong.

Likewise, the hugeness of the Brobdingnagians makes them potentially horrible. The sight of a huge cancer fills Gulliver with revulsion, as, too, does the sight of giant flies who "would sometimes alight on my victuals, and leave their loathsome excrement or spawn behind."

What do these alterations in perspective suggest? We are made to feel that perhaps all beauty or value is relative, and in the last resort of little worth. To be proud of human achievement is as absurd as to be proud of our sins. The insignificance of men in space suggests an inevitable parallel in time. Perhaps men really *are* no more than ants, playing out their fleeting tragicomedy to an uninterested or scornful void. The irony, now, is an awareness of possible cosmic insignificance. It is exploring a

wound which no amount of moral reformation would be able to heal.

In Book IV of *Gulliver* the irony completes its transformation, and is turned upon human nature itself. Swift's intensity and disgust are nowhere more striking than here.[2] This is the classic interpretative crux: and Aldous Huxley's remark, that Swift "could never forgive man for being a vertebrate mammal as well as an immortal soul," still seems to me to be the most seminal critical insight that has been offered.

The crux centres, of course, upon what we make of Swift's relationship to Gulliver. How far is Gulliver a satiric device, and how far (if at all) does he come to be a spokesman for Swift himself? The answer seems to me to be by no means clear. If we accept Gulliver as Swift's spokesman, we end in a state of despair. On this showing, it would seem that Swift has openly abandoned his positives, and that when he avows that he has "now done with all such visionary schemes" as trying to reform the Yahoos "for ever," he has passed from ironic exaggeration to sober truth. Few readers will be willing to take this view, especially when they reflect upon the dangers in store for those who identify themselves with Gul-

[2] That striking *tour-de-force A Modest Proposal* springs to mind as an exception. There, too, as Dr. Leavis has argued in his fine essay, the effect is almost wholly negative and destructive. The force of the irony is so savage that it robs its supposed positives of any power of asserting themselves. The ghastly imagery of the market and the slaughter-house ceases to sound like satiric exaggeration, and appals us with the sense of actuality. Man, we feel, really *is* as brutal and sordid as this. Theories that he might be otherwise are merely an added torment, so energetically is his inhumanity realized, so impotent is the theoretic norm in the face of this reality.

A necessary conflict seems, too, to be exposed between our ideals of humanity and rational behaviour, and the actual motives of competition and self-interest which move society. Society can no more really be expected to change for the better than Yahoos can be expected to turn into Houyhnhnms. The law of love is absolutely incompatible with things as they are.

liver too readily. And yet, if we reject this, what is the alternative view to be? Swift leads us very skilfully to follow Gulliver step by step. If at some point we depart from his view of himself we have to depart also from the Houyhnhnms: who seem, however, to be an incarnation of Swift's actual positives, and the very standard against which the Yahoos are tried and found wanting. What happens in Book IV is that Gulliver is converted gradually to an admiration of the Houyhnhnms, and then to an acceptance of their judgements upon himself and his kind. The result of this enlightenment is that he comes to realize also the unattainability of such an ideal for himself. He sinks into bitterness and misanthropy, and ends, as a result of his contact with the ideal, far more unpleasant and unconstructive than he was before. At some stage, it seems, he has taken the wrong turning: but where has the mistake occurred?

The construction of the Book is of great interest. Gulliver first of all comes across the Yahoos, and is instantly repelled by them. "Upon the whole, I never beheld in all my travels so disagreeable an animal, or one against which I naturally conceived so strong an antipathy." Soon after this, he encounters the noble horses, and is equally strongly impressed, this time in their favour. Almost at once, he starts to discover between himself and the Yahoos an appalling resemblance: "my horror and astonishment are not to be described, when I observed, in this abominable animal, a perfect human figure." At this stage, it is the physical resemblance which disturbs him. But later, as he falls under the influence of the Houyhnhnms, he comes also to accept a moral resemblance. And this is at the core of the satire.

The cleverness of Swift's technique is that at first the horses are only sketched in. They are clean, kindly, rational, but apart from seeing them through Gulliver's eyes we learn little in detail about them. Gulliver is first "amazed to see . . . in brute beasts . . . behaviour . . . so orderly and ra-

tional, so acute and judicious." But almost at once he finds that they regard *him* as the "brute beast," and with somewhat more justice, "For they looked upon it as a prodigy, that a brute animal should discover such marks of a rational creature." From this moment, the Houyhnhnms start to insinuate into Gulliver's mind a vision of himself that becomes increasingly more repellent. They begin by rejecting his claim to be truly rational, speaking of "those appearances of reason" in him, and deciding that he has been taught to "imitate" a "rational creature." When they compare him with the Yahoos, Gulliver at first objects, acknowledging "some resemblance," but insisting that he cannot account for "their degenerate and brutal nature." The Houyhnhnms will have none of this, however, deciding that if Gulliver does differ, he differs for the worse. "He said, I differed indeed from other Yahoos, being much more cleanly, and not altogether so deformed; but in point of real advantage, he thought I differed for the worse." The reason for this judgement—a reason which Gulliver himself comes to accept—is that his "appearance of reason" is a fraud; and that what seems reason in him is no more than a faculty which makes him *lower* than the Yahoos.

. . . when a creature pretending to reason, could be capable of such enormities, he dreaded, lest the corruption of that faculty, might be worse than brutality itself. He seemed therefore confident, that instead of reason, we were only possessed of some quality fitted to increase our natural vices.

Up to this point, the reader might feel fairly confident that he sees what is happening. The Houyhnhnms really are ideal, and Gulliver's conversion to their point of view is the lesson we should be learning. The contemptuous view of mankind formed by the Houyhnhnms is the main satiric charge. The view that man is a Yahoo and cannot become a Houyhnhnm is satiric exaggeration: near enough to the truth to shake us, but not intended to be taken literally. We shall be "betrayed" if we identify ourselves with Gulliver at the points where the horses scorn him, but safe enough if we accept his conversion at their hands.

This, I fancy, is what many readers are led to feel: and to my mind, in so leading them, Swift sets his most subtle trap of all. The real shock comes in the middle of Chapter VIII, when Gulliver turns, at long last, to give us a more detailed description of the horses. We have already been aware, perhaps, of certain limitations in them: they have a limited vocabulary, limited interests, and an attitude to life that seems wholly functional. But Gulliver has explained all these limitations as virtues, and persuaded us to see them as a sign of grace. No doubt, we feel, these horses *are* noble savages of some kind, and their simplicity a condition and a reward of natural harmony. It remains for the fuller account to show us two further truths about the horses: the first, that they are not human at all, so that their way of life is wholly irrelevant as a human ideal; and the second, that their supposedly rational way of life is so dull and impoverished that we should not wish to emulate them even if we could.

Their society, for instance, is stoic in appearance. They accept such inevitable calamities as death calmly; they eat, sleep and exercise wisely: they believe in universal benevolence as an ideal, and accordingly have no personal ties or attachments. The family is effectually abolished: marriage is arranged by friends as "one of the necessary actions in a reasonable being"; husband and wife like one another, and their children, just as much and as little as they like everyone else. Sex is accepted as normal, but only for the purpose of procreation. Like all other instincts, it is regarded as entirely functional, and has no relevance beyond the begetting of a standard number of offspring. They have no curiosity: their language, their arts and their sciences are purely functional, and restricted to the bare necessities of harmonious social existence. Life is lived "without jealousy, fondness,

quarrelling or discontent"; and it is lived in tribal isolation, since they are "cut off from all commerce with other nations."

This impoverished and devitalized society is the one which Gulliver uncritically accepts as an ideal, and on the strength of which he sinks into a most negative and unedifying misanthropy. And yet, so plausibly does Swift offer this as the ideal of Reason and Nature which his own age believed in, so cunningly does he lead us to think that this is the positive against which a satiric account of the Yahoos is functioning, that the trick is hard to detect. Even the fact that Gulliver is in an escapist frame of mind is not immediately apparent, unless we are on the alert. We see at once, it is true, that the Houyhnhnms are not *like* men: that physically Gulliver might be a monkey but is nothing like a horse, and that this physical placing is linked with a moral one. Yet we assume that this placing is only one more satiric technique: and it is with a distinct shock that we realize that it exists at a more fundamental level than any *moral* amendment on the part of a man could resolve. The Houyhnhnms are literally not human: they are inaccessible to Gulliver not because they are morally superior, but because they are physically non-existent. They are mental abstractions disguised as animals: but they are no more animals, really, than the medieval angels were, and nothing like any human possibility, bad or good.

The horses have, in fact, no passions at all. Their "virtue" is not a triumph over impulse and temptation, but a total immunity from these things—and an immunity which is also, by its very nature, an absence of life and vitality. They have no compulsive sexual impulses, no sensuous pleasures, no capacity for any degree of human love. They have no wishes and fears, and scarcely any ideas. If they are incapable of human bestiality they are even less capable of human glory or sublimity; and it is only because Swift prevents us from thinking of humanity as anything other than a real or potential Yahoo that this is not at once immediately apparent.

What is the true force of Book IV, then? Swift seems to my mind, to have posed, in new form, and with appalling consequences, the old riddle of man's place as the microcosm. Instead of relating him to the angels and the beasts, he relates him to the Houyhnhnms and the Yahoos. The Houyhnhnm is as non-bodily and abstract, in its essential nature, as an angel, the Yahoo a beast seen in its most disgusting lights. As for man, represented by Gulliver, he is left in a disastrous microcosmic vacuum. Instead of having his own distinctive place, he has to *be* one or the other of the extremes. Swift drives a wedge between the intellectual and the emotional, makes one good, the other evil, and pushes them further apart, as moral opposites, than any except the most extreme Puritans have usually done. The result is the kind of tormenting and bitter dilemma which always lies in wait for those who do this and, to quote Huxley again (a writer temperamentally very similar to Swift himself), who cannot "forgive man for being a vertebrate mammal as well as an immortal soul." The ideal is unattainable, the vicious alternative inescapable, and both are so unattractive that one is at a loss to decide which one dislikes the more.

Once again, then, the irony intended for moral satire has undergone a metamorphosis: and starting as an attempt to improve man, ends by writing him off as incurable.

But how far did Swift intend this to be so? This is the question which now becomes relevant, and the answer cannot, I think, be a straightforward one. My own feeling is that we are faced with a split between conscious intention and emotional conviction, of a kind which modern criticism has familiarized us with in Milton. Perhaps Swift really did intend a simple moral purpose, and was not consciously betraying his reader into despair. And yet, the unpleasantness of the Yahoos is realized so powerfully, and any supposed alternative is so palpably non-existent, that he

must have been to some degree aware of his dilemma. He must have known that men do, for better or worse, have bodily desires, and that the Houyhnhnms were therefore an impossible ideal. He must have known, too, being a man, that Houyhnhnms were both very limited and very unattractive. And in identifying Reason and Nature with them, he must have been aware that he was betraying his own positives and those of his age: leaving the Yahoos in triumphant possession of all the reality and the life, and removing the possibility of any human escape by way of Reason or Nature from their predicament.

As a satire, Gulliver can work normally only if we can accept the Houyhnhnms as a desirable human possibility: and this, I do not for a moment believe Swift thought we could. The very energy of the style is masochistic—a tormenting awareness of its own impotence to do, or change, anything. Swift is publicly torturing both himself and the species to which he belongs.[3]

[3] We might feel, today, that in exploring the dangers of dissociating reason from emotion, and calling the one good, the other bad, Swift really did hit on the central weakness of his age: that Book IV is still valid, in fact, as a satire upon Augustanism itself. The Augustans, at their most characteristic, disapproved of strong emotions as necessarily disruptive, subordinated even those emotions they could not exile to the stern control of "Right Reason," and found no place for "feeling" in their search for "truth." This attitude, we might decide, is doomed to failure by the actual nature of man—and Swift, by driving reason and emotion to opposite poles (with the result that man can live happily by neither) reveals just *how* impossible it is.

If we take this view, we might see Book IV as a counterpart, on the negative side, to the sort of criticism of the "Age of Reason" that Blake was later to offer, very positively, in *The Marriage of Heaven and Hell*. Such a view, however, is very paradoxical, since Swift can certainly not have intended anything of the kind, and would have been temperamentally very averse to accepting Blake's "solution." We might, then, see Swift's *impasse* as evidence that could be used in a critique of Augustanism. But we can be sure that Swift himself would not have agreed with such a critique, even had such a possibility occurred to him.

The irony, then, intended for moral reformation, has undergone a more or less conscious metamorphosis; and the total effect of Book IV, as Dr. Leavis has insisted, is largely negative.

There are, nevertheless, before this is finally asserted, one or two compensating factors to notice. The first, often surprisingly overlooked, is that Swift cannot really have supposed his readers to be Yahoos, if only because Yahoos could not have responded at all to *Gulliver's Travels*. The deliberate obtuseness with which Gulliver prattles of his "beloved England" will register only with a reader much less obtuse. The reader must not only be betrayed but see that he has been betrayed: and in order for this to happen he must have more intelligence and more moral sense than a Yahoo. Swift knew, in any case, that his readers *were* Augustan gentlemen with ideals of human decency that he had in common with them, and that however much a case against them could be both thought and felt, the ultimate *fact* of Augustan civilization—a fact embodied in his own style as much as anywhere—was not to be denied. *Gulliver's Travels* might leave us, then, with a wholly negative attitude, but the very fact of its being written at all is positive proof that Swift's own total attitude was not negative.

This may seem commonplace: but it leads on to another consideration, equally important, which most commentators upon *Gulliver* seem oddly afraid of: namely that Swift, writing for gentlemen, intended to give pleasure by what he wrote. When Gulliver says of the Yahoos (his readers), "I wrote for their amendment, and not their approbation," there is a general readiness to accept this at its face value, and to credit Swift with a similar sternness. Sooner or later most writers about *Gulliver* hit upon the word "exuberance," and then pause doubtfully, wondering whether, if Swift is so moral and so misanthropic as we think, such a word can have any place in describing him. Yet "exuberant" he certainly is,

even in Book IV of *Gulliver*. The "vive la bagatelle," the flamboyant virtuosity of *A Tale of a Tub* is less central, but it is still to be detected, in the zest with which Gulliver describes bad lawyers, for example, and in the fantastic turns and contortions of the irony. Clearly, Swift enjoyed his control of irony: enjoyed its flexibility, its complex destructiveness, his own easy mastery of it. Clearly, too, he expects his readers to enjoy it. The irony is not *only* a battle, but a game: a civilized game, at that, since irony is by its very nature civilized, presupposing both intelligence, and at least some type of moral awareness. The "war" is a battle of wits: and if one confesses (as the present writer does) to finding *Gulliver* immensely enjoyable, need one think that Swift would really, irony apart, have been surprised or annoyed by such a reaction?

On a final balance, I fancy that we have to compromise: agreeing that *Gulliver* ends by destroying all its supposed positives, but deducing, from the exuberance of the style and the fact that it was written at all, that Swift did not really end in Gulliver's position. He was, at heart, humane, and his savage indignation against cruelty and hypocrisy in the straightforwardly satiric parts reflects a real moral concern. He was, also, iconoclastic, and disillusioned about the ultimate dignity of man at a deep level: and when irony undergoes the type of metamorphosis that has been discussed here, it is as disturbing and uprooted as any we can find. But he always, at the same time, enjoyed the technique of irony itself, both as an intellectual game, and as a guarantee of at least some civilized reality. Very often, even at the most intense moments, we may feel that pleasure in the intellectual destructiveness of the wit is of more importance to him than the moral purpose, or the misanthropy, that is its supposed *raison d'être*. Irony, by its very nature, instructs by *pleasing*: and to ignore the pleasure, and its civilized implications, is inevitably to oversimplify, and falsify the total effect.

Martin Price

Swift's Symbolic Works

SYMBOLISM AND STRUCTURE

SYMBOLS are the concrete embodiment of relationships. In Swift's sermons and tracts, symbolic patterns often emerge at the close of an argument and fix in a pictorial or dramatic analogy the relations that have been presented abstractly. In a longer work such analogies may be used repeatedly. The sun, for example, may be turned to a number of functions: like reason, it may outlast the gaudy clouds of rhetoric; like judgment, it may govern its universe with order and proportion; like divine love, it may warm and attract all that moves about it. The suggestiveness of the sun symbol is the vast range of relations it may condense into one image; it is the task of the writer to make as many of these relations as possible relevant to his work. On the other hand, a single relationship may be given a vast range of embodiments; the balance of extremes, for example, may be evoked in the ethical mean, in the architect's balance of stresses, in the stability of the middle rank of society, in the precarious stance of man in the Great Chain of Being. The wider the range of relations a symbol may represent, or the wider the range of symbols that represent a relation, the more dense the meaning of a work and the more precisely qualified. The effect is somewhat as if the author had plotted the points through which a curve might be drawn: the relation must be general enough to satisfy each of these symbols, and, once it is abstracted, it may suggest countless new ones. The finest symbols are perhaps those that resist any neat formulation into a simple meaning; rather, they may suggest the pattern of the curve or even of several possible curves through the same points without allowing their suggestiveness to be lost in a single equation.

Swift's method in his two major works is based largely on the creation of symbolic patterns, in both cases reductive patterns. In each work this reductive pattern emerges in spite of the narrator and comes to include all that he has granted the highest dignity. To this extent, there is mere transvaluation: high becomes low. But in the course of including so much of man's behavior, these reductive patterns acquire a dignity of their own, a "bad eminence" that makes man's vice and folly a thorough and terrible inversion of his true goodness. The pressure with which Swift reduces so many patterns of handsome corruption to those of the Bedlam inmate or the Yahoo gives weight and intensity to his simplification.

Even more, the simplification is not all that it seems. First of all, it provides a general pattern of incongruity by which meaning is given to a great range of detail. The ambitious amplification of the mock author of *A Tale of a Tub* and the ingenuous awe of Gulliver are both set off at every point by the underlying symbolic patterns of the book. Each event, each important word, is given a complexity of meaning that the author cannot discern. More important, the reductive patterns are not the whole truth. If two curves of quite different pattern can be drawn through the same points, at least a third seems possible.

Reprinted from *Swift's Rhetorical Art: A Study in Structure and Meaning*, Yale University Studies in English, vol. 123, New Haven, 1953, by permission of the author and the Yale University Press. Footnotes have been omitted or shortened without notice.

If we have come to see the weakness of the conventional distinction between greatness and baseness, we need not abandon either the words or the distinction but consider both anew. The eventual identification of carping and serenity (of Jack and Peter) in the *Tale* and the impossible choice of Gulliver between Houyhnhnm and Yahoo are Swift's devices for dissolving the reductive simplicity he has opposed to an uncritical complacency. A middle view is left for the reader to define.

In both *A Tale of a Tub* and *Gulliver's Travels* the symbolic pattern is freed of dependence upon abstract argument. The general meanings are implied in the pattern of event or image. In neither work is the narrative structure allowed to become so tightly coherent as to demand simple allegorical equations, although there are particular allegorical meanings among others in parts of both books. Nor, on the other hand, do Swift's symbols become vague and indefinite. The complexity lies in the conflict of rather precise patterns; in *Gulliver's Travels* the conflict is finally dramatized in the dilemma of the hero. In these works, then, we are confronted with a new situation. Instead of starting with generalities which acquire a weight of suggestion through symbolic patterns, we start almost at once with elaborate symbolic patterns and move toward apparent simplification. It is useful to compare the two works in their themes, their symbolism, and their irony. Between them they represent all of Swift's methods at their best.

COMMON THEMES

The theme of inversion is one of many in Swift, but it is an important one, a peculiar concern of his age as of our own. It is difficult to read the last books of George Orwell, for example, without being frequently reminded of Swift. And it is difficult, on the other hand, to read Plato, at least with the guidance of John Wild's recent book, *Plato's Theory of Man*, without seeing both Swift's problems and our own.

Orwell in *1984* has given us a picture of a society which must create its own past and indeed its own world. In its worship of power, it claims right as well by constantly re-creating the world to justify its own acts. History must be revised at every moment, memory must be destroyed, all threat of an objective truth must be overcome. Wild's analysis of the world's present ills is similar. He finds our chief danger in "idealism," and he sees three symptoms of its prevalence: the "absence of any faith in a real order of existence, independent of the opinions and desires of the national group"; a "scorn for reason, except as the contriver of technical instruments"; and a contempt for the rational individual.

Whatever one may think of this analysis of the modern situation, it could not have greatly displeased Swift. If there is a central preoccupation running through Swift's work, it is surely something very close to the theme Wild stresses in Plato—anatropism, the inversion of culture. The inversion may be the rule of the tryant, of a man like Callicles or Thrasymachus who considers justice a mere convention imposed by power; or it may be the guidance of the sophist, who fits all moral terms "to the fancies of the great beast and calls what it enjoys good and what vexes it bad." Within the individual it is the rule of appetite, the failure "to subdue the brutish parts of our nature to the human," the willingness "to enslave our humanity to the savagery of the beast." Wild shows the fundamental importance in Plato's work of the contrast "between the true, upward way of life, and the downward way which *thinks* it is going up."

In Swift the problem of inversion is stated as the threat of corruption—the barbarity which is "kept out with so much Difficulty, by so few Hands." [1] Society is constantly degenerating into forms which cease to effect control over the individual will and in fact are turned by the will to

[1] *The History of the Four Last Years of the Queen, Works*, Temple Scott edition, X, 126.

its own purposes. So, too, the men who rule the society fail in the virtue which alone makes them human and become instead the instruments of their own or of a party's will. Their words finally, when they lose their proper meaning, become the means of deception or domination.

In *A Tale of a Tub* Swift dramatizes the corruptions of religion and learning in two ways: the allegory embodies in the career of typical Restoration fops the history of the church in the world, and the prefaces and digressions embody in a continuous dramatic monologue the bathos and pretentious folly of the modern spirit. The monologue includes numerous symbolic accounts of the corruption of learning; they are presented as a panegyric upon the moderns, but they are written in the language of a man so obtuse and uncritical that he unwittingly betrays his case at every turn. Since Swift is concerned with the misuse of religion to serve "schemes of wealth and power," his allegory treats religion on the level of manners, as one more means of achieving self-aggrandizement or domination at the expense of reason. True religion can survive only if man serves God; when man serves himself and seeks "sublunary happiness" as an end in itself, as Swift frequently points out, he may use *nominal* Christianity as an instrument, but he has already discarded true Christianity. The three brothers of the allegory slay "certain Dragons" but soon come to the town, the *grand monde* or world of fashion. They cease, in short, to redeem the time but live for it instead, and fashion becomes Swift's principal symbol of this absorption in the world.

Much of the *Tale* is built around the contrast of the temporal or fashionable and the permanent or timeless. The Epistle to Prince Posterity first shows the inevitable conflict of Time and the ambitions of a time-bound generation. The moderns seek distinction rather than truth, and they seek it by novelty and singularity, by ignoring the universal or enduring. Though they seek to reach Posterity by evading the judgment of Time, their works vanish before they can so much as offer them. In seeking distinction, the moderns wish to *conquer* the past. "I here think fit," says the Tale Teller, "to lay hold on that great and honourable Privilege of being the *Last Writer*; I claim an absolute Authority in Right, as the *freshest Modern*, which gives me a Despotick Power over all Authors before me." (Sect. V) The result of this view is self-indulgence—private meaning, "tender wit," ephemeral achievement. The Tale Teller's demonstration of his own age's greatness collapses, and he is finally left clinging to the specious present: "what I am going to say is literally true this Minute I am writing." ("Epistle to Prince Posterity")

What is ephemeral, however, may be praised all the more as fashionable, and Swift uses clothes symbolism to present this inversion. The three coats of the brothers (the simple and plain truths of doctrine) become, in their misuse, the instruments of pride and worldly ambition. The Tale Teller is ready to systematize this, and he presents us with an inverted theology to support inverted practices and institutions. The God of the clothes philosophy is the tailor, who "daily create[s] Men, by a kind of Manufactory Operation." His creatures, which "the World calls improperly *Suits of Cloaths*," are "in Reality the most refined Species of Animals"—in fact, "Rational Creatures, or Men." The soul of man is really his celestial or outer suit, daily created anew, and its faculties are parts of dress:

Embroidery, was *Sheer wit; Gold Fringe* was *agreeable Conversation, Gold Lace* was *Repartee*, a huge long *Periwig* was *Humour*, and a *Coat full of Powder* was very good *Raillery:* All which required abundance of *Finesse* and *Delicatesse* to manage with Advantage, as well as strict Observance after Times and Fashions.

The implications are clear: when the end of man is self-love and distinction and his means singularity or fashion, he has no standards which endure, no integrity. In a sense, he has ceased to have a soul at all, for when religion and the soul cease to be regulatory and moral they have become lackeys rather than masters and no longer deserve their original names: "Is not Religion a *Cloak,* Honesty a *Pair of Shoes,* worn out in the Dirt, Self-love a *Surtout,* Vanity a *Shirt,* and Conscience a *Pair of Breeches,* which, tho' a Cover for Lewdness as well as Nastiness, is easily slipt down for the Service of both." (Sect. I)

Elsewhere, Swift deals at length with the instability of happiness as a human end. The pagan philosophers, never able to agree about the *summum bonum,* either became cynical skeptics or, for lack of any solid faith, were inclined "to fall into the vulgar pursuits of common men, to hunt after greatness and riches, to make their court, and to serve occasions." The world offers no stable end; only heavenly wisdom ("a daily vision of God") can provide it.[2] To return to the words of the *Tale,* "as human Happiness is of a very short Duration, so in those Days were human Fashions, upon which it entirely depends." (Sect. I) The very nature of fashion makes every victory a necessary defeat. The pattern of natural man for Swift, as for Hobbes, shows him endlessly acquisitive and endlessly unsatisfied.[3] Such limited self-love involves the need for superiority or pre-eminence; at best it retains the spirit of opposition, the love of party or sect. Reason seeks victory instead of truth and becomes sophistry in the process. Knowledge gives way to an imagination which can frame a gratifying image of the world. The soul itself becomes a mere image of the fashions of the day, an ever-changing garment of the body whose needs it now serves. Over all this, as Swift wrote elsewhere, hovers the threat of Time,

the instrument of judgment: "Principles, as the world goes, are little more than fashion; and the apostle tells us, that 'the fashion of this world passeth away.' "[4]

The *Tale* points throughout to a middle way that lies between opposed forms of corruption. Reason is always a balance between extremes of refinement and superficiality or, as we might put it, idle curiosity and naïve credulity. Refinement takes the form of theorizing, of finding at any expense meanings which can be built into a system. It is the typical seventeenth-century crime of wresting Scriptures carried into the realms of criticism, science, and philosophy. The piety of the Tale Teller requires that the hacks of Grub Street be revealed as *"Grubaean* Sages," their works as "Vehicles of Types and Fables" containing the "most finished and refined Systems of all Science and Arts." But the systems can only be revealed by "Untwisting or Unwinding": much industry is required to force impressive meaning from trivialities.

The systems themselves are either built, like "Edifices in the Air" out of sight and hearing, completely beyond empirical test, or they may be turned into "Oratorial Machines," devices for raising demagogues to a position from which they may dominate the crowd. So, too, the three ladies who lead the brothers away from simplicity are "at the very Top of the Fashion." In both cases height is the departure from the common forms which confers distinction and authority. Each system builder seeks to conquer all of nature, as do the moderns all of literature, and thereby to overthrow all rival systems. The Tale Teller boasts of an essay on the number three: "I have by most convincing Proofs, not only reduced the *Senses* and the *Elements* under its Banner, but brought over several Deserters from its two great Rivals *SEVEN* and *NINE*." (Sect. I) The system builder becomes, in short, the

---

[2] *On the Wisdom of this World,* Temple Scott, IV, 175, 178.

[3] "For learning, like all true merit, is easily satisfied; while the false and counterfeit is perpetually craving, and never thinks it has enough." Temple Scott, XI, 20.

[4] "Advertisement to Memoirs of Captain John Creichton," Temple Scott, XI, 167. Cf. I Corinthians 7:31.

hero in the universe of fashion. Swift places together all revolutions "in empire, philosophy, and religion." Each is achieved by the conqueror's reduction of "Multitudes to his own *Power*, his *Reasons* or his *Visions*." (Sect. IX) The patterns of conqueror, bully, and tyrant all contribute to the archetype by which proselytizing and system building are to be understood. In his account of Bedlam Swift finally shows the fundamental standard of this inverted world; madness is only heroism out of fashion.

The story of the three brothers is itself one of the typical modern systems, a reductive allegory of the history of the church from its primitive simplicity to its division and further corruption under the pretense of reformation and counterreformation. The story, however, is more than allegory; it provides a causal explanation of these corruptions in terms of personal morality. It allows Swift to study the individual motives which underlie the decay of religion, while the Tale Teller presents specious rationalization for a comparable decay in learning. Swift reduces the behavior of the churches to that of fops and gallants, while the Tale Teller refines foppery and gallantry into a mock religion.

The culmination of Swift's satiric point comes with the reduction of man to mechanism. Swift once noted that "climbing is performed in the same Posture with Creeping." [5] In the same way pretension which seeks to lift man above reason can also reduce him to the mechanism of physical causation. Man loses freedom when he surrenders the power of *rational* choice, and his visions have a way of turning out to be irrational compulsions. This is best illustrated in the fate of words: as sound replaces meanings and words are "spiritualized and refined . . . from the Dross and Grossness of Sense and Human Reason," their operation may be described in "physico-logical" terms. Words become weapons

[5] *Thoughts on Various Subjects*, Temple Scott, I, 273.

rather than symbols; they are "Bodies of much Weight and Gravity, as it is manifest from those deep *Impressions* they make and leave upon us; and therefore must be delivered from a due Altitude, or else they will neither carry a good Aim, nor fall down with a sufficient Force." (Sect. I) When words are reduced to mere forceful sound, all sound becomes operative. The uncritical audience which abandons a standard of rational communication treasures all forms of expression or stimulation. "For, the *Spirit* being the same in all, it is of no Import through what Vehicle it is convey'd." And Swift, in *The Mechanical Operation of the Spirit*, provides a picture of that preromantic personality, the evangelistic preacher of the Puritans: "A Master Work-man shall *blow his Nose so powerfully*, as to pierce the Hearts of his People, who are disposed to receive the Excrements of his Brain with the same Reverence, as the *Issue* of it. Hawking, Spitting, and Belching, the Defects of other Mens Rhetorick, are the Flowers, and Figures, and Ornaments of his."

Again, the Tale Teller readily systematizes the doctrine of the Aeolists, who value inspiration and take all eccentricity to be divine possession. Their "inspiration" is literalized to the point where they affirm "the Gift of BELCHING to be the noblest Act of a Rational Creature." (Sect. VIII) The Aeolists do not disclaim rationality but simply invert its meaning, just as the moderns do not dismiss religion but turn it into the worship of fashion. Swift makes Aeolism a substitution both of the physical for the truly rational and of self-induced disease for normal health. His scheme may be reduced to a matrix somewhat as follows:

CORRUPTION		DECENCY	
Principle	*Expression*	*Expression*	*Principle*
passion	flatulency	health	reason
display	belching	speech	communication
imagination	cant	meaning	thought
domination	sound	argument	persuasion

This scheme could be extended in several ways—for example, the kinds of effect achieved in each case, conviction or ecstasy, comprehension or titillation.[6]

Reason may be neglected by the bestial Aeolists or transcended by the sophistical system builders. Swift brings the two groups together in his digression on madness. The vapors of the brain are fed by the lower parts of the body: "Mists arise from the Earth, Steams from Dunghills, Exhalations from the Sea, and Smoak from Fire; yet all Clouds are the same in Composition, as well as Consequences: and the Fumes issuing from a Jakes, will furnish as comely and useful a Vapor, as Incense from an Altar. . . . [The vapors may be repressed sexuality, the rains a bursting storm of conquest.] The same Spirits, which in their superior Progress would conquer a Kingdom, descending upon the *Anus*, conclude in a *Fistula*." (Sect. IX) Higher and lower become transposed terms in this inverted world; the physical expression is at least less harmful than the spiritual. Both forms of expression are escapes from rational control, and all their issue in human conduct is an inversion of rational order, whether social or religious, poetic or rhetorical. In place of order man enjoys the endless whirl of fashion and the endless competition for distinction and power.

In *Gulliver's Travels* the same themes arise. They are not made fully explicit until the fourth voyage, but the whole book moves toward the final definition of man's nature. Only after the first three voyages have shown man's potential order and his actual disorder can Swift divide the rational aspect from the bestial. The Houyhnhnms are all order and reason, their only emotions the social or rational ones of friendship and benevolence; the Yahoos are all disorder and passion, competitive beasts vying for satisfaction and supremacy. In the scheme of the fourth voyage there is

[6] For the use of a matrix, see Scott Buchanan, *Symbolic Distance in Relation to Analogy and Fiction*, London, 1932.

no third kind of creature—except Gulliver himself, who can no longer bear to see what he really is—and to one of these two must be assigned the achievements upon which civilized man prides himself. The Yahoos provide Swift countless metaphors for human institutions which have grown corrupt and inverted.

These metaphors grow out of a framework of interpretation. Swift prepares us with sufficient implicit analysis of human corruption to make the final analogies possible. Two patterns are traced throughout the earlier voyages, the meanness of man's mind and the grossness of his body.

Gulliver fails to draw any connection between the physical grossness of man and his moral nature. He neglects to see that although the Brobdingnagians reveal the horror of the human animal they also exemplify the restraint of the animal by decency and reason. Swift's pattern in these books becomes clear if we look ahead to the Yahoos, in whom physical grossness and unchecked passion are combined. Decency serves as a partial corrective of human corruption; conscience is in this sense not "a Cover for Lewdness as well as Nastiness" but a restraint upon them. This accounts for Swift's constant emphasis, in the *Tale* and in the *Travels*, upon manners; Jack's refusal "to eat his Victuals like a Christian" is a rejection of the common forms in which reason finds its compromise with man's animality. Self-indulgence and filth are virtually equated.

In the third voyage Swift closes in upon the proudest achievements of man, reducing them to the very denial of a rational nature. In Laputa, he brings together speculation, pride, foppery, and conquest. Laputa, like Lilliput, is a small and ingenious power dominating a vastly larger one. The speculative mind, like that of the system builder, demands adherence; the king, in fact, "would be the most absolute Prince in the Universe." The divorce between the distracted mind and the animal body is elaborated in the division of the Laputan family into oblivious husband and incorrigibly adulterous wife. The Flying Island (whose adamantine bottom recalls the royal prerogative with which Swift had been so much concerned in the *Drapier's Letters*) is a world of pure self-indulgence, but it is also an instrument of power sought for its own sake.

In Balnibarbi below, power is sought in the name of social improvement. The earthbound disciples of the Laputans are, like the Aeolists of the *Tale*, "full of Volatile Spirits acquired in that Airy Region." Like the moderns of the *Tale*, they seek to attain permanence in haste and with ease: "A Palace may be built in a Week, of Materials so durable as to last for ever without repairing." While Lord Munodi tries to hold on to the living past, which is the universally sound, the Balnibarbians sacrifice all to the pride which they project into a utopian future. The projectors of Lagado seek to outdo nature at any cost; art must be shown not in perfecting nature but in confounding her. Mechanical operation is once more introduced as the escape from reason: the "laborious" method of attaining knowledge is evaded by the swallowing of wafers.

The remainder of the third voyage extends and intensifies the attack upon man's achievements. First, Swift turns to man's legends of himself. The conversations with the dead leave Gulliver with a sextumvirate not of conquerors but of "Destroyers of Tyrants and Usurpers, and . . . Restorers of Liberty to oppressed and injured Nations." The truly learned are winnowed from the multitude of pedants, the few deserving from the host of corrupt and successful. Intellectual systems are seen to be, as in the *Tale*, "Fashions, which . . . vary in every Age." Finally, the price of wealth and power is shown to be the surrender of virtue and liberty: "that positive, confident, restive Temper, which Virtue infused into Man, was a perpetual Clog to publick Business." Associated with moral corruption are the loss of simplicity of

"Manners, Dyet and Dress" and the growth of disease, notably the pox. The condition of the body is an index to the moral estate of man.

As if in confirmation of all that Gulliver has seen at Glubbdubdrib, the court of Luggnagg reproduces once more the pomp, tyranny, and pride of man. Here the creeping of courtiers, as in Lilliput, is made literal; it is now accompanied by the licking of dust, often poisoned at the whim of the king. The "Ceremony" which Gulliver craved in Brobdingnag here overwhelms him; "a Party of Ten Horse" is sent for conducting him and his "Retinue" (one "poor Lad") to the court. But as always Gulliver is the devotee of appearance; he is altogether uncritical of the king's poisoned dust:

> I myself heard him give Directions, that one of his Pages should be whipt, whose Turn it was to give Notice about washing the Floor after an Execution, but maliciously had omitted it; by which Neglect a young Lord of great Hopes coming to an Audience, was unfortunately poisoned, although the King at that Time had no Design against his Life. But this good Prince was so gracious, as to forgive the poor Page his Whipping, upon Promise that he would do so no more, without special Orders.

Gulliver is able to recognize immorality only when it is divorced from power and authority. The tyrant's expediency is equated with justice, his indifference with clemency.

The Struldbrugs provide the occasion for Swift to sum up all the forms of worldly aspiration: wealth, learning, historical wisdom. In each of these, given immortal life, Gulliver would wish to become supreme. By teaching and example he would prevent the "continual Degeneracy of human Nature," but he has naïve confidence in his own ability to achieve greatness without corruption. His conviction that man can be changed by history or example, or that with the gift of immortality man can achieve virtual perfection, is the dream of "sublunary Happiness," as he calls it, given free range. All that Gulliver has neglected he sees in the actual Struldbrugs, who embody in their endless lives the whole range of human corruption. "Envy and impotent Desires, are their prevailing Passions," and these passions govern hideously decayed bodies. In Gulliver's last remarks about the Struldbrugs he has come to defend the restraints placed upon them: "Otherwise, as Avarice is the necessary Consequent of old Age, those Immortals would in time become Proprietors of the whole Nation, and engross the Civil Power; which, for want of Abilities to manage, must end in the Ruin of the Publick." [7]

Here, then, is man's unlimited corruption, at once both physical and moral, and we need not look beyond Swift's own writings to find its obvious theological explanation. In a letter written about ten years later Swift composed an allegory about his "copyhold tenure" on a "poor little house of clay":

For the first thirty years of my life I am to pay nothing, only to do suit and service, and attend upon the courts, that are kept once a week or oftener. Four years after that I am to pay a rose every year, and farther than this, during the remainder of my life I am to pay a tooth . . . every two or three years, or oftener, if it be demanded; and when I have nothing else to pay, out with me is the word, and I will not be long before my person will be seized. I might have had my lease on much better terms, if it had not been the fault of my great-grandfather. He and his wife, with the advice of a bad neighbour, robbed an orchard belonging to the Lord of the Manor, and so forfeited their grand privileges; to my sorrow I am sure, but, however, I must do as well as I can. [8]

The movement from the Struldbrugs to the Yahoos is clear. The Yahoos are the culmination of the symbolic matrix Swift has created for the corruptions of man. They embody in a crude animal form most of the vices (and supposed glories) of civi-

lized man. The most concretely disgusting of all the images Swift creates, they are also the most abstract symbol of man's irrational pursuit of power at the expense of reason. Swift makes clear in the last part of the fourth voyage that the Yahoos are not man himself any more than are the Houyhnhnms. But all the institutions of men are close to the fulfillment of a Yahoo nature as long as they remain in their inverted state. Created to embody rational control, to keep man decent like the brothers' coats, they are used instead to serve man's passions and desire for power over his fellows. It is this doubleness of all man's creations, and of man's nature itself, that Swift's irony constantly explores. He is, of course, exploiting a traditional classical view:

A social instinct is implanted in all men by nature, and yet he who first founded the state was the greatest of benefactors. For man, when perfected, is the best of animals, but, when separated from law and justice, he is the worst of all; since armed injustice is the more dangerous, and he is equipped at birth with arms, meant to be used by intelligence and virtue, which he may use for the worst ends. Wherefore, if he have not virtue, he is most unholy and the most savage of animals, and the most full of lust and gluttony. [9]

But it is important to recall the full matrix into which Swift's symbols are placed for even a nominally Christian society. To men concerned with "our war with the world, the devil, and our own corrupt nature," the "most savage of animals" is not simply opposed to "the best of animals." When Swift prays he asks God to "make us hate every thing in ourselves that is unlike to thee." [10] The inversion is the greater for the greatness of the true end of man.

A COMPARISON OF METHODS

As we place the two works together, Swift's symbolic methods emerge more clearly, in their range and in their unity.

[7] Cf. Ernest Bernbaum's introduction to his edition of *Gulliver's Travels*, New York, 1920, p. xvii.
[8] *Correspondence*, ed. Ball, V, 246 (Oct. 1735).

[9] Aristotle, *Politics* (tr. Jowett), Bk. I, chap. ii, 1253ᵃ. Cf. also Aristotle, *Politics*, Bk. VII, chap. xiii, 1332ᵃ, ᵇ, on the contrast of man and animals.
[10] *An Evening Prayer*, Temple Scott, III, 315, 317.

Each of the works is recounted by an author who is the counterpart neither of Swift nor of the intelligent reader. Each author has his peculiar blindness, his own variant of the obliviousness which comes from excessive concentration on part of the truth. The two authors belong, however, to different rhetorical structures, and their characters are adapted to different satirical methods. The Tale Teller is garrulous and ingenious, full of explanations, proud of witty flights: Gulliver is spare in comment, literal minded, stolidly dedicated to factual reporting. The blindness of the Tale Teller emerges in a tissue of verbal contretemps; he is the victim of his own wit, which escapes his control and carries him along, a helpless rider, in a direction he does not intend. Gulliver's blindness becomes evident in his language as the scenes he describes demand a moral judgment he has no capacity to make; but he is primarily the victim of events. The witty analogies which led to unexpected conclusions for the Tale Teller are embodied in the concrete world Gulliver inhabits; conclusions assert themselves as encounters with strange customs and strange peoples. Gulliver is trapped by circumstances, not words, and therefore cannot escape, as the Tale Teller does, an awareness of consequences. Gulliver does change in the last part of the book and to that extent at least comes closer to being a true fictional character than any of Swift's other ironic masks.

As the character of each author differs, so does the range of allusion which Swift can introduce. The very facility of the Tale Teller makes him the echo of a multitude of authors and serves to make the *Tale* itself a destructive parody of the solemn use of false wit. The manner of Gulliver is no less a parody but of a more limited kind: he reproduces the careful observation enjoined on mariners by the Royal Society.[11] Less extravagant and pretentious than the

Tale Teller, he is less suggestive a figure, and his language contains less allusive parody. Yet the very simplicity of Gulliver allows him more readily to become a universal figure in a work whose rhetorical argument becomes increasingly general as it progresses.

Both the Tale Teller and Gulliver are versions of a typical Swiftian character—the fool who serves the knaves. The hypocrite is a more striking satirical subject in some ways, but he is too limited a figure, as superficial a representation of man as the Hobbesian image of thorough self-love or the sentimentalist's portrait of utter benevolence. The central issue for Swift is cognition. Whatever man's motives, selfish or not, a clear knowledge of his true interest will lead to virtue, and prudence will eventually become moral habit. This does not rule out a more transcendent virtue born directly of faith in God, obedience to His law, and imitation of divine virtues; but it does accept man at his worst and start from there, and it does make each man responsible for an error which common sense alone can avoid. The common dupe Swift invents, like his counterpart in the reader, is not clear-sighted in selfishness; he is neither a rebel nor a Machiavel. A man of middling virtue, he would recoil from an accurate recognition of the ends he is promoting, and Swift, of course, never allows him that recognition but demands it instead of the reader. Rather, the fool among knaves is somewhat vain, somewhat proud, and very gullible. His shortsightedness can be exaggerated, as it is in much of Swift's satire, into a prepossession that approaches insanity. This kind of man is both too dense to be morally alert and too naïve to disguise his folly. Neither the Tale Teller nor

---

11 See Ray W. Frantz, *The English Traveller and the Movement of Ideas 1660–1732, University Studies of the University of Nebraska,* 32–3

(1932–33), 15–29. Especially valuable for Swift's parody of scientific style and thought are the two articles by Marjorie H. Nicolson and Nora V. Mohler, "The Scientific Background of Swift's Voyage to Laputa" and "Swift's 'Flying Island' in the Voyage to Laputa," *Annals of Science,* 2 (1937), 299–334, 405–30.

Gulliver is the worst of his kind: each is a man seeking to defend more successful villains with a bathetic credulity. But as we can see in *A Modest Proposal,* the insanity of the fool becomes a metaphor for the guilt of responsible men.

The Tale Teller

The Tale Teller is not one of the "Wits of the present Age" like his "more successful Brethren the *Moderns.*" He is anxious to please, to be a "most devoted Servant of all *Modern* Forms," but he is somewhat uncomfortable among his younger contemporaries. Particularly does he resent the usurpation by Gresham and Will's—by the new scientists and wits—of the dignity of Grub Street. These are "revolted and new-fangled" offspring who deny the Grubean parents they have outdone. The Tale Teller, then, is a modern *manqué,* aware of some limitations, free of some caprices, but only envious rather than critical of the brighter moderns. He is more tolerable than the knaves, less arrogant, more confused. He is old-fashioned enough to claim a rational pattern for, and to give the dignity of system to, the self-indulgence and competition of the moderns.

It is in the Epistle Dedicatory to Prince Posterity that we first encounter him, seeking to claim immortality for his brethren (having resigned it for himself). He cannot see Time's verdict as the impartial judgment of reason asserting itself inevitably over a long enough expanse but only as a "peculiar Malice" toward his own age. Unable to see, as the knaves are unwilling to admit, the age's own responsibility for this "universal Ruin," the Tale Teller projects his horror and fear into an extravagant image of Time as a cruel tyrant: "Be pleased to remark the Length and Strength, the Sharpness and Hardness, of his *Nails* and *Teeth:* Consider his baneful abominable *Breath,* Enemy to Life and Matter, infectious and corrupting." But this very appeal to Posterity sets the Tale Teller off from his brethren, who scorn him as "a clown and pedant" for seeking works that have already been succeeded by fresher ones. As it turns out, he "can only avow in general . . . that we do abound in Learning and Wit; but to fix upon Particulars, is a Task too slippery for my slender Abilities." The Tale Teller suffers from an excessive respect for fact; once the rational faculty is completely divorced from the empirical by the truer moderns, or by Peter and Jack, systems can be built more freely. The guise of the fool serves much the same function as the witty construction; it allows Swift to convert an argument into its opposite.

The Tale Teller is scarcely an admirable character at any point. As a representative of a "Corporation of Poets," he is devoted to the forms of his "refined Age." For all his difficulties he is frightfully vain, both as "author of this miraculous treatise" and as the heir of man's inevitable progress. Having spent his years writing "Four-score and eleven Pamphlets . . . for the Service of six and thirty Factions," he can look back with "unspeakable Comfort" at having "passed a long Life, with a Conscience void of Offence." Yet his venality has an irresponsible innocence about it; he still offers himself as "Secretary" of the universe, willing to elucidate all mysteries for "the general Good of Mankind." (Sects. I, V) In his eagerness to defend the indefensible he becomes a throwback to another kind of devout wit. Since the slightness of modern works can be denied only if we consider these works the vehicles of hidden truths, the Tale Teller becomes much like the Christian virtuoso of the seventeenth century who reads signs of God's wisdom in the meanest of natural phenomena. It is the attitude we find constantly in Sir Thomas Browne or in Robert Boyle's *Occasional Reflections,* which Swift parodied in the *Meditation upon a Broomstick.* Lady Berkeley remarked, when Swift announced the title of the pretended meditation of Boyle, "What a strange subject! But there is no knowing what useful lessons of instruction this wonderful man may draw from things apparently the most trivial." This ingenuity has in the moderns the inverted motive of revealing the greater glory not of God but of themselves.

Appropriately, Swift recalls the equation common in the century behind him, of the extravagant doctrines of dissenters and such heresies as those of the Gnostics. Both split Christianity with schism, both are justified by the wresting of Scripture, both are instruments of pride and dominion. In placing on his title page an epigraph from Irenaeus quoting the jargon of the Gnostics, Swift allies himself with the church fathers and identifies the moderns with the speculative heretics. Even more, Swift adds a passage from Lucretius wherein new flowers, unlike any previously offered, are sought. The moderns can only turn to the variety of disease if they repudiate the health of the ancients as trite or commonplace. The Tale Teller, like the Gnostics, attempts great subtlety. In this he is akin to all possessed fools who would prove the truth of their fancies. All of them wrest Scripture in one way or another—the virtuoso forcing the evidence of nature, Bentley quarrying literary texts for historical evidence, Thomas Vaughan ceaselessly and fantastically referring "all naturals to their spirituals by the way of secret analogy." [12]

In Vaughan and the dark authors Swift found the most direct heirs of the Gnostics and also the most conspicuously nonsensical theorizers of speculative fancies. Vaughan, in words reminiscent of Donne, urged a departure from too narrow a reading of Scripture:

That which I now write must needs appear very strange and incredible to the common man, whose knowledge sticks in the bark of allegories and mystical speeches, never apprehending that which

is signified by them unto us. This, I say, must needs sound strange with such as understand the Scriptures in the literal, plain sense, considering not the scope and intention of the Divine Spirit, by whom they were first penned and delivered. [13]

Not only did Vaughan profess to reveal the mysteries in Scripture but he turned as well, for his magical doctrine, to oral tradition, as does Peter in the *Tale*. Some things, Vaughan explained, "which exceeded carnal understanding were transmitted without writing." Centuries before, Irenaeus had complained of the Gnostics that "they disregard the order and connection of the Scriptures," that they "patch together old wives' fables, and then endeavour, by violently drawing [words] away from their proper connection . . . to adapt the oracles of God to their baseless fictions." They "desert what is certain, indubitable, and true" and, like the sophists interpreting Homer, collect scattered expressions and "twist them" to their own sense. [14] Swift might have looked back beyond Irenaeus to Plato, whose attack upon rhapsode and sophist resembles Swift's treatment of inverted wit. As the sophists claimed to extract all kinds of wisdom from Homer, Swift's moderns seem to imply the presence of such wisdom in their own writings. It is only appropriate, therefore, that the moderns should scorn Homer for his inadequacy in providing a "compleat Body of all Knowledge Human, Divine, Political, and Mechanick," for his imperfect knowledge of Jacob Boehme, and for his unreliable cure for syphilis. (Sect. V)

In the spirit of modern subtlety the Tale Teller urges greater penetration (that is, credulity) upon his readers:

But the greatest Maim given to that general Reception, which the Writings of our Society have formerly received, (next to the transitory State

---

[12] Thomas Vaughan, *Anima Magica Abscondita*, in *Works*, ed. Arthur E. Waite (London, 1919), p. 116. The fullest account of the immediate background of the *Tale* and of Swift's use of it for satire and parody is in Starkman, *Swift's Satire on Learning in A Tale of a Tub*. There is a valuable discussion of Swift's use of Thomas Vaughan in pp. 45–56.

[13] Vaughan, *Anthroposophia Theomagica*, in *Works*, ed. Waite, p. 36.
[14] Irenaeus, *Against Heresies*, Bk. I, chaps. viii, ix; Bk. II, chap. xxvii, in *The Ante-Nicene Fathers*, ed. Alexander Roberts, James Donaldson, and A. C. Coxe (Buffalo, 1885), I, 326, 330, 399.

of all sublunary Things), hath been a superficial Vein among many Readers of the present Age, who will by no means be persuaded to inspect beyond the Surface and the Rind of Things; whereas, *Wisdom* is a *Fox*, who after long hunting, will at last cost you the Pains to dig out: 'Tis a *Cheese*, which by how much the richer, has the thicker, the homelier, and the coarser Coat; and whereof to a judicious Palate, the *Maggots* are the best. 'Tis a *Sack-Posset*, wherein the deeper you go, you will find it the sweeter. *Wisdom* is a *Hen*, whose *Cackling* we must value and consider, because it is attended with an *Egg*; But then, lastly, 'tis a *Nut*, which, unless you chuse with Judgment, may cost you a Tooth, and pay you with nothing but a *Worm*.

Here we can see all the devices at work. The figure of the rind and the kernel was a commonplace popular throughout the seventeenth century and long before. The Tale Teller argues from analogy, with vivacity and copiousness of wit, but his analogies gradually become less and less apt. From a praise of the reward which costs pains he turns to a praise of pains which yield a reward. The instance of the maggots throws doubt on the value of the reward, and the instance of the hen uses the reward not only to justify the means but to dignify all accompanying annoyances. Finally Swift turns to new effect a sentence he probably found in Dryden. Dryden wrote of Cleveland that "he gives us many times a hard nut to break our teeth without a kernel for our pains." It is Swift's peculiar genius to make of Dryden's sharp figure an even sharper one; he gives more than an image of futile pains, he creates revulsion as well. It is not merely folly which Swift is castigating but a perversion of values.

It is the special gift of the Tale Teller to be able to reach a damaging conclusion with no discomposure and move on with only a complacent reference to "these momentous Truths." We can see the same composed self-exposure in his encouragement to satirists: "but let them remember, it is with *Wits* as with *Razors*, which are never so apt to *cut* those they are employ'd on, as when they have *lost their Edge*. Be-

sides, those whose Teeth are too rotten to bite, are best of all others, qualified to revenge that Defect with their Breath." ("Preface") The function of razors casually shifts from shaving to cutting; it can then be blandly assumed that teeth are meant only for wounding. Again the reversal of true values is made disgusting as well as foolish: if destruction is the real purpose, the foulest means are available to the least competent.

One can find many such ironic reversals in *A Tale of a Tub*, woven together into a web of imperturbable sweet reasonableness:

> The *True Criticks* are known by their Talent of swarming about the noblest Writers, to which they are carried meerly by Instinct, as a Rat to the best Cheese, or a Wasp to the fairest Fruit. So, when the *King* is a Horse-back, he is sure to be the *dirtiest* Person of the Company, and they that make their Court best, are such as *bespatter* him most.

Nor does the author rest with these analogies; he has still another to make complete the reversal of standards:

> Lastly; A *True Critick*, in the Perusal of a Book, is like a *Dog* at a Feast, whose Thoughts and Stomach are wholly set upon what the Guests *fling away*, and consequently, is apt to *Snarl* most, when there are fewest *Bones*. (Sect. III)

This is the kind of passage which illustrates the richness of Swift's wit. The Tale Teller has no purpose but to show his talent for creating figures. But all the terms allow extension. The "feast" provides us with the suggestion not only of true nourishment (as opposed to the corrupt diet of the moderns) and pleasure but also of the decorum of hospitality. This decorum is a constant theme in Swift, we see it in the grace of the bee's flight or the decency of the brothers' original coats, just as we see the counterpart of the snarling dog in the angry spider or the rudeness of the foppish Peter. The eye for faults becomes an appetite for them, just as the raking together of the dung of Augeas' stables becomes an end in itself, and both reversals recall the worm in the nut. What other ages, the true guests, have neglected and flung away as worthless is the only diet the moderns will allow themselves. The Tale Teller's wit lacks order or purpose of its own, but it serves Swift's own rhetorical ends at every point.

A few conclusions about Swift's attitudes may be drawn from his practice in *A Tale of a Tub*. False wit can lead us wherever we want to go; reasoning by analogy can, in the hands of a fool or a sophister, be used to reach any conclusion. Speculative interpretation which thrives upon such false wit can maintain constant warfare within religion. Each zealot may battle for his own interest under the banners of whatever sanctions he can wrest from Scripture. Thus the departure from common forms and common sense makes hypocrisy possible for the conscious knaves and gives them countless gullible dupes. The same is true in the realm of politics: we can see in the *Examiner* or in the replies to Burnet and the Irish dissenters Swift's resistance to that manipulation of words which makes them a cloak for one's own ambition. One must constantly place these words in new contexts, test their application, purge them of false power. Otherwise each man becomes his own Partridge or Bickerstaff, finding what he will in the influence of the stars, winning credulity without responsibility of proof but with all the authority of supernatural wisdom. This is the implicit critique of false wit. Recognized for what it is, however, it can become a brilliant satirical device.

The most important function of the Tale Teller in the structure of the work is his gradual absorption of a vast range of folly in his panegyric and imitation. The power of the *Tale* arises not so much from a tight and economical structure as from the unpredictable extension that is given a few commanding principles. Its unity is one of "repetitive form," the "consistent maintaining of a principle under new guises." [15] Its

[15] Kenneth Burke, *Counter-Statement*, New York, 1931, p. 159.

economy comes of the deftness with which Swift makes the same symbolic pattern work again and again, each time including a new victim, who in turn represents a new field of achievement. The pattern itself is intensified more and more, from folly to bestiality, from bestiality to mechanism.

The point at which the meanings of the *Tale* become most general and inclusive is the "Digression concerning the Original, the Use and Improvement of Madness in a Commonwealth." Madness becomes the common term for all the abuses of reason and sources of greatness in the *Tale*, much as the Yahoos provide the basic pattern of civilized society in *Gulliver's Travels*. Where Gulliver is sufficiently human to be disgusted by the Yahoos, the Tale Teller glorifies madness, only regretting the waste of powers which the confinement of Bedlam represents. It is as if Gulliver were to bring home a Yahoo to be prime minister. In defending madness the Tale Teller looks upon reason with the same irrational horror he earlier showed toward Time:

then comes Reason officiously, with Tools for cutting, and opening, and mangling, and piercing, offering to demonstrate that they [bodies] are not of the same consistence quite thro'. Now, I take all this to be the last Degree of perverting Nature; one of whose Eternal Laws it is, to put her best Furniture forward.

This last phrase recalls the clothes worshippers' account of God as a tailor and "*Journey-man* Nature" as a valet to the "*vegetable* Beaux." In what follows one finds the same distortion of imagination:

And therefore, in order to save the Charges of all such expensive Anatomy for the Time to come; I do here think fit to inform the Reader, that in such Conclusions as these, Reason is certainly in the Right; and that in most Corporeal Beings, which have fallen under my Cognizance, the *Outside* has been infinitely preferable to the *In:* Whereof I have been farther convinced from some late Experiments. Last Week I saw a Woman flay'd, and you will hardly believe, how much it altered her Person for the worse. (Sect. V)

The last sentence becomes significant only through being the calm assertion of a man without normal awareness. The Tale Teller is able to equate reason with cutting, analysis with flaying, just as he has easily turned the pursuit of wisdom into the enjoyment of obscurity. All the inversions we have seen before are brought to focus here. The rind has replaced the kernel and clothes the man. The digression has overwhelmed the tale. Fancy is astride reason. The body governs the soul. Most generally, the outside has replaced the inside. So the Tale Teller can argue for contentment with "the *Films* and *Images* that fly off upon his senses from the *Superficies* of Things" and placidly expose his own argument with a conclusion that negates all his praise:

> Such a Man truly wise, creams off Nature, leaving the Sower and the Dregs for Philosophy and Reason to lap up. This is the sublime and refined Point of Felicity, called *the Possession of being well deceived*; The Serene Peaceful State of being a Fool among Knaves. (Sect. IX)

The Tale Teller has reduced the choice to carping or serenity, and from this opposition the true nature of reason has escaped. We need hardly assume that Swift accepts either alternative for himself or that he means the reader to be completely frustrated. Man is neither the beau's suit nor his dissected body. True poetry is neither the modern effusion nor the ancient fragments Bentley has collected. Proper food is neither a ragout nor the bones flung under the table, proper dress neither gold fringe nor rags, and the true church, for Swift, is neither Peter's nor Jack's. The middle way demands a harmony of outside and inside, a decent coat which always fits. To choose between inside and outside is either to seek a transcendent purity impossible for man or to settle for mere appearance to the neglect of spirit. It is by some such principle as this that Swift's symbols work in *A Tale of a Tub*. The structure of the book, by a series of ironic reversals, reduces the Tale Teller's praise of his fellows to the exposure

of a few principles of physiological compulsion. But if the drives are few, simple, and low, there is complexity enough. It lies not in the riches of wit that the Tale Teller claims but in the unfailing ingenuity of rationalization, the enormous effort exerted to escape from seeing oneself as one is and from submitting to the discipline of becoming better. The style of the Tale Teller is itself a symbol of this complexity which is really simplicity, a distortion of meanings that is no better than an incapacity for them: "it is the Nature of Rags to bear a kind of mock Resemblance to Finery; there being a sort of fluttering Appearance in both, which is not to be distinguished at a Distance, in the Dark, or by short-sighted Eyes." (Sect. X)

Lemuel Gulliver

For Lemuel Gulliver, the tradition of travel books provided Swift with a useful type, the voyager whose judgment is easily corrupted either by his pleasure in the strange or by his complacent condescension toward it. He may be the innovator finding new models or the proud patriot defying any challenge to his own or to his countrymen's superiority. In either case, a faithful report of his responses arouses sentiments in the detached reader quite different from his own. Gulliver's meticulously accurate report of the Lilliputians is altogether surface observation and produces the kind of understatement that neglects completely the overtones of an experience. This is heightened by Gulliver's casual insertion of a human scale at those moments when increments of size are the mark of Lilliputian grandeur. The emperor, Gulliver tells us, "is taller by almost the Breadth of my Nail, than any of his Court; which alone is enough to strike an Awe into the Beholders." Just as he is oblivious to these overtones of pettiness, so Gulliver can take Lilliputian dignities at their face value, especially when they are conferred on him. Suspected of adultery with Flimnap's wife, he does not recognize the incongruity of the charge.

He is simply concerned with the lady's reputation and his own: "I had the Honour to be a *Nardac,* which the Treasurer himself is not; for all the World knows he is only a *Clumglum,* a title inferior by one Degree, as that of a Marquess is to a Duke in *England;* yet I allow he preceded me in right of his Post." Even when Gulliver has been completely betrayed and considers destroying the Lilliputians, he is restrained in part by his gratitude to the little emperor for "the high Title of *Nardac* he conferred upon me."

To an extent Gulliver has the virtues of the Drapier in being a man whose understanding cannot go beyond certain limits. When the setting becomes most transparently an English one, for example, Gulliver's humble station is also invoked. In his conversations with the Houyhnhnms he shows considerable acquaintance with royal courts, but in Lilliput he is still unable to penetrate the refinements of ministers' cabals. When he learns that his eyes are to be put out and that he is to be starved to death he confesses that "having never been designed for a Courtier either by my Birth or Education, I was so ill a Judge of Things, that I could not discover the *Lenity* and Favour of this Sentence; but conceived it (perhaps erroneously) rather to be rigorous than gentle." The Lilliputians themselves are beyond difficulties of this sort. Although nothing terrifies them "so much as those Encomiums on his Majesty's Mercy," the simple reversal of meaning in court decrees is, like the constant disputes over trivial symbols, part of the logic by which they live. They are untroubled by need for rationalization of such absurdities. Gulliver is troubled but not, like the Drapier, defiant. He is too deferential toward authority to insist upon common sense.

Since the satiric distortions are postulated as the real world and Gulliver's insensibility leaves him unaware of their significance, Swift can direct special attention throughout the book to the drama of incomprehension and the problem of meaning. Gulliver's insensibility is increased, if not actually caused, by his satisfaction with man's rational powers and all they have achieved. The mind which accepts Lilliput without contempt becomes in Brobdingnag a mind which takes childish pride in feats remarkable only in that one so diminutive can perform them. Many of the feats end in disaster: the stunned linnet comes to life, Gulliver's leap does not quite clear the dung. These disasters set the pattern of the conversation with the Brobdingnagian king. There Gulliver's pride is extended to European man, whose achievements are Gulliver's own claim to importance and to rational powers. What follows is comparable to the Tale Teller's appeal to Prince Posterity. In this case the detachment of distance replaces the hostility of Time. The king makes notes as Gulliver testifies in behalf of mankind, and the panegyric supplies the evidence for an indictment. All that Gulliver neglects is what he has seen in Lilliput, the difference between the original institutions and the corrupt practices of men. The king concludes: "My little Friend *Grildrig;* you have made a most admirable Panegyrick upon your country. You have clearly proved that Ignorance, Idleness, and Vice, are the proper Ingredients for qualifying a Legislator. That Laws are best explained, interpreted, and applied by those whose Interest and Abilities lie in perverting, confounding, and eluding them." Gulliver's pride serves even more effectively than the Tale Teller's ingenuity to damn his fellows. In the manner of the Tale Teller he can shrug off "so remote a Prince's Notions of Virtue and Vice" and console himself with the superiority of the "politer Countries of *Europe.*" But the achievements of which he can boast are not merely trivial or ridiculous; the range and intensity of the satire have greatly increased. Gulliver offers the king the means of becoming "absolute Master of the Lives, the Liberties, and the Fortunes of his People." This is a rejection of all the scruples which prevented Gulliver from completing the conquest of Blefuscu, but the inconsistency is partially explained by Gulliver's experience at Lilliput. Having learned there the nature of kings and courts, he seeks to win this king's favor by appealing to his desire for power. He is awed by the learning which has "reduced *Politicks* into a *Science*," and he is unable to see its moral significance. Conversely, Gulliver can dismiss as "visionary" those few political projectors in Lagado who have a rational program.

Gulliver's change in the fourth voyage is largely an emotional conversion. Having resisted all the lessons which have confronted him in the first three voyages, he is now led into a dilemma. Although he expects to meet "Savages," he fails to recognize the Yahoos as more than intensely disagreeable animals. His antipathy is aroused before his pride can operate: he unknowingly sees the human animal for the first time without the adornment of dress or civilization. It is only when the Houyhnhnms arrange a juxtaposition that Gulliver sees with horror "in this abominable Animal, a perfect human Figure." His pride in man comes too late: "although there were few greater Lovers of Mankind, at that time, than myself; yet I confess I never saw any sensitive Being so detestable on all Accounts." Gulliver can only hope to save himself from identification with the Yahoos, and his clothes become his sole defense.

Once the secret of the clothes is revealed and Gulliver's physical identity with the Yahoos is established, he seeks to establish himself as at least a rational Yahoo. Gulliver still smarts at the application of that term to himself, but the lack of any other term in the Houyhnhnm language enforces its use. The limited experience which Swift postulates for the Houyhnhnms serves, therefore, to make the dilemma inescapable. The dilemma is as false as that created by the Tale Teller in the digression on madness. In both cases the extremes are presented as necessary alternatives, and the

mean is ignored. In this case, the false dilemma is created largely by Gulliver's pride, turning from deluded complacency only to deluded misanthropy. Allowed only the name of Yahoo, Gulliver must prove mankind rational in order to escape the stigma of complete identification with the brutes. His account of man founders almost at once; in describing his crew, he reveals a full catalogue of human vice:

> Some were undone by Law-suits; others spent all they had in Drinking, Whoring and Gaming; others fled for Treason; many for Murder, Theft, Poysoning, Robbery, Perjury, Forgery, Coining false Money; for committing Rapes or Sodomy; for flying from their Colours, or deserting to the Enemy; and most of them had broken Prison. None of these durst return to their native Countries for fear of being hanged, or of starving in a Jail; and therefore were under the Necessity of seeking a Livelihood in other Places.

Gulliver's description of Europe is one of the triumphs of the book. We are prepared for Gulliver's new antipathy to his own kind by his reference to "our barbarous *English*" language. It becomes clear by the time he has finished that he is no longer interested in saving appearances. He has given up the defense of fellow men and hopes only to be able to cast his lot with the Houyhnhnms. His pride can be saved only by winning their favor. Gulliver's account is limited, moreover, by the language in which he must speak, by the remoteness of the Houyhnhnms from all human conceptions, and by his strict adherence to truth. What follows is a picture of human institutions simplified in much the manner of the mythical Lilliput and Laputa. In this section, however, Gulliver is describing a literal Europe.

In missing the moral significance of what he has previously described, Gulliver has also missed its symbolic import; he sees the Lilliputians as a strange people but not as a representation of man's pettiness. Throughout his travels Gulliver is incapable of perceiving relationships, and Swift has deliberately placed him in a world of semiallegorical relationships. He has remained indifferent to all but appearances, never venturing to see the appearances as significant of anything but themselves. His account of Europe has the same simplification Gulliver has learned to accept without question in the symbolic world of his travels. Accustomed to moving among symbols (really, among aspects of man) as if they were solid realities, he has little difficulty in reducing reality to the same symbolic patterns. His typical understatement, in these new circumstances, becomes overstatement. All that he has seen finds its counterpart in the picture of Europe—the inversion of institutions and of the meaning of words, the limitless appetites without avowal or control, the ingenuities of intellect turned to display or rationalization, and the juxtaposition of dignity and decay, of pride and filth. But his picture presents only the comic surface of epicyclic complication, of constant reversal, and of inhuman mechanism. It is a picture which assembles all the degraded gestures with no attempt to explain their purpose or their cause. Thus Gulliver can tell the Houyhnhnm that "a *Soldier* is a *Yahoo* hired to kill in cold Blood as many of his own Species, who have never offended him, as possibly he can." This divorces the soldier from patriotism or duty and the means of killing from the end; one need not commend war to recognize it as something more than this. In places this method of distortion becomes comparable to the Lilliputian travesty or to the allegorical events of the *Tale:*

Difference in Opinions hath cost many Millions of Lives: For Instance, whether *Flesh* be *Bread*, or *Bread* be *Flesh:* Whether the Juice of a certain *Berry* be *Blood* or *Wine:* Whether *Whistling* be a Vice or a Virtue: Whether it be better to *kiss* a Post, or throw it into the Fire: What is the best Colour for a *Coat*, whether, *Black*, *White*, *Red*, or *Grey*; and whether it should be *long* or *short*, *narrow* or *wide*, *dirty* or *clean*; with many more.

Once Gulliver has presented the picture of human society drained of all nobility and even of purpose, the Houyhnhnm master can draw the relationship for him. By setting aside some of the achievements of man in "Learning, Government, Arts, Manufactures, and the like," and by amplifying the qualities of the Yahoos, the Houyhnhnm finds a "Parity" in their natures. "He went through all our Vices and Follies, and discovered many which I had never mentioned to him; by only supposing what Qualities a *Yahoo* of their Country, with a small Proportion of Reason, might be capable of exerting: And concluded, with too much Probability, how vile as well as miserable such a Creature must be." It is the simplest of relationships, the identity of man and Yahoo. The Houyhnhnm, who is unacquainted with the possibility of rational creatures other than of his own kind, is reluctant to admit a new species as long as man can be accounted for in terms of previous experience. He has no animus, therefore, in drawing the damning equation; his conclusion is the result of cool logic. Once Gulliver has come to accept this identity, he has reached the limits of his comprehension. He has no conception of a relationship that is less than identity. He can no more distinguish the corrupt Yahoo pattern from man's total behavior than he can abstract the rational pattern of the Houyhnhnms' life from their passionless embodiment of it. He has arrived at no generalizations, no lessons: he can only hope to resemble a Houyhnhnm so that he will not be taken for a Yahoo. We have seen the Tale Teller saving the world of appearance by drawing relationships which comfort his pride but distort the nature of reality. Gulliver is no less a victim of appearance in his failure to draw relationships. Thoroughly empirical, he can follow models but cannot grasp principles. Thoroughly literal, he can respond to images but not to their metaphorical significance. His world is a world of outsides, not by choice as for the Tale Teller but by necessity. Having believed that man is a rational animal, now finally convinced of his error, his solution is to worship the only thoroughly rational animal he has encountered.

The close of the book shows Gulliver suffering from a kind of inverted pride, a hatred of all humankind for the qualities which he himself shares. The encounter with Pedro de Mendez illustrates this very well; he is, according to Gulliver, a "very courteous and generous Person," but only with reluctance does Gulliver *descend* "to treat him like an Animal which had some little Portion of Reason." The final absurdity is Gulliver's affection for his horses' conversation and his intolerance of the smell and presence of his own family. As he has returned from Brobdingnag with a visual maladjustment but no moral improvement, so now he has acquired the convert's zeal for Houyhnhnm mannerisms (even to a whinnying voice and an equine gait) but with no real sense of their meaning. Yet Gulliver's madness and projector's enthusiasm do not altogether undercut his charge. This madness, in a wiser man, would be the *splendida bilis* of the satirist, the only sanity in a perverted world. One need not accept Gulliver's picture of man, but one cannot neglect the partial truth which it reveals. It is not the human animal as such he attacks in his saner moments but the animal's engrossment of the tribute due to virtue, reason, and nature:

My Reconcilement to the *Yahoo*-kind in general might not be so difficult, if they would be content with those Vices and Follies only which Nature hath entitled them to. I am not in the least provoked at the Sight of a Lawyer, a Pickpocket, a Colonel, a Fool, a Lord, a Gamester, a Politician, a Whoremonger, a Physician, an Evidence, a Suborner, an Attorney, a Traytor, or the like. This is all according to the due Course of Things: But, when I behold a Lump of Deformity, and Diseases both in Body and Mind, smitten with Pride, it immediately breaks all the Measures of my Patience; neither shall I be ever able to comprehend how such an Animal and such a Vice could tally together.

The use of "Nature" in this passage is ironic enough, but it suggests a middle view that Gulliver hardly perceives. Both the Houyhnhnms and the Yahoos live according to a nature simpler than man's— the Houyhnhnms with a rationality which no passions or appetites disturb, the Yahoos with appetites their cunning can only serve. Both are free of responsibility: the Houyhnhnm's intuition is never clouded by error, the Yahoo's grossness is disgusting but incorrigible. The responsibility of man is imposed by the presence both of conflict and of capacity for change. His moral duties are the counterpart of his industry in the world:

The motions of the sun and moon, in short, the whole system of the universe . . . are in the utmost degree of regularity and perfection; but wherever God hath left to man the power of interposing a remedy by thought or labour, there he hath placed things in a state of imperfection, on purpose to stir up human industry, without which life could stagnate, or indeed rather could not subsist at all.[16]

Pride, of all vices, most robs man of the clear self-knowledge which awakens his sense of responsibility, and it is appropriate that Gulliver attack it. But it is notable that even as he attacks it Gulliver is its victim. The irony is sustained to the last. Gulliver, who began with a pride in man that found him above criticism, ends with a pride in pure reason that finds man insupportable. Even as he warns men of the vice of pride, he entreats "those who have any Tincture of this absurd Vice, that they will not presume to appear in my Sight." Gulliver plans, he tells us, "to behold my Figure often in a Glass, and thus if possible to habituate myself by Time to tolerate the Sight of a human Creature." The obvious injunction is one that Auden has framed in a similar case of illusion and resultant despair:

16 *Thoughts on Various Subjects*, Temple Scott, I, 279.

O look, look in the mirror,
    O look in your distress;
Life remains a blessing
    Although you cannot bless.

O stand, stand at the window
    As the tears scald and start;
You shall love your crooked neighbor
    With your crooked heart.[17]

Throughout the four voyages a rhetorical pattern is prepared by linkages between apparently discrete events. Gulliver does not connect these events and so cannot learn from experience, but the pattern is evident to the reader. The "utopian" sections, for example, are clearly an embodiment of reason but not necessarily the only possible embodiment or that best suited to the human animal. They serve as a standard of rational behavior if not as a model for human practice. This rational pattern, a neglected possibility in Lilliput, is repeated again and again—with modifications in Brobdingnag, by suggestion in the estate of Lord Munodi and the historical visions of Glubbdubdrib, explicitly in the life of the Houyhnhnms.[18] We are pre-

pared to see rationality in a static, simple society and to associate motion and force with irrational programs of conquest. The physical horror of the body is introduced, without much awareness, by Gulliver in the first voyage; it becomes his preoccupation in Brobdingnag and is constantly evoked throughout the third voyage. We are prepared for the wedding of irrational conquest with physical grossness in the filthy and competitive Yahoos. There is, then, in *Gulliver's Travels* a weaving together of motifs not unlike that of *A Tale of a Tub.* In the *Tale* we are constantly shocked by new linkages blandly discovered by the ingenious Tale Teller. In the *Travels* the linkages remain implicit. A matrix is prepared unobtrusively instead of explicitly; its full range is revealed not gradually but suddenly, and its revelation affects Gulliver profoundly, as the Tale Teller is never affected. The difference in method can be likened to the differences we have seen on the level of style. *A Tale of a Tub* is close to the false wit of the poems. The witty transformations are made openly; the surprise comes largely from unpredictable extravagance being turned to aptness. *Gulliver's Travels* resembles the works in the plain style which seem to be doing one thing while they accomplish another, whose apparent flatness is designed to distract us from their rhetorical complexity. Both works are ironical, but the irony is much more in command of *Gulliver's Travels* than of the *Tale;* it is not sacrificed to local effects of wit, and it has acquired dramatic force. *A Tale of a Tub* is a more inventive work and perhaps richer in suggestion, but it lacks the rhetorical precision which steadily prepares the enormous weight of meaning that is carried in the final symbols of *Gulliver's Travels.*

[17] W. H. Auden, "As I Walked Out One Evening," *Collected Poetry,* New York, 1945, p. 198.
[18] There has been a tendency in recent critics to find the Houyhnhnms inherently ludicrous. Swift's rational horses are clearly no model for man, and it seems as much beside the point to deny the appeal of their life as to follow Gulliver in succumbing to it. The Houyhnhnms are, of course, entirely "natural": they are unaware of "things . . . above our reason" such as Swift treats in his sermon *On the Trinity.* Their life is, like that of animals guided by "unerring" instinct, both more orderly and less complex than that of man. See Pope, *An Essay on Man,* ed. Mack, Epistle III, line 83, and note to lines 83–98, p. 100. It is important to see Gulliver's folly in taking the Houyhnhnms as a model for man, but there is a danger of multiplying ironies. If we consider the Houyhnhnm life ludicrous in itself, we are likely to fall into the Mandevillian celebration of a corrupt world for its richness and complexity. Most versions of heaven show it as simpler than the world, and Shaw's Satan, for one, makes much of that disagreeable fact. The pattern of *Gulliver's Travels*

as a whole makes the Houyhnhnms the culmination of the rationality suggested in the three earlier voyages. In revealing the "inside," Swift has divested it entirely; we can look back to the mediation of "inside" and "outside" of Brobdingnag as a possible model.

William Butler Yeats

"Preface" to *The Words upon the Window-pane*

SOMEBODY said the other night that Dublin was full of clubs—he himself knew four—that met in cellars and garrets and had for their object our general improvement. He was scornful, said that they had all begun by drawing up a programme and passing a resolution against the censorship and would never do anything else. When I began my public life Dublin was full of such clubs that passed resolutions and drew up programmes, and though the majority did nothing else some helped to find an audience for a school of writers. The fall of Parnell had freed imagination from practical politics, from agrarian grievance and political enmity, and turned it to imaginative nationalism, to Gaelic, to the ancient stories, and at last to lyrical poetry and to drama. Political failure and political success have had the same result except that to-day imagination is turning full of uncertainty to something it thinks European, and whether that something will be "arty" and provincial, or a form of life, is as yet undiscoverable. Hitherto we have walked the road, but now we have shut the door and turned up the lamp. What shall occupy our imagination? We must, I think, decide among these three ideas of national life: that of Swift; that of a great Italian of his day; that of modern England. If the Garrets and the Cellars listen I may throw light upon the matter, and I hope if all the time I seem thinking of something else I shall be forgiven. I must speak of things that come out of the common consciousness, where every thought is like a bell with many echoes.

My little play *The Words upon the Window-pane* came to me amidst considerations such as these, as a reward, as a moment of excitement. John O'Leary read, during an illness, the poems of Thomas Davis, and though he never thought them good poetry they shaped his future life, gave him the moral simplicity that made him so attractive to young men in his old age, but we can no longer permit life to be shaped by a personified ideal, we must serve with all our faculties some actual thing. The old service was moral, at times lyrical; we discussed perpetually the character of public men and never asked were they able and well-informed, but what would they sacrifice? How many times did I hear on the lips of J. F. Taylor these words: "Holy, delicate white hands"? His patriotism was a religion, never a philosophy. More extreme in such things than Taylor and O'Leary, who often seemed to live in the eighteenth century, to acknowledge its canons alone in literature and in the arts, I turned from Goldsmith and from Burke because they had come to seem a part of the English system, from Swift because I acknowledged, being a romantic, no verse between Cowley and Smart's *Song to David*, no prose between Sir Thomas Browne and the *Conversations* of Landor. But now I read Swift for months together, Burke and Berkeley less often but always with excitement, and Goldsmith lures and waits. I collect materials for my thought and work, for some identification of my beliefs with the nation itself, I seek an image of the modern mind's discovery of

The essay published here is Part I of the "Preface" to *The Words upon the Window-pane* in *Wheels and Butterflies*, London, 1934. Reprinted by permission of Mrs. W. B. Yeats, Macmillan and Co., Ltd., London, and The Macmillan Co., New York.

itself, of its own permanent form, in that one Irish century that escaped from darkness and confusion. I would that our fifteenth, sixteenth, or even our seventeenth century had been the clear mirror, but fate decided against us.

Swift haunts me; he is always just round the next corner. Sometimes it is a thought of my great-great-grandmother, a friend of that Archbishop King who sent him to England about the "First Fruits," sometimes it is S. Patrick's, where I have gone to wander and meditate, that brings him to mind, sometimes I remember something hard or harsh in O'Leary or in Taylor, or in the public speech of our statesmen, that reminds me by its style of his verse or prose. Did he not speak, perhaps, with just such an intonation? This instinct for what is near and yet hidden is in reality a return to the sources of our power, and therefore a claim made upon the future. Thought seems more true, emotion more deep, spoken by someone who touches my pride, who seems to claim me of his kindred, who seems to make me a part of some national mythology, nor is mythology mere ostentation, mere vanity if it draws me onward to the unknown; another turn of the gyre and myth is wisdom, pride, discipline. I remember the shudder in my spine when Mrs. Patrick Campbell said, speaking words Hofmannsthal put into the mouth of Electra, "I too am of that ancient race":

> Swift has sailed into his rest:
> Savage indignation there
> Cannot lacerate his breast.
> Imitate him if you dare,
> World-besotted traveller; he
> Served human liberty.

"In Swift's day men of intellect reached the height of their power, the greatest position they ever attained in society and the State. . . . His ideal order was the Roman Senate, his ideal men Brutus and Cato; such an order and such men had seemed possible once more." The Cambridge undergraduate into whose mouth I have put

these words may have read similar words in Oliver, "the last brilliant addition to English historians," for young men such as he read the newest authorities; probably Oliver and he thought of the influence at Court and in public life of Swift and of Leibniz, of the spread of science and of scholarship over Europe, its examination of documents, its destruction of fables, a science and a scholarship modern for the first time, of certain great minds that were medieval in their scope but modern in their freedom. I must, however, add certain thoughts of my own that affected me as I wrote. I thought about a passage in the Grammont *Memoirs* where some great man is commended for his noble manner, as we commend a woman for her beauty or her charm; a famous passage in the *Appeal from the New to the Old Whigs* commending the old Whig aristocracy for their intellect and power and because their doors stood open to like-minded men; the palace of Blenheim, its pride of domination that expected a thousand years, something Asiatic in its carved intricacy of stone.

"Everything great in Ireland and in our character, in what remains of our architecture, comes from that day . . . we have kept its seal longer than England." The overstatement of an enthusiastic Cambridge student, and yet with its measure of truth. The battle of the Boyne overwhelmed a civilisation full of religion and myth, and brought in its place intelligible laws planned out upon a great blackboard, a capacity for horizontal lines, for rigid shapes, for buildings, for attitudes of mind that could be multiplied like an expanding bookcase: the modern world, and something that appeared and perished in its dawn, an instinct for Roman rhetoric, Roman elegance. It established a Protestant aristocracy, some of whom neither called themselves English [1] nor looked with con-

---

[1] Nor were they English: the newest arrivals soon intermarried with an older stock, and that older stock had intermarried again and again with Gaelic Ireland. All my childhood the Coopers of

tempt or dread upon conquered Ireland. Indeed the battle was scarcely over when Molyneux, speaking in their name, affirmed the sovereignty of the Irish Parliament.[2] No one had the right to make our laws but the King, Lords and Commons of Ireland; the battle had been fought to change not an English but an Irish Crown; and our Parliament was almost as ancient as that of England. It was this doctrine [3] that Swift uttered in the fourth *Drapier Letter* with such astringent eloquence that it passed from the talk of study and parlour to that of road and market, and created the political nationality of Ireland. Swift found his nationality through the *Drapier Letters,* his convictions came from action and passion, but Berkeley, a much younger man, could find it through contemplation. He and his fellow-students but knew the war through the talk of the older men. As a boy of eighteen or nineteen he called the Irish people "natives" as though he were in some

Markree, County Sligo, represented such rank and fashion as the County knew, and I had it from my friend the late Bryan Cooper that his supposed Cromwellian ancestor being childless adopted an O'Brien; while local tradition thinks that an O'Brien, promised the return of her confiscated estate if she married a Cromwellian soldier, married a Cooper and murdered him three days after. Not, however, before he had founded a family. The family of Yeats, never more than small gentry, arrived, if I can trust the only man among us who may have seen the family tree before it was burnt by Canadian Indians, "about the time of Henry VII." Ireland, divided in religion and politics, is as much one race as any modern country.
[2] "Until 1691 Roman Catholics were admitted by law into both Houses of Legislature in Ireland" (MacNeill's *Constitutional and Parliamentary History of Ireland*, p. 10).
[3] A few weeks ago the hierarchy of the Irish Church addressed, without any mandate from Protestant Ireland, not the Irish people as they had every right to, even in the defence of folly, but the Imperial Conference, and begged that the Irish Courts might remain subservient to the Privy Council. Terrified into intrigue where none threatened, they turned from Swift and Molyneux. I remind them that when the barons of the Irish Court of Exchequer obeyed the English Privy Council in 1719 our ancestors clapped them into gaol. (1931.)

foreign land, but two or three years later, perhaps while still an undergraduate, defined the English materialism of his day in three profound sentences, and wrote after each that "we Irishmen" think otherwise— "I publish . . . to know whether other men have the same ideas as we Irishmen" —and before he was twenty-five had fought the Salamis of the Irish intellect. The Irish landed aristocracy, who knew more of the siege of Derry and the battle of the Boyne delineated on vast tapestries for their House of Lords by Dublin Huguenots than of philosophy, found themselves masters of a country demoralised by generations of war and famine and shared in its demoralisation. In 1730 Swift said from the pulpit that their houses were in ruins and no new building anywhere, that the houses of their rack-ridden tenants were no better than English pigsties, that the bulk of the people trod barefoot and in rags. He exaggerated, for already the Speaker, Connolly, had built that great house at Celbridge where slate, stone and furniture were Irish, even the silver from Irish mines; the new Parliament House had perhaps been planned; and there was a general stir of life. The old age of Berkeley passed amid art and music, and men had begun to boast that in these no country had made such progress; and some dozen years after Berkeley's death Arthur Young found everywhere in stately Georgian houses scientific agriculturalists, benefactors of their countryside, though for the half-educated, drunken, fire-eating, impoverished lesser men he had nothing but detestation. Goldsmith might have found likeable qualities, a capacity for mimicry [4] perhaps, among these lesser men, and Sir Jonah Barrington made them his theme, but, detestable or not, they were out of fashion. Miss Edgeworth described her *Castle Rackrent* upon the title-page of its first edition as "the habits of the Irish

[4] He wrote that he had never laughed so much at Garrick's acting as at somebody in an Irish tavern mimicking a Quaker sermon.

squirearchy before 1782." A few years more and the country people would have forgotten that the Irish aristocracy was founded like all aristocracies upon conquest, or rather, would have remembered, and boasted in the words of a medieval Gaelic poet, "We are a sword people and we go with the sword." Unhappily the lesson first taught by Molyneux and Swift had been but half learnt when the test came—country gentlemen are poor politicians—and Ireland's "dark insipid period" began. During the entire eighteenth century the greatest land-owning family of the neighbourhood I best knew in childhood sent not a single man into the English army and navy, but during the nineteenth century one or more in every generation; a new absenteeism, foreseen by Miss Edgeworth, began; those that lived upon their estates bought no more fine editions of the classics; separated from public life and ambition they sank, as I have heard Lecky complain, "into grass farmers." Yet their genius did not die out; they sent everywhere administrators and military leaders, and now that their ruin has come —what resolute nation permits a strong alien class within its borders?—I would, remembering obscure ancestors that preached in their churches or fought beside their younger sons over half the world, and despite a famous passage of O'Grady's, gladly sing their song.

"He foresaw the ruin to come, Democracy, Rousseau, the French Revolution; that is why he hated the common run of men,—'I hate lawyers, I hate doctors,' he said, 'though I love Dr. So-and-so and Judge So-and-so,'—that is why he wrote *Gulliver*, that is why he wore out his brain, that is why he felt *saeva indignatio*, that is why he sleeps under the greatest epitaph in history." The *Discourse of the Contests and Dissensions between the Nobles and the Commons in Athens and Rome*, published in 1703 to warn the Tory Opposition of the day against the impeachment of Ministers, is Swift's one philosophical work.

All States depend for their health upon a right balance between the One, the Few, and the Many. The One is the executive, which may in fact be more than one—the Roman republic had two Consuls—but must for the sake of rapid decision be as few as possible; the Few are those who through the possession of hereditary wealth, or great personal gifts, have come to identify their lives with the life of the State, whereas the lives and ambitions of the Many are private. The Many do their day's work well, and so far from copying even the wisest of their neighbours affect "a singularity" in action and in thought; but set them to the work of the State and every man Jack is "listed in a party," becomes the fanatical follower of men of whose characters he knows next to nothing, and from that day on puts nothing into his mouth that some other man has not already chewed and digested. And furthermore, from the moment of enlistment thinks himself above other men and struggles for power until all is in confusion. I divine an Irish hatred of abstraction likewise expressed by that fable of Gulliver among the inventors and men of science, by Berkeley in his *Commonplace Book*, by Goldsmith in the satire of *The Good-Natured Man*, in the picturesque, minute observation of *The Deserted Village*, and by Burke in his attack upon mathematical democracy. Swift enforced his moral by proving that Rome and Greece were destroyed by the war of the Many upon the Few; in Rome, where the Few had kept their class organisation, it was a war of classes, in Greece, where they had not, war upon character and genius. Miltiades, Aristides, Themistocles, Pericles, Alcibiades, Phocion, "impeached for high crimes and misdemeanours . . . were honoured and lamented by their country as the preservers of it, and have had the veneration of all ages since paid justly to their memories." In Rome parties so developed that men born and bred among the Few were compelled to join one party or the other and to flatter and bribe. All civilisations must end in some such way, for the Many obsessed by emotion create a multitude of religious sects but give themselves at last to some one master of bribes and flatteries and sink into the ignoble tranquillity of servitude. He defines a tyranny as the predominance of the One, the Few, or the Many, but thinks that of the Many the immediate threat. All States at their outset possess a ruling power seated in the whole body as that of the soul in the human body, a perfect balance of the three estates, the king some sort of chief magistrate, and then comes "a tyranny: first either of the Few or the Many; but at last infallibly of a single person." He thinks the English balance most perfect in the time of Queen Elizabeth, but that in the next age a tyranny of the Many produced that of Cromwell, and that, though recovery followed, "all forms of government must be mortal like their authors," and he quotes from Polybius, "those abuses and corruptions, which in time destroy a government, are sown along with the very seeds of it" and destroy it "as rust eats away iron, and worms devour wood." Whether the final tyranny is created by the Many—in his eyes all Caesars were tyrants—or imposed by foreign power, the result is the same. At the fall of liberty came "a dark insipid period through all Greece"—had he Ireland in his mind also?—and the people became, in the words of Polybius, "great reverencers of crowned heads."

Twenty-two years later Giambattista Vico published that *Scienza Nuova* which Mr. James Joyce is expounding or symbolising in the strange fragments of his *Work in Progress*. He was the opposite of Swift in everything, an humble, peaceful man, son of a Neapolitan bookseller and without political opinions; he wrote panegyrics upon men of rank, seemed to admire all that they did, took their gratuities and yet kept his dignity. He thought civilisation passed through the phases Swift has described, but that it was harsh and terrible until the Many prevailed, and its joints cracked and loosened, happiest when some one man, surrounded by able subordinates, dismissed the Many to their private business, that its happiness lasted some generations until, sense of the common welfare lost, it grew malicious and treacherous, fell into "the barbarism of reflection," and after that into an honest, plain barbarism accepted with relief by all and started upon its round again. Rome had conquered surrounding nations because those nations were nearer than it to humanity and happiness; was not Carthage already almost a democratic state when destruction came? Swift seemed to shape his narrative upon some clairvoyant vision of his own life, for he saw civilisation pass from comparative happiness and youthful vigour to an old age of violence and self-contempt, whereas Vico saw it begin in penury like himself and end as he himself would end in a long inactive peace. But there was a greater difference; Swift, a practical politician in everything he wrote, ascribed its rise and fall to virtues and vices all could understand, whereas the philosophical Vico ascribed them to "the rhythm of the elemental forms of the mind," a new idea that would dominate philosophy. Outside Anglo-Saxon nations where progress, impelled by moral enthusiasm and the Patent Office, seems a perpetual straight line, this "circular movement," as Swift's master, Polybius, called it, has long been the friend and enemy of public order. Both Sorel and Marx, their eyes more Swift's than Vico's, have preached a return to a primeval state, a beating of all down into a single class that a new civilisation may arise with its Few, its Many, and its One. Students of contemporary Italy, where Vico's thought is current through its influence upon Croce and Gentile, think it created, or in part created, the present government of one man surrounded by just such able assistants as Vico foresaw. Some philosopher has added this further thought: the classes rise out of the matrix, create all mental and bodily riches, sink back, as Vico saw civilisation rise and sink, and government is there to keep the ring and see to it that combat never ends. These thoughts in the next few generations, as elaborated by Oswald Spengler, who has followed Vico without essential change, by Flinders Petrie, by the German traveller Frobenius, by Henry Adams, and perhaps by my friend Gerald Heard, may affect the masses. They have already deepened our sense of tragedy and somewhat checked the naïver among those creeds and parties who push their way to power by flattering our moral hopes. Pascal thought there was evidence for and against the existence of God, but that if a man kept his mind in suspense about it he could not live a rich and active life, and I suggest to the Cellars and Garrets that though history is too short to change either the idea of progress or the eternal circuit into scientific fact, the eternal circuit may best suit our preoccupation with the soul's salvation, our individualism, our solitude. Besides we love antiquity, and that other idea—progress—the sole religious myth of modern man, is only two hundred years old.

Swift's pamphlet had little effect in its day; it did not prevent the impeachment and banishment a few years later of his own friends; and although he was in all probability the first—if there was another "my small reading cannot trace it"—to describe in terms of modern politics the discord of parties that compelled revolutionary France, as it has compelled half a dozen nations since the war, to accept the "tyranny" of a "single person," it was soon forgotten; but for the understanding of Swift it is essential. It shows that the defence of liberty boasted upon his tombstone did not come from political disappointment (when he wrote it he had suffered none); and what he meant by liberty. Gulliver, in those travels written twenty years later, calls up from the dead "a sextumvirate to which all the ages of the world cannot add a seventh": Epaminondas and Socrates, who suffered at the hands of the Many; Brutus, Junius Brutus, Cato the Younger, Thomas More, who fought the tyranny of the One; Brutus with Caesar still his inseparable friend, for a man may be a tyrant without personal guilt.

Liberty depended upon a balance within the State, like that of the "humours" in a human body, or like that "unity of being" Dante compared to a perfectly proportioned human body, and for its sake Swift was prepared to sacrifice what seems to the modern man liberty itself. The odds were a hundred to one, he wrote, that "violent zeal for the truth" came out of "petulancy, ambition, or pride." He himself might prefer a republic to a monarchy, but did he open his mouth upon the subject would be deservedly hanged. Had he religious doubts he was not to blame so long as he kept them to himself, for God had given him reason. It was the attitude of many a modern Catholic who thinks, though upon different grounds, that our civilisation may sink into a decadence like that of Rome. But sometimes belief itself must be hidden. He was devout; had the Communion Service by heart; read the Fathers and prayed much, yet would not press the mysteries of his faith upon any unwilling man. Had not the early Christians kept silent about the divinity of Christ; should not the missionaries to China "soften" it? He preached as law commanded; a man could save his soul doubtless in any religion which taught submission to the Will of God, but only one State could protect his body; and how could it protect his body if rent apart by those cranks and sectaries mocked in his *Tale of a Tub?* Had not French Huguenots and English Dissenters alike sinned against the State? Except at those moments of great public disturbance, when a man must choose his creed or his king, let him think his own thoughts in silence.

What was this liberty bought with so much silence, and served through all his life with so much eloquence? "I should think," he wrote in the *Discourse,* "that the saying, *vox populi, vox dei* ought to be understood of the universal bent and current of a people, not of the bare majority of a few representatives, which is often procured by little arts, and great industry and application; wherein those who engage in the pursuits of malice and revenge are much more sedulous than such as would prevent them." That *vox populi* or "bent and current," or what we even more vaguely call national spirit, was the sole theme of his *Drapier Letters;* its right to express itself as it would through such men as had won or inherited general consent. I doubt if a mind so contemptuous of average men thought, as Vico did, that it found expression also through all individual lives, or asked more for those lives than protection from the most obvious evils. I remember J. F. Taylor, a great student of Swift, saying "individual liberty is of no importance, what matters is national liberty."

The will of the State, whether it build a cage for a dead bird or remain in the bird itself, must always, whether interpreted by Burke or Marx, find expression through some governing class or company identified with that "bent and current," with those "elemental forms," whether by interest or training. The men of Swift's day would have added that class or company must be placed by wealth above fear and toil, though Swift thought every properly conducted State must limit the amount of wealth the individual could possess. But the old saying that there is no wisdom without leisure has somewhat lost its truth. When the physical world became rigid; when curiosity inherited from the Renaissance, and the soul's anxiety inherited from the Middle Ages, passed, man ceased to think; his work thought in him. Spinoza, Leibniz, Swift, Berkeley, Goethe, the last typical figure of the epoch, recognised no compulsion but the "bent and current" of their lives; the Speaker, Connolly, could still call out a posse of gentlemen to design the façade of his house, and though Berkeley thought their number too great, that

work is still admired; Swift called himself a poor scholar in comparison with Lord Treasurer Harley. Unity of being was still possible though somewhat over-rationalised and abstract, more diagram than body; whereas the best modern philosophers are professors, their pupils compile notebooks that they may be professors some day; politicians stick to their last or leave it to plague us with platitudes; we poets and artists may be called, so small our share in life, "separated spirits," words applied by the old philosophers to the dead. When Swift sank into imbecility or madness his epoch had finished in the British Isles, those "elemental forms" had passed beyond him; more than the "great Ministers" had gone. I can see in a sort of nightmare vision the "primary qualities" torn from the side of Locke, Johnson's ponderous body bent above the letter to Lord Chesterfield, some obscure person somewhere inventing the spinning-jenny, upon his face that look of benevolence kept by painters and engravers, from the middle of the eighteenth century to the time of the Prince Consort, for such as he, or, to simplify the tale—

> Locke sank into a swoon;
> The Garden died;
> God took the spinning-jenny
> Out of his side.

"That arrogant intellect free at last from superstition": the young man's overstatement full of the unexamined suppositions of common speech. I saw Asia in the carved stones of Blenheim, not in the pride of great abstract masses, but in that humility of flower-like intricacy—the particular blades of the grass; nor can chance have thrown into contiguous generations Spinoza and Swift, an absorption of the whole intellect in God, a fakir-like contempt for all human desire; "take from her," Swift prayed for Stella in sickness, "all violent desire whether of life or death"; the elaboration and spread of Masonic symbolism, its God made in the image of a Christopher Wren;

Berkeley's declaration, modified later, that physical pleasure is the *Summum Bonum,* Heaven's sole reality, his counter-truth to that of Spinoza.

In judging any moment of past time we should leave out what has since happened; we should not call the Swift of the *Drapier Letters* nearer truth because of their influence upon history than the Swift who attacked in *Gulliver* the inventors and logicians; we should see certain men and women as if at the edge of a cliff, time broken away from their feet. Spinoza and the Masons, Berkeley and Swift, speculative and practical intellect, stood there free at last from all prepossessions and touched the extremes of thought; the Gymnosophists of Strabo close at hand, could they but ignore what was harsh and logical in themselves, or the China of the Dutch cabinet-makers, of the *Citizen of the World:* the long-settled rule of powerful men, no great dogmatic structure, few great crowded streets, scattered unprogressive communities, much handiwork, wisdom wound into the roots of the grass.

"I have something in my blood that no child must inherit." There have been several theories to account for Swift's celibacy. Sir Walter Scott suggested a "physical defect," but that seems incredible. A man so outspoken would have told Vanessa the truth and stopped a tragic persecution, a man so charitable have given Stella the protection of his name. The refusal to see Stella when there was no third person present suggests a man that dreaded temptation; nor is it compatible with those stories still current among our country people of Swift sending his servant out to fetch a woman, and dismissing that servant when he woke to find a black woman at his side. Lecky suggested dread of madness—the theory of my play—of madness already present in constant eccentricity; though, with a vagueness born from distaste of the theme, he saw nothing incompatible between Scott's theory and his own. Had Swift dreaded transmitting madness he might well have

been driven to consorting with the nameless barren women of the streets. Somebody else suggests syphilis contracted doubtless between 1699 when he was engaged to Varina and some date soon after Stella's arrival in Ireland. Mr. Shane Leslie thinks that Swift's relation to Vanessa was not platonic,[5] and that whenever his letters speak of a cup of coffee they mean the sexual act; whether the letters seem to bear him out I do not know, for those letters bore me; but whether they seem to or not he must, if he is to get a hearing, account for Swift's relation to Stella. It seems certain that Swift loved her though he called it by some other name, and she him, and that it was platonic love.

> Thou, Stella, wert no longer young,
> When first for thee my harp was strung,
> Without one word of Cupid's darts,
> Of killing eyes or bleeding hearts;
> With friendship and esteem possest,
> I ne'er admitted Love a guest.
> In all the habitudes of life,
> The friend, the mistress, and the wife,
> Variety we still pursue,
> In pleasure seek for something new;
> Or else comparing with the rest,
> Take comfort that our own is best;
> The best we value by the worst,
> As tradesmen show their trash at first;
> But his pursuits are at an end,
> Whom Stella chooses for a friend.

If the relation between Swift and Vanessa was not platonic there must have been some bar that affected Stella as well as Swift. Dr. Delaney is said to have believed that Swift married Stella in 1716 and found in some exchange of confidences that they were brother and sister, but Sir William Temple was not in Ireland during the year that preceded Swift's birth, and so far as we know Swift's mother was not in England.

There is no satisfactory solution. Swift, though he lived in great publicity, and

---

[5] Rossi and Hone take the same view, though uncertain about the coffee. When I wrote, their book had not appeared.

wrote and received many letters, hid two things which constituted perhaps all that he had of private life: his loves and his religious beliefs.

"Was Swift mad? Or was it the intellect itself that was mad?" The other day a scholar in whose imagination Swift has a pre-eminence scarcely possible outside Ireland said: "I sometimes feel that there is a black cloud about to overwhelm me, and then comes a great jet of life; Swift had that black cloud and no jet. He was terrified." I said, "Terrified perhaps of everything but death," and reminded him of a story of Dr. Johnson's.[6] There was a reward of £500 for the identification of the author of the *Drapier Letters*. Swift's butler, who had carried the manuscript to the printer, stayed away from work. When he returned Swift said, "I know that my life is in your hands, but I will not bear, out of fear, either your insolence or negligence." He dismissed the butler, and when the danger had passed he restored him to his post, re-

[6] Sheridan has a different version, but as I have used it merely to illustrate an argument I leave it as Dr. Johnson told it.

warded him, and said to the other servants, "No more Barclay, henceforth Mr. Barclay." "Yes," said my friend, "he was not afraid of death but of life, of what might happen next; that is what made him so defiant in public and in private and demand for the State the obedience a Connacht priest demands for the Church." I have put a cognate thought into the mind of John Corbet. He imagines, though but for a moment, that the intellect of Swift's age, persuaded that the mechanicians mocked by Gulliver would prevail, that its moment of freedom could not last, so dreaded the historic process that it became in the half-mad mind of Swift a dread of parentage: "Am I to add another to the healthy rascaldom and knavery of the world?" Did not Rousseau within five years of the death of Swift publish his *Discourse upon Arts and Sciences* and discover instinctive harmony not in heroic effort, not in Cato and Brutus, not among impossible animals—I think of that noble horse Blake drew for Hayley—but among savages, and thereby beget the sans-culottes of Marat? After the arrogance of power the humility of a servant.

George Orwell

Politics vs. Literature: An Examination of *Gulliver's Travels*

IN *Gulliver's Travels* humanity is attacked or criticized, from at least three different angles, and the implied character of Gulliver himself necessarily changes somewhat in the process. In Part I he is the typical eighteenth-century voyager, bold, practical and unromantic, his homely outlook skilfully impressed on the reader by the biographical details at the beginning, by his age (he is a man of forty, with two children, when his adventures start), and by the inventory of the things in his pockets, especially his spectacles, which make several appearances. In Part II he has in general the same character, but at moments when the story demands it he has a tendency to develop into an imbecile who is capable of boasting of "our noble Country, the Mistress of Arts and Arms, the Scourge of France," etc., etc., and at the same time of betraying every available scandalous fact about the country which he professes to love. In Part III he is much as he was in Part I, though, as he is consorting chiefly with courtiers and men of learning, one has the impression that he has risen in the social scale. In Part IV he conceives a horror of the human race which is not apparent, or only intermittently apparent, in the earlier books, and changes into a sort of unreligious anchorite whose one desire is to live in some desolate spot where he can devote himself to meditating on the goodness of the Houyhnhnms. However, these inconsistencies are forced upon Swift by the fact that Gulliver is there chiefly to provide a contrast. It is necessary, for instance, that he should appear sensible in Part I and at least intermittently silly in Part II, because in both books the essential maneuver is the same, i.e. to make the human being look ridiculous by imagining him as a creature six inches high. Whenever Gulliver is not acting as a stooge there is a sort of continuity in his character, which comes out especially in his resourcefulness and his observation of physical detail. He is much the same kind of person, with the same prose style, when he bears off the warships of Blefuscu, when he rips open the belly of the monstrous rat, and when he sails away upon the ocean in his frail coracle made from the skins of Yahoos. Moreover, it is difficult not to feel that in his shrewder moments Gulliver is simply Swift himself, and there is at least one incident in which Swift seems to be venting his private grievance against contemporary Society. It will be remembered that when the Emperor of Lilliput's palace catches fire, Gulliver puts it out by urinating on it. Instead of being congratulated on his presence of mind, he finds that he has committed a capital offence by making water in the precincts of the palace, and

> I was privately assured, that the Empress, conceiving the greatest Abhorrence of what I had done, removed to the most distant Side of the Court, firmly resolved that those buildings should never be repaired for her Use; and, in the Presence of her chief Confidents, could not forbear vowing Revenge.

According to Professor G. M. Trevelyan (*England under Queen Anne*), part of the reason for Swift's failure to get preferment was that the Queen was scandalized by the *Tale of a Tub*—a pamphlet in which Swift

From *Shooting an Elephant and Other Essays*, copyright, 1945, 1946, 1949, 1950, by Sonia Brownell Orwell. Reprinted by permission of Harcourt, Brace & World, Inc.

probably felt that he had done a great service to the English Crown, since it scarifies the Dissenters and still more the Catholics while leaving the Established Church alone. In any case no one would deny that *Gulliver's Travels* is a rancorous as well as a pessimistic book, and that especially in Parts I and III it often descends into political partisanship of a narrow kind. Pettiness and magnanimity, republicanism and authoritarianism, love of reason and lack of curiosity, are all mixed up in it. The hatred of the human body with which Swift is especially associated is only dominated in Part IV, but somehow this new preoccupation does not come as a surprise. One feels that all these adventures, and all these changes of mood, could have happened to the same person, and the inter-connection between Swift's political loyalties and his ultimate despair is one of the most interesting features of the book.

Politically, Swift was one of those people who are driven into a sort of perverse Toryism by the follies of the progressive party of the moment. Part I of *Gulliver's Travels*, ostensibly a satire on human greatness, can be seen, if one looks a little deeper, to be simply an attack on England, on the dominant Whig Party, and on the war with France, which—however bad the motives of the Allies may have been—did save Europe from being tyrannized over by a single reactionary power. Swift was not a Jacobite nor strictly speaking a Tory, and his declared aim in the war was merely a moderate peace treaty and not the outright defeat of England. Nevertheless there is a tinge of quislingism in his attitude, which comes out in the ending of Part I and slightly interferes with the allegory. When Gulliver flees from Lilliput (England) to Blefuscu (France) the assumption that a human being six inches high is inherently contemptible seems to be dropped. Whereas the people of Lilliput have behaved towards Gulliver with the utmost treachery and meanness, those of Blefuscu behave generously and straightforwardly, and indeed

this section of the book ends on a different note from the all-round disillusionment of the earlier chapters. Evidently Swift's animus is, in the first place, against *England*. It is "your Natives" (i.e. Gulliver's fellow-countrymen) whom the King of Brobdingnag considers to be "the most pernicious Race of little odious vermin that Nature ever suffered to crawl upon the surface of the Earth," and the long passage at the end, denouncing colonization and foreign conquest, is plainly aimed at England, although the contrary is elaborately stated. The Dutch, England's allies and target of one of Swift's most famous pamphlets, are also more or less wantonly attacked in Part III. There is even what sounds like a personal note in the passage in which Gulliver records his satisfaction that the various countries he has discovered cannot be made colonies of the British Crown:

> The *Houyhnhnms*, indeed, appear not to be so well prepared for War, a Science to which they are perfect Strangers, and especially against missive Weapons. However, supposing myself to be a Minister of State, I could never give my advice for invading them. . . . Imagine twenty thousand of them breaking into the midst of an *European* army, confounding the Ranks, overturning the Carriages, battering the Warriors' Faces into Mummy, by terrible Yerks from their hinder hoofs. . . .

Considering that Swift does not waste words, that phrase, "battering the warriors' faces into mummy," probably indicates a secret wish to see the invincible armies of the Duke of Marlborough treated in a like manner. There are similar touches elsewhere. Even the country mentioned in Part III, where "the Bulk of the People consist, in a Manner, wholly of Discoverers, Witnesses, Informers, Accusers, Prosecutors, Evidences, Swearers, together with their several subservient and subaltern Instruments, all under the Colours, the Conduct, and Pay of Ministers of State," is called Langdon, which is within one letter of being an anagram of England. (As the early editions of the book contain misprints, it may perhaps have been intended as a complete anagram.) Swift's *physical* repulsion from humanity is certainly real enough, but one has the feeling that his debunking of human grandeur, his diatribes against lords, politicians, court favorites, etc., has mainly a local application and springs from the fact that he belonged to the unsuccessful party. He denounces injustice and oppression, but he gives no evidence of liking democracy. In spite of his enormously greater powers, his implied position is very similar to that of the innumerable silly-clever Conservatives of our own day —people like Sir Alan Herbert, Professor G. M. Young, Lord Elton, the Tory Reform Committee or the long line of Catholic apologists from W. H. Mallock onwards: people who specialize in cracking neat jokes at the expense of whatever is "modern" and "progressive," and whose opinions are often all the more extreme because they know that they cannot influence the actual drift of events. After all, such a pamphlet as *An Argument to prove that the Abolishing of Christianity*, etc., is very like "Timothy Shy" having a bit of clean fun with the Brains Trust, or Father Ronald Knox exposing the errors of Bertrand Russell. And the ease with which Swift has been forgiven—and forgiven, sometimes, by devout believers—for the blasphemies of *A Tale of a Tub* demonstrates clearly enough the feebleness of religious sentiments as compared with political ones.

However, the reactionary cast of Swift's mind does not show itself chiefly in his political affiliations. The important thing is his attitude towards Science, and, more broadly, towards intellectual curiosity. The famous Academy of Lagado, described in Part III of *Gulliver's Travels*, is no doubt a justified satire on most of the so-called scientists of Swift's own day. Significantly, the people at work in it are described as "Projectors," that is, people not engaged in disinterested research but merely on the look-out for gadgets which will save labor and bring in money. But there is no sign—

indeed, all through the book there are many signs to the contrary—that "pure" science would have struck Swift as a worth-while activity. The more serious kind of scientist has already had a kick in the pants in Part II, when the "Scholars" patronized by the King of Brobdingnag try to account for Gulliver's small stature:

> After much Debate, they concluded unanimously that I was only *Relplum Scalcath*, which is interpreted literally, *Lusus Naturae*; a Determination exactly agreeable to the modern philosophy of *Europe*, whose Professors, disdaining the old Evasion of *Occult Causes*, whereby the followers of *Aristotle* endeavoured in vain to disguise their Ignorance, have invented this wonderful Solution of All Difficulties, to the unspeakable Advancement of human Knowledge.

If this stood by itself one might assume that Swift is merely the enemy of *sham* science. In a number of places, however, he goes out of his way to proclaim the uselessness of all learning or speculation not directed towards some practical end:

> The learning of [the Brobdingnagians] is very defective, consisting only in Morality, History, Poetry, and Mathematics, wherein they must be allowed to excel. But, the last of these is wholly applied to what may be useful in Life, to the improvement of Agriculture, and all mechanical Arts so that among us it would be little esteemed. And as to Ideas, Entities, Abstractions, and Transcendentals, I could never drive the least Conception into their Heads.

The Houyhnhnms, Swift's ideal beings, are backward even in a mechanical sense. They are unacquainted with metals, have never heard of boats, do not, properly speaking, practise agriculture (we are told that the oats which they live upon "grow naturally"), and appear not to have invented wheels.[1] They have no alphabet, and evidently have not much curiosity about the physical world. They do not believe that any inhabited country exists be-

1 Houyhnhnms too old to walk are described as being carried in "sledges" or in "a kind of vehicle, drawn like a sledge." Presumably these had no wheels.

side their own, and though they understand the motions of the sun and moon, and the nature of eclipses, "this is the utmost progress of their *Astronomy*." By contrast, the philosophers of the flying island of Laputa are so continuously absorbed in mathematical speculations that before speaking to them one has to attract their attention by flapping them on the ear with a bladder. They have catalogued ten thousand fixed stars, have settled the periods of ninety-three comets, and have discovered in advance of the astronomers of Europe, that Mars has two moons—all of which information Swift evidently regards as ridiculous, useless and uninteresting. As one might expect, he believes that the scientist's place, if he has a place, is in the laboratory, and that scientific knowledge has no bearing on political matters:

What I . . . thought altogether unaccountable, was the strong Disposition I observed in them towards News and Politics, perpetually enquiring into Public Affairs, giving their judgments in Matters of State, and passionately disputing every inch of a Party Opinion. I have, indeed, observed the same Disposition among most of the Mathematicians I have known in *Europe*, though I could never discover the least Analogy between the two Sciences; unless those people suppose, that, because the smallest Circle hath as many Degrees as the largest, therefore the Regulation and Management of the World require no more Abilities, than the Handling and Turning of a Globe.

Is there not something familiar in that phrase "I could never discover the least analogy between the two sciences"? It has precisely the note of the popular Catholic apologists who profess to be astonished when a scientist utters an opinion on such questions as the existence of God or the immortality of the soul. The scientist, we are told, is an expert only in one restricted field: why should his opinions be of value in any other? The implication is that theology is just as much an exact science as, for instance, chemistry, and that the priest is also an expert whose conclusions on certain subjects must be accepted. Swift in effect makes the same claim for the politician, but he goes one better in that he will not allow the scientist—either the "pure" scientist or the *ad-hoc* investigator —to be a useful person in his own line. Even if he had not written Part III of *Gulliver's Travels*, one could infer from the rest of the book that, like Tolstoy and like Blake, he hates the very idea of studying the processes of Nature. The "Reason" which he so admires in the Houyhnhnms does not primarily mean the power of drawing logical inferences from observed facts. Although he never defines it, it appears in most contexts to mean either common sense—i.e. acceptance of the obvious and contempt for quibbles and abstractions— or absence of passion and superstition. In general he assumes that we know all that we need to know already, and merely use our knowledge incorrectly. Medicine, for instance, is a useless science, because if we lived in a more natural way, there would be no diseases. Swift, however, is not a simple-lifer or an admirer of the Noble Savage. He is in favor of civilization and the arts of civilization. Not only does he see the value of good manners, good conversation, and even learning of literary and historical kind, he also sees that agriculture, navigation and architecture need to be studied and could with advantages be improved. But his implied aim is a static, incurious civilization—the world of his own day, a little cleaner, a little saner, with no radical change and no poking into the unknowable. More than one would expect in anyone so free from accepted fallacies, he reveres the past, especially classical antiquity, and believes that modern man has degenerated sharply during the past hundred years.[2] In the island of sorcerers,

---

[2] The physical decadence which Swift claims to have observed may have been a reality at that date. He attributes it to syphilis, which was a new disease in Europe and may have been more virulent than it is now. Distilled liquors, also, were a novelty in the seventeenth century and must have led at first to a great increase in drunkenness.

where the spirits of the dead can be called
up at will:

> I desired that the Senate of *Rome* might appear
> before me in one large chamber, and a modern
> Representative in Counterview, in another. The
> first seemed to be an Assembly of Heroes and
> Demy-Gods, the other a Knot of Pedlars, Pick-
> pockets, Highwaymen and Bullies.

Although Swift uses this section of Part
III to attack the truthfulness of recorded
history, his critical spirit deserts him as
soon as he is dealing with Greeks and Ro-
mans. He remarks, of course, upon the corruption of imperial Rome, but he has an
almost unreasoning admiration for some
of the leading figures of the ancient world:

> I was struck with profound Veneration at the
> sight of *Brutus*, and could easily discover the
> most consummate Virtue, the greatest Intrepidity
> and Firmness of Mind, the truest Love of his
> Country, and general Benevolence for Mankind,
> in every Lineament of his Countenance. . . . I
> had the honour to have much Conversation with
> *Brutus*, and was told, that his Ancestors *Junius*,
> *Socrates*, *Epaminondas*, *Cato* the younger, *Sir
> Thomas More*, and himself, were perpetually to-
> gether: a *Sextumvirate*, to which all the Ages of
> the World cannot add a seventh.

It will be noticed that of these six people,
only one is a Christian. This is an important point. If one adds together Swift's pessimism, his reverence for the past, his incuriosity and his horror of the human
body, one arrives at an attitude common
among religious reactionaries—that is,
people who defend an unjust order of Society by claiming that this world cannot
be substantially improved and only the
"next world" matters. However, Swift
shows no sign of having any religious beliefs, at least in any ordinary sense of the
words. He does not appear to believe seriously in life after death, and his idea of
goodness is bound up with republicanism,
love of liberty, courage, "benevolence"
(meaning in effect public spirit), "reason"
and other pagan qualities. This reminds
one that there is another strain in Swift,

not quite congruous with his disbelief in
progress and his general hatred of humanity.

To begin with, he has moments when he
is "constructive" and even "advanced."
To be occasionally inconsistent is almost
a mark of vitality in Utopia books, and
Swift sometimes inserts a word of praise
into a passage that ought to be purely satirical. Thus, his ideas about the education
of the young are fathered on to the Lilliputians, who have much the same views on
this subject as the Houyhnhnms. The Lilliputians also have various social and legal
institutions (for instance, there are old age
pensions, and people are rewarded for
keeping the law as well as punished for
breaking it) which Swift would have liked
to see prevailing in his country. In the
middle of this passage Swift remembers
his satirical intention and adds, "In relating these and the following Laws, I
would only be understood to mean the original Institutions, and not the most scandalous Corruptions into which these people
are fallen by the degenerate Nature of
Man": but as Lilliput is supposed to represent England, and the laws he is speaking
of have never had their parallel in England,
it is clear that the impulse to make constructive suggestions has been too much
for him. But Swift's greatest contribution
to political thought in the narrower sense
of the words, is his attack especially in
Part III, on what would now be called
totalitarianism. He has an extraordinarily
clear pre-vision of the spy-haunted "police
State," with its endless heresy-hunts and
treason trials, all really designed to neu-
tralize popular discontent by changing it
into war hysteria. And one must remember
that Swift is here inferring the whole from
a quite small part, for the feeble govern-
ments of his own day did not give him illustrations ready-made. For example, there is
the professor at the School of Political
Projectors who "shewed me a large Paper
of Instructions for discovering Plots and
Conspiracies," and who claimed that one

can find people's secret thoughts by examining their excrement:

> Because Men are never so serious, thoughtful, and intent, as when they are at Stool, which he found by frequent Experiment: for in such Conjunctures, when he used meerly as a trial to consider what was the best Way of murdering the King, his Ordure would have a tincture of Green; but quite different when he thought only of raising an Insurrection, or burning the Metropolis.

The professor and his theory are said to have been suggested to Swift by the—from our point of view—not particularly astonishing or disgusting fact that in a recent State trial some letters found in somebody's privy had been put in evidence. Later in the same chapter we seem to be positively in the middle of the Russian purges:

> In the Kingdom of Tribnia, by the Natives called Langdon . . . the Bulk of the People consist, in a Manner, wholly of Discoverers, Witnesses, Informers, Accusers, Prosecutors, Evidences, Swearers. . . . It is first agreed, and settled among them, what suspected Persons shall be accused of a Plot: Then, effectual Care is taken to secure all their Letters and Papers, and put the Owners in Chains. These papers are delivered to a Sett of Artists, very dexterous in finding out the mysterious Meanings of Words, Syllables, and Letters. . . . Where this method fails, they have two others more effectual, which the Learned among them call *Acrostics* and *Anagrams. First,* they can decypher all initial Letters into political Meanings: Thus: N shall signify a Plot, B a Regiment of Horse, L a Fleet at Sea: Or, *Secondly,* by transposing the Letters of the Alphabet in any suspected Paper, they can lay open the deepest Designs of a discontented Party. So, for Example if I should say in a Letter to a Friend, *Our Brother Tom has just got the Piles,* a skilful Decypherer would discover that the same Letters, which compose that Sentence, may be analysed in the following Words: *Resist—a Plot is brought Home—The Tour.* And this is the anagrammatic method.

Other professors at the same school invent simplified languages, write books by machinery, educate their pupils by inscribing the lesson on a wafer and causing them to swallow it, or propose to abolish individuality altogether by cutting off part of the brain of one man and grafting it on to the head of another. There is something queerly familiar in the atmosphere of these chapters, because, mixed up with much fooling, there is a perception that one of the aims of totalitarianism is not merely to make sure that people will think the right thoughts, but actually to make them *less conscious.* Then, again, Swift's account of the Leader who is usually to be found ruling over a tribe of Yahoos, and of the "favorite" who acts first as a dirty-worker and later as a scapegoat, fits remarkably well into the pattern of our own times. But are we to infer from all this that Swift was first and foremost an enemy of tyranny and a champion of the free intelligence? No: his own views, so far as one can discern them, are not markedly liberal. No doubt he hates lords, kings, bishops, generals, ladies of fashion, orders, titles and flummery generally, but he does not seem to think better of the common people than of their rulers, or to be in favor of increased social equality, or to be enthusiastic about representative institutions. The Houyhnhnms are organized upon a sort of caste system which is racial in character, the horses which do the menial work being of different colors from their masters and not interbreeding with them. The educational system which Swift admires in the Lilliputians takes hereditary class distinctions for granted, and the children of the poorest classes do not go to school, because "their Business being only to till and cultivate the Earth . . . therefore their Education is of little Consequence to the Public." Nor does he seem to have been strongly in favor of freedom of speech and the Press, in spite of the toleration which his own writings enjoyed. The King of Brobdingnag is astonished at the multiplicity of religious and political sects in England, and considers that those who hold "opinions prejudicial to the public" (in the context this seems to mean simply heretical opinions), though they need not be obliged to change them, ought to be obliged to conceal them: for "as it was Tyranny in any Government to require the first, so it was weakness not to enforce the second." There is a subtler indication of Swift's own attitude in the manner in which Gulliver leaves the land of the Houyhnhnms. Intermittently, at least, Swift was a kind of anarchist, and Part IV of *Gulliver's Travels* is a picture of an anarchistic Society, not governed by law in the ordinary sense, but by the dictates of "Reason," which are voluntarily accepted by everyone. The General Assembly of the Houyhnhnms "exhorts" Gulliver's master to get rid of him, and his neighbors put pressure on him to make him comply. Two reasons are given. One is that the presence of this unusual Yahoo may unsettle the rest of the tribe, and the other is that a friendly relationship between a Houyhnhnm and a Yahoo is "not agreeable to Reason or Nature, or a Thing ever heard of before among them." Gulliver's master is somewhat unwilling to obey, but the "exhortation" (a Houyhnhnm, we are told, is never *compelled* to do anything, he is merely "exhorted" or "advised") cannot be disregarded. This illustrates very well the totalitarian tendency which is explicit in the anarchist or pacifist vision of Society. In a Society in which there is no law, and in theory no compulsion, the only arbiter of behavior is public opinion. But public opinion, because of the tremendous urge to conformity in gregarious animals, is less tolerant than any system of law. When human beings are governed by "thou shalt not," the individual can practise a certain amount of eccentricity: when they are supposedly governed by "love" or "reason," he is under continuous pressure to make him behave and think in exactly the same way as everyone else. The Houyhnhnms, we are told, were unanimous on almost all subjects. The only question they ever *discussed* was how to deal with the Yahoos. Otherwise there was no room for disagreement among them, because the truth is always either self-evident, or else

it is undiscoverable and unimportant. They had apparently no word for "opinion" in their language, and in their conversations there was no "difference of sentiments." They had reached, in fact, the highest stage of totalitarian organization, the stage when conformity has become so general that there is no need for a police force. Swift approves of this kind of thing because among his many gifts neither curiosity nor good-nature was included. Disagreement would always seem to him sheer perversity. "Reason," among the Houyhnhnms, he says, "is not a Point Problematical, as with us, where men can argue with Plausibility on both Sides of a Question; but strikes you with immediate Conviction; as it must needs do, where it is not mingled, obscured, or discoloured by Passion and Interest." In other words, we know everything already, so why should dissident opinions be tolerated? The totalitarian Society of the Houyhnhnms, where there can be no freedom and no development, follows naturally from this.

We are right to think of Swift as a rebel and iconoclast, but except in certain secondary matters, such as his insistence that women should receive the same education as men, he cannot be labelled "Left." He is a Tory anarchist, despising authority while disbelieving in liberty, and preserving the aristocratic outlook while seeing clearly that the existing aristocracy is degenerate and contemptible. When Swift utters one of his characteristic diatribes against the rich and powerful, one must probably, as I said earlier, write off something for the fact that he himself belonged to the less successful party, and was personally disappointed. The "outs," for obvious reasons, are always more radical than the "ins." [3]

[3] At the end of the book, as typical specimens of human folly and viciousness, Swift names "a Lawyer, a Pickpocket, a Colonel, a Fool, a Lord, a Gamester, a Politician, a Whore-master, a Physician, an Evidence, a Suborner, an Attorney, a Traitor, or the like." One sees here the irresponsible violence of the powerless. The list lumps together those who break the conventional code, and

But the most essential thing in Swift is his inability to believe that life—ordinary life on the solid earth, and not some rationalized, deodorized version of it—could be made worth living. Of course, no honest person claims that happiness is *now* a normal condition among adult human beings; but perhaps it *could* be made normal, and it is upon this question that all serious political controversy really turns. Swift has much in common—more, I believe, than has been noticed—with Tolstoy, another disbeliever in the possibility of happiness. In both men you have the same anarchistic outlook covering an authoritarian cast of mind; in both a similar hostility to Science, the same impatience with opponents, the same inability to see the importance of any question not interesting to themselves; and in both cases a sort of horror of the actual process of life, though in Tolstoy's case it was arrived at later and in a different way. The sexual unhappiness of the two men was not of the same kind, but there was this in common, that in both of them a sincere loathing was mixed up with a morbid fascination. Tolstoy was a reformed rake who ended by preaching complete celibacy, while continuing to practise the opposite into extreme old age. Swift was presumably impotent, and had an exaggerated horror of human dung: he also thought about it incessantly, as is evident throughout his works. Such people are not likely to enjoy even the small amount of happiness that falls to most human beings and, from obvious motives, are not likely to admit that earthly life is capable of much improvement. Their incuriosity, and hence their intolerance, spring from the same root.

those who keep it. For instance, if you automatically condemn a colonel, as such, on what grounds do you condemn a traitor? Or again, if you want to suppress pickpockets, you must have laws, which means that you must have lawyers. But the whole closing passage, in which the hatred is so authentic, and the reason given for it so inadequate, is somehow unconvincing. One has the feeling that personal animosity is at work.

Swift's disgust, rancor and pessimism would make sense against the background of a "next world" to which this one is the prelude. As he does not appear to believe seriously in any such thing, it becomes necessary to construct a paradise supposedly existing on the surface of the earth, but something quite different from anything we know, with all that he disapproves of— lies, folly, change, enthusiasm, pleasure, love and dirt—eliminated from it. As his ideal being he chooses the horse, an animal whose excrement is not offensive. The Houyhnhnms are dreary beasts—this is so generally admitted that the point is not worth laboring. Swift's genius can make them credible, but there can have been very few readers in whom they have excited any feeling beyond dislike. And this is not from wounded vanity at seeing animals preferred to men; for, of the two, the Houyhnhnms are much liker to human beings than are the Yahoos, and Gulliver's horror of the Yahoos, together with his recognition that they are the same kind of creature as himself, contains a logical absurdity. This horror comes upon him at his very first sight of them. "I never beheld," he says, "in all my Travels, so disagreeable an Animal, nor one against which I naturally conceived so strong an Antipathy." But in comparison with what are the Yahoos disgusting? Not with the Houyhnhnms, because at this time Gulliver has not seen a Houyhnhnm. It can only be in comparison with himself, i.e. with a human being. Later, however, we are to be told that the Yahoos *are* human beings, and human society becomes insupportable to Gulliver because all men are Yahoos. In that case why did he not conceive his disgust of humanity earlier? In effect we are told that the Yahoos are fantastically different from men, and yet are the same. Swift has overreached himself in his fury, and is shouting at his fellow-creatures: "You are filthier than you are!" However, it is impossible to feel much sympathy with the Yahoos, and it is not because they oppress the Yahoos that the Houyhnhnms are unattractive. They are unattractive because the "Reason" by which they are governed is really a desire for death. They are exempt from love, friendship, curiosity, fear, sorrow and—except in their feelings towards the Yahoos, who occupy rather the same place in their community as the Jews in Nazi Germany—anger and hatred. "They have no Fondness for their Colts or Foles, but the Care they take, in educating them, proceeds entirely from the Dictates of *Reason.*" They lay store by "Friendship" and "Benevolence," but "these are not confined to particular Objects, but universal to the whole Race." They also value conversation, but in their conversations there are no differences of opinion, and "nothing passed but what was useful, expressed in the fewest and most significant Words." They practise strict birth control, each couple producing two offspring and thereafter abstaining from sexual intercourse. Their marriages are arranged for them by their elders, on eugenic principles, and their language contains no word for "love," in the sexual sense. When somebody dies they carry on exactly as before, without feeling any grief. It will be seen that their aim is to be as like a corpse as is possible while retaining physical life. One or two of their characteristics, it is true, do not seem to be strictly "reasonable" in their own usage of the word. Thus, they place a great value not only on physical hardihood but on athleticism, and they are devoted to poetry. But these exceptions may be less arbitrary than they seem. Swift probably emphasizes the physical strength of the Houyhnhnms in order to make clear that they could never be conquered by the hated human race, while a taste for poetry may figure among their qualities because poetry appeared to Swift as the antithesis of Science, from his point of view the most useless of all pursuits. In Part III he names "Imagination, Fancy, and Invention" as desirable faculties in which the Laputan mathematicians (in spite of their love of music) were wholly lacking. One must remember that although Swift was an admirable writer of comic verse, the kind of poetry he thought valuable would probably be didactic poetry. The poetry of the Houyhnhnms, he says—

must be allowed to excel (that of) all other Mortals; wherein the Justness of their Similes, and the Minuteness, as well as exactness, of their Descriptions, are, indeed, inimitable. Their Verses abound very much in both of these; and usually contain either some exalted Notions of Friendship and Benevolence, or the Praises of those who were Victors in Races, and other bodily Exercises.

Alas, not even the genius of Swift was equal to producing a specimen by which we could judge the poetry of the Houyhnhnms. But it sounds as though it were chilly stuff (in heroic couplets, presumably), and not seriously in conflict with the principles of "Reason."

Happiness is notoriously difficult to describe, and pictures of a just and well-ordered Society are seldom either attractive or convincing. Most creators of "favorable" Utopias, however, are concerned to show what life could be like if it were lived more fully. Swift advocates a simple refusal of life, justifying this by the claim that "Reason" consists in thwarting your instincts. The Houyhnhnms, creatures without a history, continue for generation after generation to live prudently, maintaining their population at exactly the same level, avoiding all passion, suffering from no diseases, meeting death indifferently, training up their young in the same principles—and all for what? In order that the same process may continue indefinitely. The notions that life here and now is worth living, or that it could be made worth living, or that it must be sacrificed for some future good, are all absent. The dreary world of the Houyhnhnms was about as good a Utopia as Swift could construct, granting that he neither believed in a "next world" nor could get any pleasure out of certain normal activities. But it is not really set up as something desirable in itself, but as the justification for another attack on humanity. The aim, as usual, is to humiliate Man by reminding him that he is weak and ridiculous, and above all that he stinks, and the ultimate motive, probably, is a kind of envy, the envy of the ghost for the living, of the man who knows he cannot be happy for the others who—so he fears—may be a little happier than himself. The political expression of such an outlook must be either reactionary or nihilistic, because the person who holds it will want to prevent Society from developing in some direction in which his pessimism may be cheated. One can do this either by blowing everything to pieces, or by averting social change. Swift ultimately blew everything to pieces in the only way that was feasible before the atomic bomb—that is, he went mad—but, as I have tried to show, his political aims were on the whole reactionary ones.

From what I have written it may have seemed that I am *against* Swift, and that my object is to refute him and even to belittle him. In a political and moral sense I am against him, so far as I understand him. Yet curiously enough he is one of the writers I admire with least reserve, and *Gulliver's Travels,* in particular, is a book which it seems impossible for me to grow tired of. I read it first when I was eight—one day short of eight, to be exact, for I stole and furtively read the copy which was to be given me next day on my eighth birthday—and I have certainly not read it less than half a dozen times since. Its fascination seems inexhaustible. If I had to make a list of six books which were to be preserved when all others were destroyed, I would certainly put *Gulliver's Travels* among them. This raises the question: what is the relationship between agreement with a writer's opinions, and enjoyment of his work?

If one is capable of intellectual detachment, one can *perceive* merit in a writer whom one deeply disagrees with, but *enjoyment* is a different matter. Supposing that

there is such a thing as good or bad art, then the goodness or badness must reside in the work of art itself—not independently of the observer, indeed, but independently of the mood of the observer. In one sense, therefore, it cannot be true that a poem is good on Monday and bad on Tuesday. But if one judges the poem by the appreciation it arouses, then it can certainly be true, because appreciation or enjoyment is a subjective condition which cannot be commanded. For a great deal of his waking life, even the most cultivated person has no aesthetic feelings whatever, and the power to have aesthetic feelings is very easily destroyed. When you are frightened, or hungry, or are suffering from toothache or sea-sickness, *King Lear* is no better from your point of view than *Peter Pan.* You may know in an intellectual sense that it is better, but that is simply a fact which you remember: you will not *feel* the merit of *King Lear* until you are normal again. And aesthetic judgment can be upset just as disastrously—more disastrously, because the cause is no less readily recognized—by political or moral disagreement. If a book angers, wounds or alarms you, then you will not enjoy it, whatever its merits may be. If it seems to you a really pernicious book, likely to influence other people in some undesirable way, then you will probably construct an aesthetic theory to show that it *has* no merits. Current literary criticism consists quite largely of this kind of dodging to and fro between two sets of standards. And yet the opposite process can also happen: enjoyment can overwhelm disapproval, even though one clearly recognizes that one is enjoying something inimical. Swift, whose world-view is so peculiarly unacceptable, but who is nevertheless an extremely popular writer, is a good instance of this. Why is it that we don't mind being called Yahoos, although firmly convinced that we are *not* Yahoos?

It is not enough to make the usual answer that of course Swift was wrong, in fact he was insane, but he was "a good writer." It is true that the literary quality of a book is to some small extent separable from its subject-matter. Some people have a native gift for using words, as some people have a naturally "good eye" at games. It is largely a question of timing and of instinctively knowing how much emphasis to use. As an example near at hand, look back at the passage I quoted earlier, starting "In the Kingdom of Tribnia, by the Natives called Langdon." It derives much of its force from the final sentence: "And this is the anagrammatic Method." Strictly speaking this sentence is unnecessary, for we have already seen the anagram decyphered, but the mock-solemn repetition, in which one seems to hear Swift's own voice uttering the words, drives home the idiocy of the activities described, like the final tap to a nail. But not all the power and simplicity of Swift's prose, nor the imaginative effort that has been able to make not one but a whole series of impossible worlds more credible than the majority of history books—none of this would enable us to enjoy Swift if his world-view were truly wounding or shocking. Millions of people, in many countries, must have enjoyed *Gulliver's Travels* while more or less seeing its anti-human implications: and even the child who accepts Parts I and II as a simple story gets a sense of absurdity from thinking of human beings six inches high. The explanation must be that Swift's world-view is felt to be *not* altogether false—or it would probably be more accurate to say, not false all the time. Swift is a diseased writer. He remains permanently in a depressed mood which in most people is only intermittent, rather as though someone suffering from jaundice or the after-effects of influenza should have the energy to write books. But we all know that mood, and something in us responds to the expression of it. Take, for instance, one of his most characteristic works, *The Lady's Dressing Room:* one might add the kindred poem, *Upon a Beautiful Young Nymph Going to Bed.* Which is truer, the viewpoint expressed in these poems, or the viewpoint implied in Blake's phrase, "The naked female human form divine"? No doubt Blake is nearer the truth, and yet who can fail to feel a sort of pleasure in seeing that fraud, feminine delicacy, exploded for once? Swift falsifies his picture of the world by refusing to see anything in human life except dirt, folly and wickedness, but the part which he abstracts from the whole does exist, and it is something which we all know about while shrinking from mentioning it. Part of our minds—in any normal person it is the dominant part—believes that man is a noble animal and life is worth living: but there is also a sort of inner self which at least intermittently stands aghast at the horror of existence. In the queerest way, pleasure and disgust are linked together. The human body is beautiful: it is also repulsive and ridiculous, a fact which can be verified at any swimming pool. The sexual organs are objects of desire and also of loathing, so much so that in many languages, if not in all languages, their names are used as words of abuse. Meat is delicious, but a butcher's shop makes one feel sick: and indeed all our food springs ultimately from dung and dead bodies, the two things which of all others seem to us the most horrible. A child, when it is past the infantile stage but still looking at the world with fresh eyes, is moved by horror almost as often as by wonder—horror of snot and spittle, of the dogs' excrement on the pavement, the dying toad full of maggots, the sweaty smell of grown-ups, the hideousness of old men, with their bald heads and bulbous noses. In his endless harping on disease, dirt and deformity, Swift is not actually inventing anything, he is merely leaving something out. Human behavior, too, especially in politics, is as he describes it, although it contains other more important factors which he refuses to admit. So far as we can see, both horror and pain are necessary to the continuance of life on this planet, and it is therefore open to pessimists like Swift to say: "If horror and pain must always be with us, how can life be significantly improved?" His attitude is in effect the Christian attitude, minus the bribe of a "next world"—which, however, probably has less hold upon the minds of believers than the conviction that this world is a vale of tears and the grave is a place of rest. It is, I am certain, a wrong attitude, and one which could have harmful effects upon behavior; but something in us responds to it, as it responds to the gloomy words of the burial service and the sweetish smell of corpses in a country church.

It is often argued, at least by people who admit the importance of subject-matter, that a book cannot be "good" if it expresses a palpably false view of life. We are told that in our own age, for instance, any book that has genuine literary merit will also be more or less "progressive" in tendency. This ignores the fact that throughout history a similar struggle between progress and reaction has been raging, and that the best books of any one age have always been written from several different viewpoints, some of them palpably more false than others. In so far as a writer is a propagandist, the most one can ask of him is that he shall genuinely believe in what he is saying, and that it shall not be something blazingly silly. Today, for example, one can imagine a good book being written by a Catholic, a Communist, a Fascist, a pacifist, an anarchist, perhaps by an old-style Liberal or an ordinary Conservative: one cannot imagine a good book being written by a spiritualist, a Buchmanite or a member of the Ku Klux Klan. The views that a writer holds must be compatible with sanity, in the medical sense, and with the power of continuous thought: beyond that what we ask of him is talent, which is probably another name for conviction. Swift did not possess ordinary wisdom, but he did possess a terrible intensity of vision, capable of picking out a single hidden truth and then magnifying it and distorting it. The durability of *Gulliver's Travels* goes to show that, if the force of belief is behind it, a world-view which only just passes the test of sanity is sufficient to produce a great work of art.

Norman O. Brown

The Excremental Vision

ANY reader of Jonathan Swift knows that in his analysis of human nature there is an emphasis on, and attitude toward, the anal function that is unique in Western literature. In mere quantity of scatological imagery he may be equaled by Rabelais and Aristophanes; but whereas for Rabelais and Aristophanes the anal function is a part of the total human being which they make us love because it is part of life, for Swift it becomes the decisive weapon in his assault on the pretensions, the pride, even the self-respect of mankind. The most scandalous pieces of Swiftian scatology are three of his later poems—*The Lady's Dressing Room, Strephon and Chloe, Cassinus and Peter*—which are all variations on the theme:

> Oh! *Caelia, Caelia, Caelia* ———.

Aldous Huxley explicates, saying, "The monosyllabic verb, which the modesties of 1929 will not allow me to reprint, rhymes with 'wits' and 'fits.' " [1] But even more disturbing, because more comprehensively metaphysical, is Swift's vision of man as Yahoo, and Yahoo as excrementally filthy beyond all other animals, in the fourth part of *Gulliver's Travels*. Nor is the anal theme a new feature in Swift's mature or later period; it is already adumbrated in *A Tale of a Tub*, that intoxicated overflow of youthful genius and fountainhead of the entire Swiftian apocalypse. The understanding of Swift therefore begins with the recognition that Swift's anatomy of human nature, in its entirety and at the most profound and profoundly disturbing level, can be called "The Excremental Vision."

[1] Huxley, *Do What You Will*, p. 94.

"The Excremental Vision" is the title of a chapter in Middleton Murry's book (1954) on Jonathan Swift. The credit for recognizing the central importance of the excremental theme in Swift belongs to Aldous Huxley. In an essay in *Do What You Will* (1929) he says, "Swift's greatness lies in the intensity, the almost insane violence of that 'hatred of the bowels' which is the essence of his misanthropy and which underlies the whole of his work." Murry deserves credit for his arresting phrase, which redirects criticism to the central problem in Swift. Aldous Huxley's essay had no effect on Quintana's book *The Mind and Art of Jonathan Swift* (1936), which perfectly illustrates the poverty of criticism designed to domesticate and housebreak this tiger of English literature. Quintana buries what he calls the "noxious compositions" in a general discussion of Swift's last phase as a writer, saying, "From scatology one turns with relief to the capital verses entitled *Helter Skelter, or The Hue and Cry after the Attorneys going to ride the Circuit,* which exhibits Swift's complete mastery of vigorous rhythm." The excremental theme in the fourth part of *Gulliver's Travels* is dismissed as bad art (criticism here, as so often, functioning as a mask for moral prejudice): "The sensationalism into which Swift falls while developing the theme of bestiality. . . . Had part IV been toned down, *Gulliver's Travels* would have been a finer work of art." It is reassuring to know that English literature is expounded at our leading universities by men who, like Bowdler, know how to improve the classics. The history of Swiftian criticism, like the his-

From *Life against Death: The Psychoanalytical Meaning of History*, by Norman O. Brown. Copyright 1959 by Wesleyan University. Reprinted by permission of Wesleyan University Press. Footnotes have been omitted or shortened without notice.

tory of psychoanalysis, shows that repression weighs more heavily on anality than on genitality. Psychoanalytical theorems on the genital function have become legitimate hypotheses in circles which will not listen to what Freud has to say about anality, or to what Swift had to say (and who yet write books on *The Mind and Art of Jonathan Swift*).

Even Huxley and Murry, though they face the problem, prove incapable of seeing what there is to see. After admitting into consciousness the unpleasant facts which previous criticism had repressed, they proceed to protect themselves and us against the disturbing impact of the excremental vision by systematic distortion, denunciation, and depreciation. It is a perfect example, in the field of literary criticism, of Freud's notion that the first way in which consciousness becomes conscious of a repressed idea is by emphatically denying it. The basic device for repudiating the excremental vision is, of course, denunciation. Huxley adopts a stance of intellectual superiority—"the absurdity, the childish silliness, of this refusal to accept the universe as it is given." Murry, echoing that paradoxically conservative philosopher of sexuality, D. H. Lawrence, adopts a stance of moral superiority—"so perverse, so unnatural, so mentally diseased, so humanly *wrong*." The transparently emotional character of their reaction to Swift is then masked as a psychoanalytical diagnosis; the excremental vision is a product of insanity. Huxley speaks of the "obsessive preoccupation with the visceral and excrementitious subject," "to the verge of insanity," and suggests a connection between it and the "temperamental coldness" of Swift's relations to Stella and Vanessa, implying a disturbance in the genital function.

Murry's attempt to transform Huxley's suggestions into a full-dress biography is a case study in perverted argumentation. The texts of the "noxious compositions" and the fourth part of *Gulliver* are crudely distorted, as we shall see later, so as to transform Swift's misanthropy into misogyny; then the entire excremental vision can be explained away as an attempt to justify his genital failure (with Varina, Vanessa, and Stella) by indicting the filthiness of the female sex. It is falsely insinuated that the excremental vision is restricted to Swift's latest phase. This insinuation not only has the advantage of suggesting that there is a Swiftian vision which is not excremental (on this point Huxley is more tough-minded than Murry); it has the further advantage of linking the excremental vision with Swift's final mental breakdown. The fact that the mental breakdown came ten years later (1742) will not stop anyone ignorant of psychopathology and determined to lobotomize Swift's scatology; the chronological gap is filled by an enthusiastic vision of Swift's mental breakdown as God's punishment for the scatology. The fact that the excremental theme is already prominent in the fourth part of *Gulliver* (1723) is explained away by a little psychoanalytical jargon buttressed by a little flight of historical imagination: "Evidently the whole complex was working in Swift's mind when he wrote the fourth part of *Gulliver*. . . . Its emergence at that moment may have been the outcome of a deep emotional upheaval caused by the death of Vanessa." The prominence of the same complex in the *Letter of Advice to a Young Poet* (1721), two years before the death of Vanessa, is ignored. Murry's amateur diagnosis finds the origin of the entire complex in Swift's rejection by Varina (1696). It is therefore essential to his thesis to regard *A Tale of a Tub* (1696–1698) as uninfected by the complex. Murry sustains this interpretation by averting his eyes from the prominence of anality in the *Tale* and by interpreting the whole book as wonderful tomfoolery which is not to be taken seriously—that is, by a notion of comedy which denies meaning to wit.

If the duty of criticism toward Jonathan Swift is to judge him insane, criticism should be turned over to the psychoanalysts.

They have risen to the occasion and have shown that they can be counted on to issue a medical certificate of insanity against genius. Their general verdict is substantially the same as that of Huxley and Murry, with the addition of some handsome new terminology. Thus Ferenczi (1926): "From the psychoanalytical standpoint one would describe his neurotic behaviour as an inhibition of normal potency, with a lack of courage in relation to women of good character and perhaps with a lasting aggressive tendency towards women of a lower type. This insight into Swift's life surely justifies us who come after him in treating the phantasies in *Gulliver's Travels* exactly as we do the free associations of neurotic patients in analysis, especially when interpreting their dreams." Karpman (1942): "It is submitted on the basis of such a study of *Gulliver's Travels* that Swift was a neurotic who exhibited psychosexual infantilism, with a particular showing of coprophilia, associated with misogyny, misanthropy, mysophilia and mysophobia." Greenacre (1955): "One gets the impression that the anal fixation was intense and binding, and the genital demands so impaired or limited at best that there was a total retreat from genital sexuality in his early adult life, probably beginning with the unhappy relationship with Jane Waring, the first of the goddesses." [2]

In developing their diagnosis, the psychoanalysts, as might be expected, trace the origin of Swift's neurosis to his earliest childhood. If the psychoanalytical theory of the neuroses is correct, we must abandon Murry's attempt to isolate the excremental vision as a late excrescence; we must also abandon Murry's thesis (interconnected with his attempt to salvage part of Swift

for respectability) that until he was rejected by her, Swift's love for Varina (Jane Waring) was "the healthy natural love of a naturally passionate, and naturally generous nature." We shall have to return to Huxley's more tough-minded literary judgment that Swift *is* the excremental vision, and to his more tough-minded psychological judgment that Swift's sexuality was structurally abnormal from the start. And the biographical evidence, most carefully analyzed by Greenacre, supplies more than enough confirmation. Swift lost his father before he was born; was kidnaped from his mother by his nurse at the age of one; was returned to his mother only three years later, only to be abandoned by his mother one month after his return to her at the psychoanalytically crucial Oedipal period. By psychoanalytical standards such a succession of infantile traumata must establish more than a predisposition to lifelong neurosis.

The case, then, would appear to be closed. The psychoanalytical experts concur with the critics that Swift was mad and that his works should be read only as documents in a case history. Not just the fourth part of *Gulliver* and the "noxious compositions" but all of Swift. For if we cry "insane" to the objectionable parts of Swift, in all honesty we must hand the case over to the psychoanalysts. But after psychoanalytical scrutiny, there is nothing left of Swift that is not objectionable. We must not underestimate the ability of psychoanalysis to uncover the real meaning of symbols. For example, a psychoanalytical comment on Gulliver as a little man in a little boat on the island of Brobdingnag says that "the common symbolism of the man in the boat as the clitoris suggests the identification with the female phallus thought to be characteristic of the male transvestite." Similarly, psychoanalysis leaves the Dean's character without a shred of integrity. "Swift showed marked anal characteristics (his extreme personal immaculateness, secretiveness, intense ambition, pleas-

[2] S. Ferenczi, *Final Contributions to the Problems and Methods of Psycho-analysis*, London, 1955, p. 59; B. Karpman, "Neurotic Traits of Jonathan Swift," *Psychoanalytic Review*, XXIX (1942), p. 132; P. Greenacre, "The Mutual Adventures of Jonathan Swift and Lemuel Gulliver," *Psychoanalytic Quarterly*, XXIV (1955), p. 60.

ure in less obvious dirt [sc. satire], stubborn vengefulness in righteous causes) which indicate clearly that early control of the excretory function was achieved under great stress and perhaps too early." [3]

At this point common humanity revolts. If personal immaculateness, ambition, and the championship of righteous causes are neurotic traits, who shall 'scape whipping? And certainly no genius will escape if this kind of psychoanalysis is turned loose on literary texts. Common humanity makes us turn in revulsion against Huxley, Murry, and the psychoanalysts. By what right do they issue certificates of lunacy? By virtue of their own pre-eminent sanity? Judged for sanity and truthfulness, *Gulliver's Travels* will not suffer in comparison with the works of Murry and Huxley. Only Swift could do justice to the irony of Huxley condemning Swift for misanthropic distortion in a volume of essays devoted to destroying the integrity not only of Swift, but also of St. Francis and Pascal. Nor is the sanity of psychoanalysts—and their interpretations of what a man in a boat signifies—utterly beyond question. Only Swift could do justice to the irony of psychoanalysts, whose capacity for finding the anus in the most unlikely places is notorious, condemning Swift for obsessive preoccupation with anality. Fortunately Swift is not himself speechless in the face of these accusations of insanity:

> He gave the little Wealth he had
> To build a House for Fools and Mad.
> *(Verses on the Death of Dr. Swift)*

In Dr. Swift's mental hospital there is a room for Huxley and Murry; their religious eccentricities are prefigured under the name of Jack, the prototype of religious enthusiasm in *A Tale of a Tub*. For Huxley, as for Jack, it later came to pass that "it was for certain reported that he had run out of his Wits. In a short time after, he appeared abroad, and confirmed the Report by falling into the oddest Whimsies that ever a

[3] Karpman, *op. cit.*

sick Brain conceived." Swift has also prepared a room for the psychoanalysts with their anal complex; for are they not prophetically announced in *The Mechanical Operation of the Spirit* as those "certain Fortune-tellers in Northern America, who have a Way of reading a Man's Destiny, by peeping in his Breech"?

The argument thus ends in a bedlamite babel filling the air with mutual accusations of madness. If we resist the temptation to stop our ears and run away, if we retain a psychiatric interest and a clinical detachment, we can only conclude that the accusations are all justified; they are all mad. And the crux of their madness is their proud insistence that everybody except themselves—Huxley, Murry, the psychoanalysts—is mad. We can only save ourselves from their madness by admitting that we are all mad. Psychoanalysis deserves the severest strictures, because it should have helped mankind to develop this kind of consciousness and this kind of humility. Freud saw psychoanalysis as the third great wound, comparable to the Newtonian and Darwinian revolutions, inflicted by science on human narcissism. The Epigoni of Freud have set themselves up as a proud elect exempt from the general damnation. As we have argued elsewhere, the proper aim of psychoanalysis is the diagnosis of the universal neurosis of mankind, in which psychoanalysis is itself a symptom and a stage, like any other phase in the intellectual history of mankind.

If we reorient psychoanalysis in this direction, then a different method for the application of psychoanalysis to Swift (or any other literary figure) is in order. We no longer try to explain away Swift's literary achievements as mere epiphenomena on his individual neurosis. Rather we seek to appreciate his insight into the universal neurosis of mankind. Then psychoanalysis becomes a method not for explaining away but for explicating Swift. We are not disturbed by the fact that Swift had his individual version of the universal human neurosis; we are not even disturbed by the thought that his individual neurosis may have been abnormally acute, or by the thought that his abnormality may be inseparable from his art.

Intense suffering may be necessary, though not sufficient, for the production of genius; and psychoanalysis has never thought through its position towards the age-old tradition of an affinity between genius and madness. Perhaps there is that "necessity of doctors and nurses *who themselves are sick*" of which Nietzsche spoke. Psychoanalysis is then not less necessary for the study of Swift, but more so, though in a different way. It is necessary in order to sustain the requisite posture of humility —about ourselves, about mankind, and toward genius. It is also necessary in order to take seriously the Swiftian exploration of the universal neurosis of mankind. The thesis of this chapter is that if we are willing to listen to Swift we will find startling anticipations of Freudian theorems about anality, about sublimation, and about the universal neurosis of mankind. To anticipate objections, let me say that Swiftian psychoanalysis differs from the Freudian in that the vehicle for the exploration of the unconscious is not psychoanalysis but wit. But Freud himself recognized, in *Wit and the Unconscious*, that wit has its own way of exploring the universal neurosis of mankind.

Psychoanalysis is apparently necessary in order to explicate the "noxious compositions"; at least the unpsychoanalyzed neurotic appears to be incapable of correctly stating what these poems are about. These are the poems which provoke Murry to ecstasies of revulsion—"nonsensical and intolerable," "so perverse, so unnatural, so mentally diseased, so humanly *wrong*." What Murry is denouncing is the proposition that woman is abominable because she is guilty of physical evacuation. We need not consider whether the proposition deserves such denunciation, for the simple reason that it comes from Murry's imagi-

nation, not Swift's. Murry, like Strephon and the other unfortunate men in the poems, loses his wits when he discovers that Caelia -----, and thus unconsciously bears witness to the truth of Swift's psychological insight. Any mind that is at all open to the antiseptic wisdom of psychoanalysis will find nothing extraordinary about the poems, except perhaps the fact that they were written in the first half of the eighteenth century. For their real theme—quite obvious on a dispassionate reading—is the conflict between our animal body, appropriately epitomized in the anal function, and our pretentious sublimations, more specifically the pretensions of sublimated or romantic-Platonic love. In every case it is a "goddess," "so divine a Creature," "heavenly Chloe," who is exposed; or rather what is exposed is the illusion in the head of the adoring male, the illusion that the goddess is all head and wings, with no bottom to betray her sublunary infirmities.

The peculiar Swiftian twist to the theme that Caelia ----- is the notion that there is some absolute contradiction between the state of being in love and an awareness of the excremental function of the beloved. Before we dismiss this idea as the fantasy of a diseased mind, we had better remember that Freud said the same thing. In an essay written in 1912 surveying the disorder in the sexual life of man, he finally concludes that the deepest trouble is an unresolved ambivalence in the human attitude toward anality: [4]

We know that at its beginning the sexual instinct is divided into a large number of components—or rather it develops from them—not all of which can be carried on into its final form; some have to be suppressed or turned to other uses before the final form results. Above all, the corophilic elements in the instinct have proved incompatible with our aesthetic ideas, probably since the time when man developed an upright posture and so removed his organ of smell from the ground; further, a considerable proportion of

[4] *Collected Papers*, New York and London, 1924–50, IV, 215.

the sadistic elements belonging to the erotic instinct have to be abandoned. All such developmental processes, however, relate only to the upper layers of the complicated structure. The fundamental processes which promote erotic excitation remain always the same. Excremental things are all too intimately and inseparably bound up with sexual things; the position of the genital organs—*inter urinas et faeces*—remains the decisive and unchangeable factor. The genitals themselves have not undergone the development of the rest of the human form in the direction of beauty; they have retained their animal cast; and so even today love, too, is in essence as animal as it ever was.

Again, in *Civilization and Its Discontents,* Freud pursues the thought that the deepest cause of sexual repression is an organic factor, a disbalance in the human organism between higher and lower functions:[5]

The whole of sexuality and not merely anal erotism is threatened with falling a victim to the organic repression consequent upon man's adoption of the erect posture and the lowering in value of the sense of smell; so that since that time the sexual function has been associated with a resistance not susceptible of further explanation, which puts obstacles in the way of full satisfaction and forces it away from its sexual aim towards sublimations and displacements of libido. . . . All neurotics, and many others too, take exception to the fact that "*inter urinas et faeces nascimur.*" . . . Thus we should find, as the deepest root of the sexual repression that marches with culture, the organic defense of the new form of life that began with the erect posture.

Those who, like Middleton Murry, anathematize Swift's excremental vision as unchristian might ponder the quotation from St. Augustine that Freud uses in both these passages.

That Swift's thought is running parallel with Freud's is demonstrated by the fact that a fuller explication of the poems would have to use the terms "repression" and "sublimation." It is of course not igno-

[5] *Civilization and Its Discontents,* London, 1930, p. 78n.

rance but repression of the anal factor that creates the romantic illusions of Strephon and Cassinus and makes the breakthrough of the truth so traumatic. And Swift's ultimate horror in these poems is at the thought that sublimation—that is to say, all civilized behavior—is a lie and cannot survive confrontation with the truth. In the first of his treatments of the theme (*The Lady's Dressing Room,* 1730) he reasons with Strephon that sublimation is still possible:

Should I the Queen of Love refuse,
Because she rose from stinking Ooze?

Strephon should reconcile himself to—

Such Order from Confusion sprung,
Such gaudy Tulips rais'd from Dung.

But in *Strephon and Chloe* (1731) sublimation and awareness of the excremental function are presented as mutually exclusive, and the conclusion is drawn that sublimation must be cultivated at all costs, even at the cost of repression:

Authorities both old and recent
Direct that Women must be decent:
And, from the Spouse each Blemish hide
More than from all the World beside . . .
On Sense and Wit your Passion found,
By Decency cemented round.

In *Cassinus and Peter,* the last of these poems, even this solution is exploded. The life of civilized sublimation, epitomized in the word "wit," is shattered because the excremental vision cannot be repressed. The poem tells of two undergraduates—

Two College Sophs of *Cambridge* growth
Both special Wits, and Lovers both—

and Cassinus explains the trauma which is killing him:

Nor wonder how I lost my Wits;
Oh! *Caelia, Caelia, Caelia* sh—.

That blessed race of horses, the Houyhnhnms, are free from the illusions of romantic-Platonic love, or rather they are free from love. "Courtship, Love, Presents, Joyntures, Settlements, have no place in their thoughts; or Terms whereby to express them in their Language. The young Couple meet and are joined, merely because it is the Determination of their Parents and Friends: it is what they see done every Day; and they look upon it as one of the necessary Actions in a reasonable Being." If the Houyhnhnms represent a critique of the genital function and genital institutions of mankind, the Yahoos represent a critique of the anal function.

The Yahoos represent the raw core of human bestiality; but the essence of Swift's vision and Gulliver's redemption is the recognition that the civilized man of Western Europe not only remains Yahoo but is worse than Yahoo—"a sort of Animals to whose Share, by what Accident he could not conjecture, some small Pittance of *Reason* had fallen, whereof we made no other use than by its Assistance to aggravate our *natural* Corruptions, and to acquire new ones which Nature had not given us." And the essence of the Yahoo is filthiness, a filthiness distinguishing them not from Western European man but from all other animals: "Another Thing he wondered at in the *Yahoos*, was their strange Disposition to Nastiness and Dirt; whereas there appears to be a natural Love of Cleanliness in all other Animals." The Yahoo is physically endowed with a very rank smell— "the Stink was somewhat between a *Weasel* and a *Fox*"—which, heightened at mating time, is a positive attraction to the male of the species. The recognition of the rank odor of humanity stays with Gulliver after his return to England: "During the first Year I could not endure my Wife or Children in my Presence, the very Smell of them was intolerable"; when he walked the street, he kept his nose "well stopt with Rue, Lavender, or Tobacco-leaves." The Yahoo eating habits are equally filthy: "There was nothing that rendered the *Yahoos* more odious, than their undistinguishing Appetite to devour everything that

came in their Way, whether Herbs, Roots, Berries, corrupted Flesh of Animals, or all mingled together."

But above all the Yahoos are distinguished from other animals by their attitude towards their own excrement. Excrement to the Yahoos is no mere waste product but a magic instrument for self-expression and aggression. This attitude begins in infancy: "While I held the odius Vermin in my Hands, it voided its filthy Excrements of a yellow liquid Substance, all over my Cloaths." It continues in adulthood: "Several of this cursed Brood getting hold of the Branches behind, leaped up into the Tree, from whence they began to discharge their Excrements on my Head." It is part of the Yahoo ritual symbolizing the renewal of society: when the old leader of the herd is discarded, "his Successor, at the Head of all the *Yahoos* in that District, Young and Old, Male and Female, come in a Body, and discharge their Excrements upon him from Head to Foot." Consequently, in the Yahoo system of social infeudation, "this *Leader* had usually a Favourite as *like himself* as he could get, whose Employment was to *lick his Master's Feet and Posteriors, and drive the Female* Yahoos *to his Kennel*." This recognition that the human animal is distinguished from others as the distinctively excremental animal stays with Gulliver after his return to England, so that he finds relief from the oppressive smell of mankind in the company of his groom: "For I feel my Spirits revived by the Smell he contracts in the Stable." Swift does not, as Huxley says he does, hate the bowels, but only the human use of the bowels.

This demonic presentation of the excremental nature of humanity is the great stumbling block in *Gulliver's Travels*—an aesthetic lapse, crude sensationalism, says Quintana; a false libel on humanity, says Middleton Murry, "for even if we carry the process of stripping the human to the limit of imaginative possibility, we do not arrive at the Yahoo. We might arrive at his cruelty and malice; we should never arrive at his nastiness and filth. That is a gratuitous degradation of humanity; not a salutary, but a shocking one." But if we measure Swift's correctness not by the conventional and complacent prejudices in favor of human pride which are back of Quintana's and Murry's strictures, but by the ruthless wisdom of psychoanalysis, then it is quite obvious that the excremental vision of the Yahoo is substantially identical with the psychoanalytical doctrine of the extensive role of anal erotism in the formation of human culture.

According to Freudian theory the human infant passes through a stage—the anal stage—as a result of which the libido, the life energy of the body, gets concentrated in the anal zone. This infantile stage of anal erotism takes the essential form of attaching symbolic meaning to the anal product. As a result of these symbolic equations the anal product acquires for the child the significance of being his own child or creation, which he may use either to obtain narcissistic pleasure in play, or to obtain love from another (feces as gift), or to assert independence from another (feces as property), or to commit aggression against another (feces as weapon). Thus some of the most important categories of social behavior (play, gift, property, weapon) originate in the anal stage of infant sexuality and—what is more important —never lose their connection with it. When infantile sexuality comes to its catastrophic end, non-bodily cultural objects inherit the symbolism originally attached to the anal product, but only as second-best substitutes for the original (sublimations). Sublimations are thus symbols of symbols. The category of property is not simply transferred from feces to money; on the contrary, money is feces, because the anal erotism continues in the unconscious. The anal erotism has not been renounced or abandoned but repressed.

One of the central ambiguities in psychoanalytical theory is the question of whether the pregenital infantile organizations of the libido, including the anal organization, are biologically determined. We have elsewhere taken the position that they are not biologically determined but are constructed by the human ego, or rather that they represent that distortion of the human body which *is* the human ego. If so, then psychoanalysis concurs with Swift's thesis that anal erotism—in Swift's language, "a strange Disposition to Nastiness and Dirt" —is a specifically human privilege; on the other hand, psychoanalysis would differ from Swift's implication that the strange Disposition to Nastiness and Dirt is biologically given. It comes to the same thing to say that Swift errs in giving the Yahoos no "Pittance of Reason" and in assigning to Reason only the transformation of the Yahoo into the civilized man of Western Europe. If anal organization is constructed by the human ego, then the strange Disposition to Nastiness and Dirt is a primal or infantile manifestation of human Reason. Swift also anticipates Freud in emphasizing the connection between anal erotism and human aggression. The Yahoos' filthiness is manifested primarily in excremental aggression: psychoanalytical theory stresses the interconnection between anal organization and human aggression to the point of labeling this phase of infantile sexuality the anal-sadistic phase. Defiance, mastery, will to power are attributes of human reason first developed in the symbolic manipulation of excrement and perpetuated in the symbolic manipulation of symbolic substitutes for excrement.

The psychoanalytical theory of anal erotism depends on the psychoanalytical theory of sublimation. If money etc. are not feces, there is not much reason for hypothesizing a strange human fascination with excrement. By the same token it is hard to see how Swift could have come by his anticipation of the doctrine of anal erotism if he did not also anticipate the doctrine of sublimation. Full credit for perceiving this goes to William Empson. Referring to *A*

Tale of a Tub and its appendix, *The Me-chanical Operation of the Spirit,* Empson writes:[6]

It is the same machinery, in the fearful case of Swift, that betrays not consciousness of the audience but a doubt of which he may himself have been unconscious. "Everything spiritual and valuable has a gross and revolting parody, very similar to it, with the same name. Only unremitting judgement can distinguish between them"; he set out to simplify the work of judgement by giving a complete set of obscene puns for it. The conscious aim was the defense of the Established Church against the reformers' Inner Light; only the psychoanalyst can wholly applaud the result. Mixed with his statement, part of what he satirized by pretending (too convincingly) to believe, the source of his horror, was "everything spiritual is really material; Hobbes and the scientists have proved this; all religion is really a perversion of sexuality."

The source of Swift's horror, according to Empson, is the discovery of that relation between higher and lower, spiritual and physical, which psychoanalysis calls sublimation. Swift hit upon the doctrine of sublimation as a new method for the psychological analysis of religion, specifically religious enthusiasm. His new method sees religious enthusiasm as the effect of what he calls the "Mechanical Operation of the Spirit." At the outset he distinguishes his psychology of religion from traditional naturalistic psychology, which treats religious enthusiasm as "the Product of Natural Causes, the effect of strong Imagination, Spleen, violent Anger, Fear, Grief, Pain, and the like." If you want a distinctive label for Swift's new psychology of religion, it can only be called psychoanalysis. The first step is to define religious enthusiasm as "a lifting up of the Soul or its Faculties above Matter." Swift then proceeds to the fundamental proposition that "the Corruption of the Senses is the Generation of the Spirit." By corruption of the senses Swift means repression, as is quite clear from his explanation:

[6] *Some Versions of Pastoral,* London, 1935, p. 60.

Because the Senses in Men are so many Avenues to the Fort of Reason, which in this Operation is wholly block'd up. All Endeavours must be therefore used, either to divert, bind up, stupify, fluster, and amuse the Senses, or else to justle them out of their Stations; and while they are either absent, or otherwise employ'd or engaged in a Civil War against each other, the Spirit enters and performs its Part.

The doctrine that repression is the cause of sublimation is vividly implied in the analogy which Swift sets up for the "Mechanical Operation of the Spirit":

Among our Ancestors, the Scythians, there was a Nation, call'd Longheads, which at first began by a Custom among Midwives and Nurses, of molding, and squeezing, and bracing up the Heads of Infants; by which means, Nature shut out at one Passage, was forc'd to seek another, and finding room above, shot upwards, in the Form of a Sugar-Loaf.

Swift affirms not only that the spirit is generated by repression of bodily sensuousness, but also, as is implied by the analogy of the Scythian Longheads, that the basic structure of sublimation is, to use the psychoanalytical formula, displacement from below upward. Displacement from below upward, conferring on the upper region of the body a symbolic identity with the lower region of the body, is Swift's explanation for the Puritan cult of large ears: the ear is a symbolic penis. According to psychoanalysis, displacement of the genital function to another organ is the basic pattern in conversion hysteria. "Conversion hysteria genitalizes those parts of the body at which the symptoms are manifested"; maidenly blushing, for example, is a mild case of conversion hysteria—that is, a mild erection of the entire head.[7] According to Swift's analysis of the Puritans, "The Proportion of largeness, was not only lookt upon as an Ornament of the Outward Man, but as a Type of Grace in the Inward. Besides, it is held by Naturalists, that if there

[7] S. Ferenczi, *Further Contributions to the Theory and Technique of Psycho-analysis,* New York, 1955, p. 90.

be a Protuberancy of Parts in the *Superiour* Region of the Body, as in the Ears and Nose, there must be a Parity also in the *Inferior*." Hence, says Swift, the devouter Sisters "lookt upon all such extraordinary Dilatations of that Member, as Protrusions of Zeal, or spiritual Excrescencies" and also "in hopes of conceiving a suitable Offspring by such a Prospect."[8] By this road Swift arrives at Freud's theorem on the identity of what is highest and lowest in human nature. In Freud's language: "Thus it is that what belongs to the lowest depths in the minds of each one of us is changed, through this formation of the ideal, into what we value highest in the human soul."[9] In Swift's language:

> Whereas the mind of Man, when he gives the Spur and Bridle to his Thoughts, doth never stop, but naturally sallies out into both extreams of High and Low, of Good and Evil; His first Flight of Fancy, commonly transports Him to Ideas of what is most Perfect, finished and exalted; till having soared out of his own Reach and Sight, not well perceiving how near the Frontiers of Height and Depth, border upon each other; With the same Course and Wing, he falls down plum into the lowest Bottom of Things; like one who travels the *East* into the *West;* or like a strait Line drawn by its own Length into a Circle.
> (*Tale of a Tub,* Sect. VIII)

Such is the demonic energy with which Swift pursues his vision that twice, once in Section VIII of *A Tale of a Tub* and again in *The Mechanical Operation of the Spirit,* he arrives at the notion of the unity of those opposites of all opposites, God and the Devil. Men, "pretending . . . to extend the Dominion of one Invisible Power, and contract that of the other, have discovered a gross Ignorance in the Natures of Good and Evil, and most horribly confounded the Frontiers of both. After Men have lifted up the Throne of their Divinity to the *Coelum Empyraeum;* . . . after they have sunk their *Principle* of *Evil* to the lowest Center I laugh aloud, to see these Reasoners,

at the same time, engaged in wise Dispute, about certain walks and Purlieus, whether they are in the Verge of God or the Devil, seriously debating, whether such and such Influences come into Men's Minds, from above or below, or whether certain Passions and Affections are guided by the Evil Spirit or the Good . . . Thus do Men establish a Fellowship of Christ with Belial, and such is the Analogy they make between *cloven Tongues,* and *cloven Feet.*" Empson has shown how and by what law of irony the partially disclaimed thought is Swift's own thought.

As we have argued elsewhere, psychoanalysis finds far-reaching resemblances between a sublimation and a neurotic symptom. Both presuppose repression; both involve a displacement resulting from the repression of libido from the primary erogenous zones. Thus the psychoanalytic theory of sublimation leads on to the theory of the universal neurosis of mankind. In the words of Freud:[10]

> The neuroses exhibit on the one hand striking and far-reaching points of agreement with . . . art, religion and philosophy. But on the other hand they seem like distortions of them. It might be maintained that a case of hysteria is a caricature of a work of art, that an obsessional neurosis is a caricature of religion and that a paranoic delusion is a caricature of a philosophical system.

Swift develops his doctrine of the universal neurosis of mankind in the "Digression concerning the Original, the Use and Improvement of Madness in a Commonwealth," in *A Tale of a Tub.* Here Swift attributes to Madness "the greatest Actions that have been performed in the World, under the Influence of Single Men; which are, *the Establishment of New Empires by Conquest: the Advance and Progress of New Schemes in Philosophy; and the contriving, as well as the propagating of New Religions.*" Psychoanalysis must regret the omission of art, but applaud the addition

---

[8] *Tale of a Tub,* Sect. XI.
[9] *The Ego and the Id,* London, 1927, p. 48.
[10] *Standard Edition of the Complete Psychological Works,* London, 1954– , XIII, 73.

of politics, to Freud's original list; Freud himself added politics in his later writings. And Swift deduces the universal neurosis of mankind from his notion of sublimation; in his words:

For the *upper Region* of Man, is furnished like the *middle Region* of the Air; The Materials are formed from Causes of the widest Difference, yet produce at last the same Substance and Effect. Mists arise from the Earth, Steams from Dunghils, Exhalations from the Sea, and Smoak from Fire; yet all Clouds are the same in Composition, as well as Consequences: and the Fumes issuing from a Jakes, will furnish as comely and useful a Vapour, as Incense from an Altar. Thus far, I suppose, will easily be granted me; and then it will follow, that as the Face of Nature never produces Rain, but when it is overcast and disturbed, so Human Understanding, seated in the Brain, must be troubled and overspread by vapours, ascending from the lower Faculties, to water the Invention, and render it fruitful.

After a witty review of kings, philosophers, and religious fanatics Swift concludes: "If the *Moderns* mean by *Madness*, only a Disturbance or Transposition of the Brain, by force of certain *Vapours* issuing up from the lower Faculties; then has this *Madness* been the Parent of all these mighty Revolutions, that have happened in *Empire*, in *Philosophy*, and in *Religion*." And Swift ends the Digression on Madness with a humility and consistency psychoanalysis has never known, by applying his own doctrine to himself:

Even I myself, the Author of these momentous Truths, am a Person, whose Imaginations are hard-mouthed, and exceedingly disposed to run away with his *Reason*, which I have observed from long Experience to be a very light Rider, and easily shook off; upon which account, my Friends will never trust me alone, without a solemn Promise, to vent my Speculations in this, or the like manner, for the universal Benefit of Human kind.

Swift, as we have seen, sees in sublimation, or at least certain kinds of sublimation, a displacement upward of the genital

function. So much was implied in his attribution of genital significance to the Puritans' large ears. He makes a similar, only more elaborately obscene, derivation of the nasal twang of Puritan preachers. He also speaks of "certain Sanguine Brethren of the first Class," that "in the Height and *Orgasmus* of their Spiritual exercise it has been frequent with them *****; immediately after which they found the *Spirit* to relax and flag of a sudden with the Nerves, and they were forced to hasten to a Conclusion." Swift explains all these phenomena in *The Mechanical Operation of the Spirit* with his notion of sublimation:

The Seed or Principle, which has ever put Men upon *Visions* in Things *Invisible*, is of a corporeal Nature. . . . The Spinal Marrow, being nothing else but a Continuation of the Brain, must needs create a very free Communication between the Superior Faculties and those below: And thus the *Thorn in the Flesh* serves for a *Spur* to the *Spirit*.

Not only the genital function but also the anal function is displaced upward, according to Swift. The general theorem is already stated, in *A Tale of a Tub*, Sect. IX, in the comparison of the upper Region of Man to the middle Region of the Air, in which "the Fumes issuing from a Jakes, will furnish as comely and useful a Vapour, as Incense from an Altar." The idea is developed in the image of religious enthusiasts as Aeolists, or worshipers of wind. Swift is here punning on the word "spirit," and as Empson says, "The language plays into his hands here, because the spiritual words are all derived from physical metaphors." Psychoanalysis, of course, must regard language as a repository of the psychic history of mankind, and the exploration of words, by wit or poetry or scientific etymology, as one of the avenues into the unconscious. At any rate, Swift's wit, pursuing his "Physico-logical Scheme" for satirical anatomy, "dissecting the Carcass of Humane Nature," asks where all this windy preaching comes from, and his answer gives all the emphasis of obscenity to the anal factor:

> At other times were to be seen several Hundreds link'd together in a circular Chain, with every Man a Pair of Bellows applied to his Neighbour's Breech, by which they blew up each other to the Shape and Size of a *Tun;* and for that Reason, with great Propriety of Speech, did usually call their Bodies, their *Vessels.* When by these and the like Performances, they were grown sufficiently replete, they would immediately depart, and disembogue for the Public Good, a plentiful share of their Acquirements into their Disciples Chaps.

Another method of inspiration involves a Barrel instead of a Bellows:

> Into this *Barrel,* upon Solemn Days, the Priest enters; where, having before duly prepared himself by the methods already described, a secret Funnel is also convey'd from his Posteriors, to the Bottom of the Barrel, which admits of new Supplies Inspiration from a *Northern* Chink or Crany. Whereupon, you behold him swell immediately to the Shape and Size of his *Vessel.* In this posture he disembogues whole Tempests upon his Auditory, as the Spirit from beneath gives him Utterance; which issuing *ex adytis,* and *penetralibus,* is not performed without much Pain and Gripings. (*Tale of a Tub,* Sect. VIII)

Nor is Swift's vision of sublimated anality limited to religious preaching or *A Tale of a Tub.* In *Strephon and Chloe* the malicious gossip of women is so explained:

> You'd think she utter'd from behind
> Or at her Mouth were breaking Wind.

And more generally, as Greenacre observes, there is throughout Swift "a kind of linking of the written or printed word with the excretory functions." When Swift writes in a letter to Arbuthnot, "Let my anger break out at the end of my pen," the psychoanalytically uninitiated may doubt the psychoanalytical interpretation. But Swift makes references to literary polemics (his own literary form) as dirt-throwing (compare the Yahoos). More generally, in *A Meditation upon a Broomstick,* "mortal man is a broomstick," which "raiseth a mighty Dust where there was none before;

sharing deeply all the while in the very same Pollutions he pretends to sweep away." In the *Letter of Advice to a Young Poet,* he advocates the concentration of writers in a Grub Street, so that the whole town be saved from becoming a sewer: "When writers of all sizes, like freemen of cities, are at liberty to throw out their filth and excrementitious productions, in every street as they please, what can the consequence be, but that the town must be poisoned and become such another jakes, as by report of great travellers, Edinburgh is at night." This train of thought is so characteristically Swift's that in the *Memoirs of Martinus Scriblerus,* now thought to have been written by Pope after talks with Arbuthnot and Swift, the story of Scriblerus' birth must be an inspiration of Swift's: "Nor was the birth of this great man unattended with prodigies: he himself has often told me, that on the night before he was born, Mrs. Scriblerus dreamed she was brought to bed of a huge ink-horn, out of which issued several large streams of ink, as it had been a fountain. This dream was by her husband thought to signify that the child should prove a very voluminous writer." Even the uninitiated will recognize the fantasy, discovered by psychoanalysis, of anal birth.

It would be wearisome to rehearse the parallels to Swift in psychoanalytical literature. The psychoanalysts, alas, think they can dispense with wit in the exploration of the unconscious. Fenichel in his encyclopedia of psychoanalytical orthodoxy, *The Psychoanalytic Theory of Neurosis,* refers to the "anal-erotic nature of speech" without intending to be funny. Perhaps it will suffice to quote from Ferenczi's essay on the proverb "Silence is golden" (for Ferenczi the proverb itself is one more piece of evidence on the anal character of speech): [11]

> That there are certain connections between anal erotism and speech I had already learnt from

[11] *Further Contributions,* p. 251.

Professor Freud, who told me of a stammerer all whose singularities of speech were to be traced to anal phantasies. Jones too has repeatedly indicated in his writings the displacement of libido from anal activities to phonation. Finally I too, in an earlier article ("On Obscene Words") was able to indicate the connection between musical voice-culture and anal erotism.

Altogether Ernest Jones' essay on "Anal-Erotic Character Traits" leaves us with the impression that there is no aspect of higher culture uncontaminated by connections with anality. And Swift leaves us with the same impression. Swift even anticipates the psychoanalytical theorem that an anal sublimation can be decomposed into simple anality. He tells the story of a furious conqueror who left off his conquering career when "the *Vapour* or *Spirit,* which animated the Hero's Brain, being in perpetual Circulation, seized upon that Region of the Human Body, so renown'd for furnishing the *Zibeta Occidentalis,* and gathering there into a Tumor, left the rest of the World for that Time in Peace" (*Tale of a Tub,* Sect. IX).

The anal character of civilization is a topic which requires sociological and historical as well as psychological treatment. Swift turns to the sociology and history of anality in a poem called *A Panegyrick on the Dean.* The poem is written as if by Lady Acheson, the lady of the house at Market Hill where Swift stayed in 1729–1730. In the form of ironic praise, it describes Swift's various roles at Market Hill, as Dean, as conversationalist with the ladies, as Butler fetching a bottle, from the cellar, as Dairymaid churning Butter. But the Dean's greatest achievement at Market Hill was the construction of "Two Temples of magnifick Size," where—

> In sep'rate Cells the He's and She's
> Here pay their vows with *bended Knees,*

to the "gentle Goddess *Cloacine.*" As he built the two outhouses, Swift seems to

have meditated on the question of why we are ashamed of and repress the anal function:

> Thee bounteous Goddess *Cloacine,*
> To Temples why do we confine?

The answer he proposes is that shame and repression of anality did not exist in the age of innocence (here again we see how far wrong Huxley's notion of Swift's "hatred of the bowels" is):

> When *Saturn* ruled the Skies alone
> That *golden* Age, to *Gold* unknown;
> This earthly Globe to thee assign'd
> Receiv'd the Gifts of all Mankind.

After the fall—the usurpation of Jove—came "*Gluttony* with greasy Paws," with her offspring "lolling *Sloth,*" "Pale *Dropsy,*" "lordly *Gout,*" "wheezing *Asthma,*" "voluptuous *Ease,* the Child of *Wealth*"—

> This bloated Harpy sprung from Hell
> Confin'd Thee Goddess to a Cell.

The corruption of the human body corrupted the anal function and alienated the natural Cloacine:

> . . . unsav'ry Vapours rose,
> Offensive to thy nicer Nose.

The correlative doctrine in psychoanalysis is of course the equation of money and feces. Swift is carried by the logic of the myth (myth, like wit, reaches into the unconscious) to make the same equation: the age of innocence, "the *golden* Age, to *Gold* unknown," had another kind of gold. The golden age still survives among the Swains of Northern Ireland—

> Whose Off'rings plac't in golden Ranks,
> Adorn our Chrystal River's Banks.

But the perspectives now opening up are too vast for Swift or for us:

> But, stop ambitious Muse, in time;
> Nor dwell on Subjects too sublime.

Arthur E. Case

Personal and Political Satire in *Gulliver's Travels*

No ONE who reads a modern annotated edition of *Gulliver's Travels* can fail to observe the abundance of the commentary upon the first and third voyages and the comparative scarcity of it in connection with the second and fourth. The reason for this, of course, is that the first and third voyages are primarily satiric in tone, with frequent references to contemporary persons and events in western Europe. On the other hand, since Brobdingnag and Houyhnhnmland are in differing degrees Utopian commonwealths, Swift has no desire to identify their ruling classes with those of his own country. There are a few scattered exceptions which are worth remark. The maids of honor at the court of George I regarded the account of their Brobdingnagian counterparts (2.5.6, 7) [1] as a direct insult. King George himself is ridiculed as a foreigner in a not too cautious passage in the second chapter of the same voyage (2.2.2), and again in the fourth voyage as one of the beggarly German princes who hire out troops (4.5.5). And in the descriptions of Europe which Gulliver gives to the King of Brobdingnag and to his master Houyhnhnm there are, in the midst of much general satire, a few attacks on identifiable individuals.

Most of these references, however, seem to be incidental and opportunistic. It is not strange, perhaps, that the personal attacks in the two primarily satiric voyages have generally been held to be equally planless —a sort of literary Donnybrook Fair, in which Swift followed the good old Irish maxim, "Whenever you see a head, hit it!"

[1] References are to book, chapter, and paragraph.

Consequently no one has been greatly disturbed by allegorical interpretations of the first voyage which identify Gulliver now as Oxford, now as Bolingbroke, and now as Swift himself. As the careers of both of the first two politicians undoubtedly contribute incidents to Gulliver's career, the burden of proof lies on the shoulders of anyone who argues that the political allegory is consistent.

Consistency can be obtained, however, by supposing that Gulliver's career in Lilliput represents the joint political fortunes of Oxford and Bolingbroke during the latter half of Queen Anne's reign, when the two men shared the leadership of the Tory party. This device permits Swift to make use of the most dramatic incidents from the life of each man, and at the same time to avoid too close a parallel with the life of either.

The allegory is exactly coincidental with Gulliver's residence in Lilliput and Blefuscu. It begins with the hero's shipwreck and captivity, which correspond to the temporary fall from power of Oxford and Bolingbroke (then Robert Harley and Henry St. John) in 1708, when the Whigs, led by Godolphin and Marlborough, secured control of the Cabinet and the House of Commons. These events take place in the first chapter of the voyage, in which the nature of the allegory is not yet so clearly apparent. Looking back from later chapters, however, it is possible to extract a number of probable allusions to events of the years 1708–1710. Gulliver is pictured as having been caught off guard; as contemplating violence against his enemies, then as deciding upon submission as the

Reprinted from *Four Essays on "Gulliver's Travels,"* Princeton, 1945, pp. 69–96, by permission of the Princeton University Press.

more prudent course, and later as regarding this submission as a tacit promise binding him in honor not to injure his captors even when it lies within his power to do so. It is hardly necessary to point out the parallel between this conduct and that of the Tory leaders toward the Whigs.

In the second chapter we are introduced to the Emperor and to another simplification of history. Swift is telling a story which began in the reign of Anne and ended in that of George I. To supply Lilliput with an Empress and an Emperor reigning successively would have been to make the author's meaning dangerously plain: it was safer to make them husband and wife. For the same reason the Emperor was described as being almost the exact antithesis of George:

> He is taller by almost the breadth of my Nail, than any of his Court, which alone is enough to strike an Awe into the Beholders. His Features are strong and masculine, with an *Austrian* Lip and arched Nose, his Complexion olive, his Countenance erect, his Body and Limbs well proportioned, all his Motions graceful, and his Deportment majestick. He was then past his Prime, being twenty-eight Years and three Quarters old, of which he had reigned about seven, in great Felicity, and generally victorious. . . . His Dress was very plain and simple, and the Fashion of it between the *Asiatic* and the *European*; but he had on his Head a light Helmet of Gold, adorned with Jewels, and a Plume on the Crest. He held his Sword drawn in his Hand, to defend himself, if I should happen to break loose; it was almost three Inches long, the Hilt and Scabbard were Gold enriched with Diamonds. His Voice was shrill, but very clear and articulate, and I could distinctly hear it when I stood up.   (1.2.3.)

When one recalls George's thick and ungainly form, his bad taste in dress, and his guttural and unintelligible pronunciation of the little English he knew, it becomes clear that Swift is employing with unusual effectiveness the same technique that Pope was to use a few years later when he caricatured George II in the *Epistle to Augustus*. "Praise undeserved is scandal in disguise."

The most important event in the second chapter is the making of the inventory of Gulliver's possessions by a committee appointed by the Emperor. This, probably, stands for the investigation, by a committee of Whig lords, of one William Gregg, a clerk in Harley's office who had been guilty of treasonable correspondence with France. No evidence was found to implicate Harley in the affair, and he, of course, strenuously protested his innocence and his loyalty. This is reflected in a sentence describing what took place at the reading of the inventory. "In the mean time [the Emperor] ordered three thousand of his choicest Troops (who then attended him) to surround me at a distance, with their Bows and Arrows just ready to discharge: but I did not observe it, for my Eyes were wholly fixed upon his Majesty." (1.2.10.)

With the third chapter events begin to move more rapidly. Gulliver's gentleness and good behavior impress the Emperor and the populace favorably, and he becomes more and more importunate for his release. This is opposed only by Skyresh Bolgolam, a cabinet minister who, when finally overborne by the other authorities, manages at least to provide that Gulliver's liberty shall be hedged about with restrictions. This corresponds to a series of political developments which culminated early in 1711. The Tories gradually won their way back into public favor: the Queen had always been inclined toward them. The identity of Skyresh Bolgolam has been a matter of dispute. William Cooke Taylor thought he might be the Duke of Argyle, whom Swift had offended by his attacks on the Scotch. Sir Charles Firth pointed out that Bolgolam was described as being "of a morose and sour Complection," and proposed the name of the Earl of Nottingham, because there was mutual enmity between Swift and the Earl. Swift had, indeed, been the instrument of fixing upon the Earl the sobriquet of "Dismal." Both these identifications rest, however, upon the supposition that Gulliver is Swift, and both men had good reason for hating the author, whereas Gulliver protests (1.3.8) that Bolgolam's hatred arose "without any provocation." Now Nottingham was also an enemy of Harley, on no better ground than that the latter had succeeded him in office in 1704. Moreover, while the Earl never proposed anything resembling a set of conditions on which Swift might be allowed liberty, he did, in 1711, execute a political maneuver which could easily have been interpreted in these terms with regard to Harley. On the latter's rise to power as Chancellor of the Exchequer (in effect Prime Minister) Nottingham proposed in the House of Lords an amendment to the royal address which stipulated that no peace with France should be made which left Spain and the Indies in the possession of the House of Bourbon. This was an open attempt to restrict the powers of the new Tory administration, and to embarrass them by the implication that they could not be trusted to safeguard the interests of England. Harley and St. John felt it prudent not to oppose this amendment, and it was consequently carried. This is expressed allegorically by Gulliver's remark, "I swore and subscribed to these Articles with great Chearfulness and Content, although some of them were not so honourable as I could have wished; which proceeded wholly from the Malice of *Skyresh Bolgolam* the High Admiral: . . ." (1.3.19.)

The articles to which Gulliver swore are not all of the same kind. Most of them are amusing provisions arising out of the difference in size between him and the Lilliputians. But two are connected with the underlying narrative. The first provides that Gulliver shall not leave Lilliput without the Emperor's license given under the great seal. The sixth requires Gulliver to be the Emperor's ally against Blefuscu, and to do his utmost to destroy the enemy's fleet. The true significance of these stipulations does not appear until much later.

The fourth chapter is explanatory and preparatory. Swift takes an opportunity,

in describing Gulliver's visit to the palace, to emphasize the Queen's complaisance toward Gulliver, or, in other words, Queen Anne's inclination toward the Tories. The chief interest of the chapter, however, lies in the detailed account of the political situation in Lilliput and the events which led up to it. There is no special significance in the fact that the narrator is Reldresal, whose identity and relationship to the allegory do not become clear until the seventh chapter. He first explains the party system, admitting that the High-Heels (Tories) exceed in number his own party, the Low-Heels (Whigs), though the latter, through the Emperor's favor, are in power: he also admits a fear that the heir to the crown (the Prince of Wales, later George II) is partial to the High-Heels, though he tries to retain the friendship of both sides. Reldresal also expounds the religious differences of the day under the guise of the dispute between the Big-Endians and the Small-Endians (Roman Catholics and Protestants). The trouble began, he relates, with the reigning Emperor's great-grandfather, who, when his son was a boy, published an edict commanding his subjects to break their eggs at the smaller end because his son had cut his fingers in breaking an egg at the larger end, according to primitive custom. The great-grandfather is Henry VIII; the son, presumably, Elizabeth, who was declared illegitimate by the Pope; the edict, Henry's proclamation of himself as head of the national church. The choice of the symbol of the egg may have been guided by a desire to refer to the Eucharist, the nature of which was the chief theological point at issue in the great schism. Reldresal reviews the controversy, in the course of which "one Emperor [Charles I] lost his Life, and another [James II] his Crown." This all leads naturally to an explanation of international relations with Blefuscu (France), which is represented as harboring and encouraging Big-Endian exiles who have fled thither after unsuccessful rebellions. This is as

close as Swift comes to a reference to the
Jacobite movement, but it was close enough
to leave contemporary readers in no doubt
as to his meaning. Finally, the War of the
Spanish Succession is described as "a
bloody War [that] hath been carried on
between the two Empires for six and thirty
Moons with various Success." Swift, as a
Tory, has no desire to exalt the Duke of
Marlborough, or to make it appear that
England, in 1711, was clearly superior to
France in arms: consequently Reldresal's
account ends upon this note, with the further addition that Lilliput is in imminent
danger from attack by Blefuscu, and that
the Emperor relies upon Gulliver (the Tory
administration) to save the country.

The fifth chapter brings the crisis. For
dramatic purposes Swift condenses into a
short space of time happenings which his-
torically took up more than two years. The
first concern of Harley and St. John, on
obtaining power, was peace with France.
The war had become increasingly a Whig
war, from which Marlborough gained military prestige and the commercial interests
foresaw the destruction of France's international trade, to their own profit. The
Tories, on the other hand, did not anticipate any advantages from a continuation
of hostilities, which they believed could
not be carried to the point of a decisive
English victory. They could not negotiate
openly with France, however, because the
war was still generally popular, and the
Whigs might raise the cry (as they did
later) that the Tories were robbing England of the fruits of victory by granting
the enemy easy terms. But secret negotiations also involved difficulties. England was
bound by treaties not to make peace without the consent of her allies, and the ministry had no right, under English law, to
enter into discussions of the peace terms
without special royal authority granted
under the great seal. Despite all this the
administration did begin negotiations in
secret, justifying this action on the ground
that peace was necessary for the welfare

of England. Eventually, in 1713, both countries signed a treaty at Utrecht, by the
terms of which France gained more than
the military situation warranted, but did
agree, among other things, to dismantle the
port of Dunkirk, one of the chief threats
to English naval supremacy.

Swift's symbolical representation of these
events is masterly. He avoids any celebration of Marlborough's military genius by
making the victory over Blefuscu a naval
triumph, standing for the demolition of the
defenses of Dunkirk. The Whig desire for
a crushing defeat of France is pictured as
a malicious and despotic wish of the Emperor to humiliate and tyrannize over "a
Free and Brave People." The collusion of
the Tories with the French, as charged by
their opponents, is explained and defended
as common politeness on Gulliver's part
toward the diplomatic representatives of a
foreign power.

The chapter concludes with an episode
which seems unconnected with what has
preceded it. When one understands its real
meaning, however, the chapter becomes the
most completely unified in the voyage. The
story of the fire in the royal palace is
Swift's defense of the Tories' illegal negotiation of the peace. What Swift wanted
was an instance of an emergency met by an
act technically illegal, but clearly justifiable
because of the dangerous circumstances.
Gulliver's method of extinguishing the fire
answered the purpose admirably. Critics of
Swift have often complained that the allegory is needlessly gross, but this is unfair.
There was more than one reason for Harley's fall from power. Almost from the time
of his accession to the chancellorship he had
begun to lose the personal, though not the
political favor of the Queen. He had a
weakness for the bottle, and pride of place
combined with a contempt for Anne's intellect led him on more than one occasion
to appear drunk in her presence and to use
language which she felt was an affront to
her dignity. Swift was aware of all this.
While he was in Yorkshire in the dark days

of the early summer of 1714, Erasmus Lewis had written to him from London:

I have yours of the 25th. You judge very right; it is not the going out, but the manner, that enrages me. The Queen has told all the Lords the reasons of her parting with [Harley, now Earl of Oxford], viz. that he neglected all business; that he was seldom to be understood; that when he did explain himself, she could not depend upon the truth of what he said; that he never came to her at the time she appointed; that he often came drunk; that lastly, to crown all, he behaved himself toward her with ill manner, indecency, and disrespect. *Pudet haec opprobria nobis,* etc.

The brilliance of Swift's symbolism is now clear. In a single action he embodied both the political and the personal charges against Oxford. Gulliver saved the palace, though his conduct was both illegal and indecent: Oxford saved the state, in return for which incidental illegalities and indecencies should have been overlooked. But prudery was stronger than gratitude. "I was privately assured," says Gulliver, "the Empress conceiving the greatest Abhorrence of what I had done, removed to the most distant side of the Court, firmly resolved that those Buildings should never be repaired for her Use; and in the presence of her chief Confidents, could not forbear vowing Revenge." (1.5.10.) In plain terms, Queen Anne dispensed with Oxford's services and vowed never to make use of them again.

At this point Swift, to heighten suspense, interpolates a chapter on general conditions of life in Lilliput, which, while it contains a number of isolated satiric references, does not advance the main plot. This is resumed at the beginning of the seventh chapter with the secret visit to Gulliver of "a considerable Person at Court to whom [Gulliver] had been very serviceable at a time when he lay under the highest Displeasure of his Imperial Majesty." The considerable person was no less than the Duke of Marlborough. Early in 1715 Bolingbroke heard rumors that the victorious

Whigs intended to impeach him, together with Oxford and other Tory leaders, of high treason. Relying on old friendship he inquired about the truth of these rumors from Marlborough, who, seeing an opportunity to get revenge for his dismissal four years earlier, so played upon Bolingbroke's fears that he fled to France. It is upon Bolingbroke's adventures that the story of Gulliver in Lilliput is based from this point onward, since Oxford, with more courage, remained to stand his trial and to be freed.

The tale of what was in store for Bolingbroke, as translated into Lilliputian terms, was sufficiently disquieting. Gulliver's enemies are listed as Skyresh Bolgolam; Flimnap, the High Treasurer; Limtoc, the General; Lalcon, the Chamberlain; and Balmuff, the Grand Justiciary. These represent Whigs or independent Tories who displayed their hostility to the Oxford-Bolingbroke administration either by speaking against it in Parliament or by acting as members of the Committee of Secrecy which, early in 1715, investigated the conduct of the ministry in the negotiation of the peace. Bolgolam has already been identified as the Earl of Nottingham, whose hatred of Oxford has been explained. Flimnap was Robert Walpole, the rising leader of the Whigs and chairman of the Committee of Secrecy. Limtoc the General, Lalcon the Chamberlain, and Balmuff the Grand Justiciary were, respectively, General Stanhope, Secretary of State for War; the Duke of Devonshire, Lord Steward; and Lord Cowper, Lord Chancellor. The second of these identifications is a little doubtful because there was in the British cabinet an official entitled Lord Chamberlain, but in 1715 this minister was the Duke of Shrewsbury, a mild man who took no active part in the attack on the defeated ministry.

All of the four articles of impeachment are counterparts of actual charges made against Oxford and Bolingbroke. The first accuses Gulliver of illegally extinguishing the fire in the palace (the ministry's technically unlawful negotiation of the

Peace of Utrecht). The second dwells on Gulliver's refusal to subjugate Blefuscu completely (the granting of easy terms of peace to France). The third attacks the friendliness of Gulliver and the Blefuscudian ambassadors (the secret understanding between the Tory administration and the French diplomats). The fourth asserts that Gulliver intends to visit Blefuscu with only verbal license from the Emperor (a repetition of the first charge, with special reference to the failure of Oxford to procure a license under the great seal to negotiate the peace). The second and fourth articles contain allusions to the sixth and first provisions, respectively, of the agreement by which Gulliver was set at liberty.

The report of the council at which Gulliver's fate was debated is mordantly ironic. His bitterest enemies demand that he be put to a painful and ignominious death. The Emperor is more merciful, remembering Gulliver's former services: and Reldresal, Principal Secretary of State for Private Affairs and Gulliver's "true Friend," proposes and eventually carries a more "lenient" motion. Gulliver is merely to be blinded, after which, if the council finds it expedient, he may easily be starved to death. Blinding is the equivalent of barring Oxford and Bolingbroke from political activity for the remainder of their lives. Reldresal's pretended friendship is a reference to the behavior of Charles, Viscount Townshend, Secretary of State in the Whig cabinet, whom the Tory leaders at first regarded as a friend at court after their fall, but whose sincerity they came to distrust. The "mercy" of the Emperor is a fling at the execution of a number of the leaders of the rebellion of 1715 shortly after the House of Lords, in an address to George I, had praised his "endearing tenderness and clemency." Gulliver's reaction to this clemency is illuminating in its indication of the attitude of Oxford and Bolingbroke toward the Hanoverian dynasty as Swift wished it to be understood:

And as to myself, I must confess, having never been designed for a Courtier either by my Birth or Education, I was so ill a Judge of Things, that I could not discover the Lenity and Favour of this Sentence, but conceived it (perhaps erroneously) rather to be rigorous than gentle. I sometimes thought of standing my Tryal, for although I could not deny the Facts alledged in the several Articles, yet I hoped they would admit of some Extenuations. But having in my Life perused many State-Tryals, which I ever observed to terminate as the Judges thought fit to direct, I durst not rely on so dangerous a Decision, in so critical a Juncture, and against such powerful Enemies. Once I was strongly bent upon Resistance, for while I had Liberty, the whole Strength of that Empire could hardly subdue me, and I might easily with Stones pelt the Metropolis to pieces; but I soon rejected that Project with Horror, by remembering the Oath I had made to the Emperor, the Favours I received from him, and the high Title of *Nardac* he conferred upon me. Neither had I so soon learned the Gratitude of Courtiers, to persuade myself that his Majesty's present Severities acquitted me of all past Obligations. (1.7.23.)

Little more of the allegory remains to be unraveled. Gulliver prudently and secretly seeks the protection of the Emperor of Blefuscu, as Bolingbroke fled to France. Like Bolingbroke, too, Gulliver ignores a proclamation threatening to stigmatize him as a traitor unless he returns to stand trial for his alleged crimes. Here Swift breaks off: it would hardly have been politic to discuss the period during which Bolingbroke was openly Secretary of State to the Pretender. The account of Gulliver's return to Europe is, like that of his arrival in Lilliput, a narrative to be taken at its face value.

The strongest arguments in favor of this interpretation of the *Voyage to Lilliput* are its consistency and the exactness with which it follows the chronology of the events which it symbolizes. Single incidents are often open to more than one explanation: a series carries conviction in proportion to its length. There are, of course, a few cases in which Swift takes slight and unimportant liberties with chronology for the sake of simplicity. For example, he represents Gulliver as being ennobled after the capture of the fleet, whereas Oxford and Bolingbroke received their titles not after the signing of the Peace of Utrecht, but while it was still being secretly negotiated. Similarly Flimnap is represented from the beginning of the story as Prime Minister and Gulliver's most potent enemy, though Walpole did not become head of the government until 1720. Swift is careful, however, not to attribute to Walpole any act of hostility to the Tory administration for which he was not responsible.

Swift also introduces incidental satiric touches as opportunity offers wherever the events or conditions have no temporal connection with the main plot. This is especially true in the sixth chapter where, among other things, there are references to the trial of Bishop Atterbury in 1722 and 1723 (in the use of the informers Clustril and Drunlo by Flimnap, standing for Walpole's employment of the spies Pancier and Neynoe), and a gratuitous gibe, in the final paragraph, at the notorious infidelities of Walpole's wife.

The political allegory of the first voyage is primarily concerned with the defense of the conduct of the Oxford-Bolingbroke ministry, and incidentally with an attack upon the Whigs. In the third voyage the emphasis is exactly reversed. It is important to realize from the beginning that the chief purpose of the allegory is *not*, as has so often been asserted, to attack the new science, but to attack learned folly, or "pedantry," to use the word in its eighteenth-century meaning, and especially innovations and innovators in general. The focus of this attack is the Whig ministry under George I, which is accused of experimentation in the field of government, and of fostering experimenters in many other fields. Whiggery, to Swift, is the negation of that certainty which results from adherence to tried and approved procedures. In the light of this interpretation

of Swift's design it becomes evident that the third voyage is much more unified in purpose than has commonly been supposed. A very large preponderance of its specific references to contemporary persons and events is contained in the first four chapters. The key to the satire is the identification of Laputa, the flying island, which has been variously interpreted as the English court under George I, and as the whole of England. The former interpretation was the normal one until about half a century ago. Swift's own verse (in his poem *The Life and Character of Dr. Swift*) lends authority to this earlier view, for the supposed detractor of the Dean who there catalogues Swift's writings lists among them

> . . . *Libels* yet conceal'd from sight,
> Against the *Court* to show his *Spight*.
> Perhaps his *Travels*, *Part the Third*;
> A *Lye* at every *second* word;
> Offensive to a *Loyal* Ear—: . . .

In 1896, however, G. A. Aitken published in an appendix to an edition of *Gulliver's Travels* four previously unprinted paragraphs contained in the manuscript emendations in the Ford copy of the first edition. Three years later these paragraphs, which described the rebellion of Lindalino against Laputa, were restored to their proper place in the third chapter of the third voyage by G. R. Dennis, who edited the *Travels* for the Temple Scott edition. The effect of the new passage on the interpretation of the voyage was remarkable. There could be little doubt that it was an allegorical description of the controversy over Wood's halfpence, with which Swift had dealt so brilliantly in the *Drapier's Letters* only two years before *Gulliver's Travels* was published. And since Lindalino obviously stood for Dublin, it is hardly surprising that Laputa should have been taken for England as a whole, hovering over all of Ireland, or Balnibarbi. In 1919 Sir Charles Firth not only endorsed this view, but extended it to the interpretation of other parts of the third voyage, and even allowed

it to color his ideas of the fourth. In particular he suggested that Munodi was Viscount Midleton, Chancellor of Ireland from
1714 to 1725, and that Balnibarbi in the
impoverished state described in the third
chapter represented Ireland under English
domination. This theory, of course, necessi-
tates a belief that Swift changed the meaning of his symbols from time to time: for
example, Lagado is in Balnibarbi, but the
Grand Academy of Lagado is generally
identified as the Royal Society of London;
therefore Balnibarbi, of which Lagado is
the metropolis, must sometimes stand for
Ireland, and sometimes for England or
for the British Isles as a whole. Other inconsistencies involved in Sir Charles's
theory suggest themselves on further examination. From the beginning of the voyage Swift makes a good deal of the minuteness of Laputa and the relatively great
extent of the land of Balnibarbi which it
dominates. Moreover, Laputa is inhabited
only by a small number of courtiers and
their hangers-on (chiefly scientific and
musical); it is not self-supporting, but is
dependent upon sustenance drawn from
below; it travels about by a series of oblique
motions which probably symbolizes the
indirect and erratic course of Whig policy
under the ministerial clique headed by
Walpole. Lagado, the metropolis of the
kingdom, which certainly stands for London, is below and subject to Laputa. Lindalino, or Dublin, is described as the second city of the kingdom—an accurate description if the kingdom is the whole
British Isles, but not if it is Ireland alone.
Moreover, the general account of the King's
methods of suppressing insurrections which
precedes the story of Lindalino's revolt is
accurate only if Balnibarbi includes Great
Britain.

The King would be the most absolute Prince
in the Universe, if he could but prevail on a
Ministry to join with him; but these having their
Estates below on the Continent, and considering
that the Office of a Favourite hath a very uncertain Tenure, would never consent to the enslav-

ing their Country. . . . nor dare his Ministers
advise him to an Action, which as it would render them odious to the People, so it would be a
great Damage to their own Estates, which lie all
below, for the Island is the Kings Demesn.
(3.3.12.)

It is hardly necessary to point out that few
of George I's ministry held any significant
amount of Irish land, and that none of
them displayed any fear of Irish public
opinion.

If the older theory, which identified Balnibarbi as England and Laputa as the
Court, is reconsidered, it will be seen that
one slight emendation will bring it into
conformity with the account of the revolt
of Lindalino. If the continent of Balnibarbi
represents all of the British Isles, the inconsistencies in the allegory disappear.
There can be no serious doubt that Swift,
in this restored passage of Gulliver's Travels, is using the affair of Wood's halfpence
again, but this time it is for a different
purpose. In 1724, addressing Irishmen
through the Drapier's Letters, he was trying to arouse national feeling and to make
the issue one of Ireland against England.
In 1726, in a more general work, addressed
to the English more than to any other
nation, he made the issue one of tyranny
over the subject by a would-be absolute
monarch. When this is once understood it
is not difficult to find plausible counterparts in history for the various details of the
description of the Laputian method of suppressing insurrections.

The three ways of punishing a recalci-
trant city (interposing the island between
the city and the sun; pelting the city with
rocks; and completely crushing it by drop-
ping the island down upon it) represent
three degrees of severity in actual practice,
perhaps threats, accompanied by with-
drawal of court patronage; moderate civil
repressive action; and military invasion.
The reason given for the King's disinclina-
tion to proceed to the last degree of severity
is that this might endanger the adamantine
bottom of the island, which appears to

stand either for the monarchy or for the British constitution. It should be remembered that Swift believed in the theory of government which divided the power among the three estates of the realm, and which relied on a balance among them. Any estate which arrogated to itself an undue share of power was held to endanger the whole structure of the government.

The chief defenses of any city against oppression by the King and his court are thus expressed allegorically:

. . . if the Town intended to be destroyed should have in it any tall Rocks, as it generally falls out in the larger Cities, a Situation probably chosen at first with a View to prevent such a Catastrophe; or if it abound in high Spires or Pillars of Stone, a sudden Fall might endanger the Bottom or under Surface of the Island. . . .

(3.3.13.)

Of the three defenses, the "high Spires" seem least ambiguous: almost certainly these represent churches or churchmen—possibly the ecclesiastical interest generally, which rallied almost unanimously to the Irish cause. The "tall Rocks" seem to differ from the "pillars of stone" chiefly in being natural rather than creations of man, which suggests that the rocks may represent either the hereditary nobility, who constituted the second estate of the realm, or the higher ecclesiastical authorities, representing a divine rather than a man-made institution. Similarly the "Pillars of Stone" may be either self-made citizens of power and importance, or certain man-made legal institutions. In the story of the revolt of Lindalino the strong pointed rock in the middle of the city is almost certainly the combined power of the Irish Church, centered in St. Patrick's Cathedral; and the "four large Towers" presumably stand for the four most important local governmental agencies of Ireland—the Privy Council, the Grand Jury, and the two houses of the Irish Parliament. The "vast Quantity of the most combustible Fewel" collected by the inhabitants probably stands for the multitude of

incendiary pamphlets written against Wood's halfpence by Swift and others. Finally, the unsuccessful experiment made by one of the King's officers, who let down a piece of adamant from Laputa and found it so strongly drawn toward the towers and the rock that he could hardly draw it back, presumably represents the bold resistence of the Irish civil and ecclesiastical institutions to the King's measures.

That this incident could have been omitted from the text of *Gulliver's Travels* without causing an apparent break in the continuity of the story is characteristic of the structure of the third voyage, which differs markedly from that of the first. In his account of Lilliput Swift provided a climactic plot, based upon the fortunes of a particular Tory administration. In the third voyage no such plot is practicable: the history of Walpole's administration had not reached a climax in 1726, and Swift would not have wished to tell a story which could only have emphasized the success of his enemies. He therefore chose to attack the Whigs not by dramatic narrative, but by satiric portraiture. There is, consequently, no chronological scheme for the third voyage, which is a picture of conditions rather than of acts.

As in the first voyage, Swift is chary of drawing too obvious a portrait of George I. Not much is said of the physical appearance of the King of Laputa; there are, however, several references which intelligent contemporaries must have interpreted without difficulty. One is the parenthetical remark (3.2.3) about the King's "being distinguished above all his Predecessors for his Hospitality to Strangers"—a palpable hit at George's extensive appointments of Hanoverians to posts of profit in England. The last paragraph of the third chapter is still more open satire—almost dangerously open. "By a fundamental Law of this Realm," Gulliver observes, "neither the King nor either of his two elder Sons are permitted to leave the Island, nor the Queen till she is past Childbearing." No

Englishman could have failed to be reminded by this sentence that the Act of Settlement had originally forbidden the departure of the sovereign from England without the express consent of Parliament, and that George I, whose journeys to his beloved Hanover aroused the general resentment of his English subjects, had persuaded Parliament to repeal this provision of the Act in 1716. George's delight in music is parodied by the description of the Laputian King's fondness for the art. Here, however, and even more in the case of the King's supposed personal interest in science, Swift modifies the actual facts for the sake of his thesis. Under the reign of Anne men of letters had received a considerable amount of royal patronage, especially during the administration of Oxford. Under the reign of George I it seemed, especially to Tory wits who had been deprived of their posts of profit, that the pendulum had swung away from the profession of literature in the direction of musicians and experimental scientists. Patronage being, at least in theory, a personal prerogative of the King, Swift in his allegory attributed the shift in patronage to the King's inclinations. How far this shift was a fact, and, if a fact, how far it was due to conscious intention on the part of the government, are matters of secondary importance to the present inquiry. It may be said, however, that while Whig writers received some government patronage during the administration of Oxford (largely because of Swift's insistence), Tory writers got very little after the Whigs came into power in 1714. Moreover, a great wave of invention and commercial exploitation of inventions coincided with the opening years of George I's reign, and scientists, notably the astronomers Newton and Flamsteed, were given generous encouragement.

The Prince of Wales, whom Swift had once portrayed as the heir to the Lilliputian crown, with one high and one low heel, is in the third voyage aligned more definitely and sympathetically with the Tories. He is described as "a great Lord at Court, nearly related to the King, and for that reason alone used with Respect." (3.4.4.) The hostility between the Prince and his father, and his consequent unpopularity in the King's court, were, of course, common knowledge. Swift represents the Prince as one who "had great natural and acquired Parts, adorned with Integrity and Honour, but so ill an Ear for Musick, that his Detractors reported he had been often known to beat Time in the wrong Place; neither could his Tutors without extreme difficulty teach him to demonstrate the most easy Proposition in the Mathematicks." (3.4.4.) It is undoubtedly true that Prince George had a supreme contempt for academic learning, and while he probably had a better knowledge of music than Swift ascribes to him here, his interest in the art fell far below his father's: his patronage of Buononcini seems to have been motivated by a desire to annoy George I by support of a supposed rival to Handel, whom the King delighted to honor.

The Prince of Laputa is not only uninterested in the subjects which engross the attention of his father's court: he is positively interested in all the other things which they neglect. Here again Swift contrasts the theoretical Whig King with the practical Tory Prince. Alone among the Laputians the latter is anxious to learn from Gulliver the laws and customs of other countries. Alone among Laputians of rank he dispenses with the services of a flapper. He makes "very wise observations" on everything Gulliver tells him, and is loath to allow the traveler to depart, although helpful and generous when Gulliver persists in his intention. Swift makes clear the Tory hopes of the early 1720's—that Prince George on his accession to the throne might call the old Tory administration to power—through the Laputian Prince's recommendation of Gulliver to a friend of his in Lagado, the lord Munodi, who has been variously identified with Bolingbroke and Lord Midleton, but never, apparently, with Oxford, whom he actually represents. The evidence for this identification is plentiful. Munodi is described as a former governor of Lagado, which must be translated either as Lord Mayor of London or Prime Minister of England. As Swift displays no interest in the municipal government of London, the second alternative is much more probable. Munodi is represented as having been discharged from office for inefficiency by a cabal of ministers—a close parallel with Oxford's dismissal from his post in 1714 and his trial on the charge of treason between 1715 and 1717. It will be recalled that when the accusation against Oxford was finally dropped in 1717 he returned from politics to the quiet existence of a country gentleman on his estates in Herefordshire. This retirement is reflected not only in Munodi's having withdrawn from public life, but in his name, which seems to be a contraction of "*mundum odi*" —"I hate the world."

Munodi's story is a thinly veiled allegory of the results to be expected from flighty experimental Whig government as opposed to sound conservative Tory government. Balnibarbi, the inhabitants of which are occupied with financial speculation and with the exploitation of chimerical "projects," both in the city and in the country, is a symbol of the British Isles under George I and the Whigs: Munodi's private estate, managed in "the good old way," to the evident profit of its owner and the pleasure of its citizenry, represents the way of the Tory remnant, sneered at by the adherents of the newer way as reactionary. The triumph of the innovators is attributed to the conversion of weak-minded members of the governing class by the court circle in Laputa, with the result that their principles have been imported into the management of the subject continent, and a center of the new experimental culture has even been founded in Lagado. The Grand Academy no doubt stands in part for the Royal Society, and the fact that Swift in his allegory lays its creation at the door of the

court is significant as indicating the center of his interest, since the Royal Society, while it had received encouragement from the court of Charles II at the time of its foundation in 1660, certainly had more influence on the court of George I than the court had upon it.

The last detail in the history of Munodi is of particular interest, since its true significance seems never to have been pointed out by any commentator upon the *Travels*, though it must have been apparent to many of Swift's contemporaries. There was one act of Oxford's administration which laid him open to criticism as an experimenter in governmental economics—an experimenter more speculative and unsound than any Whig. The act was the sponsoring of the South Sea Company. This device for refunding the public debt of England had been urged upon Oxford by Defoe, who had finally persuaded his superior to give the company a charter in 1712, and to arrange for the exchange of governmental obligations for South Sea stock. The public was encouraged to make the exchange on the ground that the new investment was quite as safe as the old and much more profitable. The details of the great speculation and of the ultimate crash of 1720—the "South Sea year"—need not be rehearsed in detail. The crash brought with it much criticism of Oxford, and many demands that he emerge from retirement to assist in clearing up the mess for which he was responsible. Swift does what he can to rehabilitate Oxford's reputation as an economist through the allegory of the mill, near the end of the fourth chapter. Gulliver relates that there had been on Munodi's estate (England under Oxford's administration) an old mill (the old English fiscal system), turned by the current of a large river (England's income from agriculture and trade), and sufficient not only for Munodi's family (the British empire), but also for a great number of his tenants (England's allies in the War of the Spanish Succession). A club of projectors (Defoe and his abettors) proposed to destroy the old mill and substitute a new one much farther away (the South Sea Company), requiring artificial means (stockjobbing) to pump up water for its operation, on the plea that water agitated by wind and air upon a height (money put into active circulation by speculation) would turn the mill with half the current of a river whose course was more upon the level (would provide sufficient government revenues with the use of half the capital required by the old fiscal policy). Munodi, "being then not very well with the Court" (Anne had shown her displeasure at Oxford's personal behavior toward her as early as 1712), and being pressed by many of his friends, complied with the proposal. It is hardly necessary to labor the significance of the rest of the allegory. "After employing an Hundred Men for two Years, the Work miscarried, the Projectors went off, laying the blame entirely upon him, railing at him ever since, and putting others upon the same Experiment, with equal Assurance of Success, as well as equal Disappointment."

The fifth and sixth chapters of the third voyage are concerned with the Grand Academy of Lagado, generally held to stand for the Royal Society of London. That the Society was in Swift's mind cannot be doubted, but that it is the primary object of the satire in these chapters is a conclusion that deserves examination, at least. The first discrepancy in the account has to do with the physical appearance of the Academy's buildings. "This Academy," says Gulliver, "is not an entire single Building, but a Continuation of several Houses on both sides of a Street; which growing waste, was purchased and applyed to that Use." (3.5.1.) The description does not fit the buildings of the real Society, which in 1710 had moved its Museum from Arundel House to a building in Crane Court, Fleet Street, quite unlike the structure pictured by Gulliver. In the light of the emphasis placed on the Academy's school of political projectors it is not impossible that

the description should be applied rather to the rapidly expanding governmental buildings on both sides of Whitehall.

Far more interesting than the outward appearance of the Academy is the nature of the activities carried on within. Many of the Royal Society's experiments were in the realm of pure science, and were conducted for no immediately practical end. In the Academy the large majority of the projects are designed to bring about supposed improvements in commerce, medicine, or some other field of importance in daily life: what is ridiculous is that the methods, rather than the purposes of the inventors, are chimerical. Another important fact is the insistence upon the word "PROJECTORS" in the title of the Academy: it is printed in capitals, and it occurs, together with the word "projects," again and again in this section of the voyage. These words were not very frequently applied to members of the Royal Society and their exercises in the seventeenth and eighteenth centuries: the usual terms of contempt were "virtuosi" and "experiments." "Projector" was, however, a word all too familiar to Englishmen of the second decade of the eighteenth century. To them it signified a man who promoted a get-rich-quick scheme, plausible but impracticable, for the carrying out of which he levied upon the public. This latter habit seems to be alluded to twice in the fifth chapter: first, when Gulliver remarks that it is customary for the projectors to beg money from all who visit them (3.5.3), and secondly, when the inventor of the frame for writing books suggests that his operations "might be still improved, and much expedited, if the Publick would raise a Fund for making and employing five hundred such Frames in *Lagado*." (3.5.16) Speculative schemes actually floated during the first six years of the reign of George I, and especially in 1720—the "South Sea year"—were in some instances almost as illusory as those described by Swift, and may even have suggested a few of them. Companies advertising for subscriptions included one for extracting silver Colchester and elsewhere, for manuring farm from lead, and others for making bays in lands, for a more inoffensive method of emptying and cleansing "necessary houses," for bringing live sea-fish to London in specially built tank-vessels, for making salt water fresh, for planting mulberry trees and raising silk-worms in Chelsea Park, for fishing for wrecks along the Irish coast, for a wheel for perpetual motion, and, finally, for "an undertaking which shall in due course be revealed." An anonymous wag advertised for subscriptions to a company for melting down sawdust and chips and casting them into clean deal boards without cracks or knots: another group, having obtained several hundred subscriptions to a scheme almost equally vague, publicly announced that the venture had been a hoax intended to make the public more cautious, and returned the subscription money.

The school for political projectors clearly has no connection with the Royal Society: it is a satiric attack on corruption and stupidity in government, with a section at the end based upon what Swift regarded as the biased and unjust prosecution of Bishop Atterbury, in 1723, for complicity in the Jacobite plot. The paragraph on copromancy (3.6.10) arises from the putting in evidence at the trial of the Bishop of correspondence found in his closestool. The discussion of secret codes which follows has to do with the charge that the Bishop and his correspondents used the name of the Bishop's lame dog Harlequin as a symbol for the Pretender: hence the inclusion by Swift in his burlesque secret code of "*a lame Dog, an Invader.*" This code, incidentally, was one of the few passages which Motte altered out of an apparent fear that the satire was too obvious and too dangerous. His emendations, aside from a slight rearrangement, consisted of the omission of four code pairs and the alteration of another. The phrases omitted were: "a close-stool a privy council, a flock of geese a senate, . . . a codshead a——, . . . a gibbet a secretary of state": the alteration consisted of the weakening of "a buzzard a prime minister" to "a *Buzzard* a *great Statesman.*" Presumably the blank after "codshead" was to be filled in by the reader with "king." It is not difficult to understand why Motte, in 1726, preferred not to print this part of the manuscript as it stood.

The last type of code discussed is the anagram, a device which was also alleged to be used by the Jacobites. Swift's Tribnian experts, analyzing the sentence, "*Our Brother Tom has just got the Piles,*" produce the message, "*Resist; a Plot is brought Home, The Tour.*" It is not an accident that while the "a" in this message is a lower-case letter, the "T" of "The" is a capital. "The Tour" is a signature. During part of his exile in France Bolingbroke requested his friends to address him as M. La Tour. A grammarian would point out that "la tour" is a tower: a tour is "le tour": but Swift apparently did not regard this as a serious objection. Perhaps, too, he did not wish to abandon what he felt was a very appropriate anagram.

The remainder of the third voyage contains only scattering references to specific events or persons contemporary with Swift. In the seventh chapter it is sufficiently clear that the "modern representative" of assemblies, which compares so unfavorably with the senate of ancient Rome, is the British Parliament. In the next chapter the nameless ghost in Glubbdubdrib who informs Gulliver about the confounding of the commentators on Homer and Aristotle may be Sir William Temple, whose views on classical scholarship Swift had espoused so warmly in *The Battle of the Books,* but there is not enough evidence to confirm this surmise. In the following paragraph Aristotle decries the theory of gravitation propounded by Sir Isaac Newton, one of Swift's enemies. Shortly afterward occurs one of the most mysterious references in the entire *Travels.* In the midst of a series of general exposures of the true genealogies and histories of "great families" Gulliver observes that he learned in Glubbdubdrib "whence it came what *Polydore Virgil* says of a certain great House, 'Nec Vir fortis, nec Foemina Casta.'" A careful search of the works of Polydore Virgil has not brought this phrase to light: on the other hand, it is the exact converse of a much-quoted sentence, famous in that day, from the epitaph on the tomb of Margaret Cavendish, Duchess of Newcastle, born Margaret Lucas: "All the brothers were valiant, and all the sisters virtuous." (Addison quoted the phrase in *The Spectator*, June 23, 1711.) As Swift seems to have had no personal animus against the Lucases, and as that family, more than most, deserved the monumental flattery, it is possible that Swift merely borrowed and twisted an effective phrase to enforce a general satire on the nobility.

One last passage in the eighth chapter contains enough specific detail to suggest a reference to an individual. This is the paragraph which reads:

> Among the rest there was one Person whose Case appeared a little singular. He had a Youth about eighteen Years old standing by his side. He told me he had for many Years been Commander of a Ship, and in the Sea Fight at *Actium*, had the good Fortune to break through the Enemy's great Line of Battle, sink three of their Capital Ships, and take a fourth, which was the sole Cause of *Anthony's* Flight, and of the Victory that ensued; that the Youth standing by him, his only Son, was killed in the Action. He added, that upon the Confidence of some Merit, this War being at an end, he went to *Rome*, and solicited at the Court of *Augustus* to be preferred to a greater Ship, whose Commander had been killed; but without any regard to his Pretensions, it was given to a Youth who had never seen the Sea, the son of *Libertina*, who waited on one of the Emperor's Mistresses. Returning back to his own Vessels, he was charged with neglect of Duty, and the Ship was given to a Favourite Page of *Publicola* the Vice-Admiral; whereupon he retired to a poor Farm, at a great distance from *Rome*, and there ended his Life. I was so curious to know the truth of this Story, that I

desired *Agrippa* might be called, who was Admiral in that Fight. He appeared and confirmed the whole Account, but with much more Advantage to the Captain, whose Modesty had extenuated or concealed a great part of his Merit. (3.8.9.)

The general purport of the third voyage suggests that this is an allegorical account of an individual instance of Whig ingratitude toward a Tory. The two most eminent Tory "martyrs" of the day were General Webb, whose exploits had been slighted by Marlborough, and Charles Mordaunt, third Earl of Peterborough. The latter military leader, a personal friend of Swift's, had fought both on land and at sea during the War of the Spanish Succession, but after some brilliant successes in the Peninsular campaign of 1706 he disagreed with the other leaders of the Allies, and was eventually recalled to England. In 1707, on the way to Genoa, his ship was attacked by the enemy; he escaped, but a convoying ship under the command of his son was badly damaged, and the son received grave wounds which may have contributed to his death some time later. Peterborough's removal from command, and his failure to secure reinstatement, were at least partly due to the enmity of the young Emperor Charles, who succeeded him in the direction of the Peninsular campaign. Swift, in *The Conduct of the Allies*, had already taken up the cudgels for Peterborough, though without naming him explicitly:

> . . . there [in Spain] we drove on the war at a prodigious disadvantage . . . and by a most corrupt management, the only general who, by a course of conduct and fortune almost miraculous, had nearly put us into possession of the kingdom, was left wholly unsupported, exposed to the envy of his rivals, disappointed by the caprices of a young unexperienced prince, under the guidance of a rapacious German ministry, and at last called home in discontent.

The young unexperienced prince was, of course, the Emperor Charles. It seems not unlikely that he was the "youth who had never seen the sea," who displaced the

Roman hero of Gulliver's tale. The identity of the "favourite page of Publicola" does not appear.

Perhaps the most striking feature of this explanation of the personal and political allegory is that it leaves no room for an autobiographical interpretation of *Gulliver's Travels*. The various passages upon which this interpretation has rested are seen to be susceptible of other meanings more significant in themselves, and more consistent with each other and with the intent of the book. If this view is correct, Swift, so often conceived as the complete egoist, did not regard his own fortunes and misfortunes as being of equal importance with the affairs of public figures such as Oxford, Bolingbroke, and Peterborough. This is confirmed by his correspondence. Swift evidently felt that both Whigs and Tories were ungrateful to him, but his services to the Whigs were, as far as we know, relatively slight. His pamphleteering for the Tories, on the other hand, was of inestimable value, yet for years Oxford slighted him in favor of less deserving men, and finally obtained for him a post which he regarded as little else than exile, and which he accepted in a mood of bitterness. On April 16, 1713, he wrote to Stella,

> Mr Lewis tells me that D. Ormd has been to-day with Qu[een] & she was content that Dr Stearn should be Bp of Dromore and I Dean of St Patricks, but then out came Ld Tr, & sd he would not be satisfied, but that I must be Prebend of Windsor, thus he perplexes things—I expect neither; but I confess, as much as I love Engld, I am so angry at this Treatmt, that if I had my Choice I would rather have St Patricks.

That this was no passing mood is shown by his letter of July 13, 1714, written from Letcombe to John Arbuthnot when it was evident that the Tory ministry had run its race:

> Dear ——— I wonder how you came to mention that business to Lady M[asham], if I guess right, that the business is the Histor[ian]'s Place. It is in the D[uke] of Shr[ewsbury]'s gift, and he sent L[or]d Bol[ingbroke] word that though he

was under some engagement, he would give it me. Since which time I never mentioned it, though I had a memorial some months in my pocket, which I believe you saw, but I would never give it Lady M[asham] because things were embroiled with her. I would not give two pence to have it for the value of it, but I have been told by L[or]d P[eterborough] L[a]dy M[asham] and you, that the Qu[een] has a concern for her History, &c., and I was ready to undertake it. I thought L[or]d Bol[ingbroke] would have done such a trifle, but I shall not concern myself, and I should be sorry the Qu[een] should be asked for it otherwise than as what would be for her honor and reputation with posterity, etc. Pray, how long do you think I should be suffered to hold that post in the next reign? I have enclosed sent you the original memorial as I intended it; and if L[or]d Bol[ingbroke] thinks it of any moment, let him do it, but do not give him the memorial unless he be perfectly willing. For I insist again upon it, that I am not asking a favor, and there is an end of that matter, only one word more, that I would not accept it if offered, only that it would give me an opportunity of seeing those I esteem and love the little time that they will be in power. . . . I must repeat it again, that if L[or]d Bol[ingbroke] be not full as ready to give this memorial enclosed, as you are to desire him, let it drop, for in the present view of things, I am perfectly indifferent, for I think every reason for my leaving you is manifestly doubled within these 6 weeks, by your own account as well as that of others. Besides I take it perfectly ill that The Dragon, who promised me so solemnly last year to make me so easy in my debts, has never done the least thing to it. So that I can safely say I never received a penny from a minister in my life. And though I scorn to complain, yet to you I will speak it, that I am very uneasy in my Fortune, having received such accounts of my agent's management that I am likely to lose near 300 pounds, beside the heavy debts I lie under at a season of my life when I hoped to have no cares of that sort.

In the face of this ingratitude to himself, which he so clearly recognized, Swift nevertheless remained loyal to the defeated leaders, offering to accompany Oxford into retirement, and steadfastly defending both Oxford and Bolingbroke while they lay under charges of treason, even after Bolingbroke fled to France and joined the Pretender. All this was done, as Swift's letters show, in the face of a conviction that he himself could gain nothing from his friendship save, perhaps, a reputation of being himself a Jacobite traitor. Is it too difficult to suppose that he did this because of a sincere belief that the Tories' ingratitude to him was outweighed by their devotion to what were, in Swift's mind, the right principles of government?

J. C. Beckett

Swift as an Ecclesiastical Statesman

THE sincerity of Swift's religion has been a matter of controversy from his own day to ours. The gibe of his contemporary, Smedley, that he

> ... might a bishop be in time
> Did he believe in God

echoes the tradition that it was Queen Anne's pious horror of *The Tale of a Tub* which prevented Swift's elevation to the episcopal bench. This interpretation of Swift's religious position has been elaborated by later writers and as elaborately confuted. But final decision in such a dispute is impossible. The evidence of what a man really believed is bound to be of such a nature that our interpretation of it will depend upon our estimate of the man himself; and in fact all the writers on Swift's personal religion have, consciously or unconsciously, approached the subject with their minds made up.

This essay is not an attempt to refight an old battle with modern weapons. But there is an aspect of Swift's religious life which (so far as the present writer is aware) has never been clearly set out, and which, while it may serve to illuminate his personal religious convictions, can be treated independently of them. As an anglican priest Swift was not only a minister of religion, he was also an official of a large and influential organisation. How did Swift regard this organisation? What part did he take in its life? What connections can be traced between his life as a churchman and his life as a politician and a man of letters? These are some of the questions to which an answer must now be attempted.

Swift took orders in 1694, but a very brief experience of parochial life in the north of Ireland sent him back to Moor Park. He still had literary ambitions; he might hope to combine his clerical calling with some political or diplomatic office; Temple or some other patron might provide for him in England. The death of Temple in 1699 and Swift's acceptance of the vicarage of Laracor, in the diocese of Meath, early in the following year may be taken to mark the temporary abandonment of any scheme of promotion outside the regular routine of church preferment. Such preferment, if it was to equal Swift's hopes and his value of himself, could come only from the government. The circumstances of the time compelled him to look to the favour of a political party and, in the uneasy coalition which ruled England during the early years of Queen Anne, Swift's chief friends were the whigs, to whom his *Discourse of the Contests and Dissensions between the Nobles and the Commons in Athens and Rome* (published in 1701) had commended him. But though the whigs were in office they were not in power, and after a visit to England in 1703-4 Swift remained in Ireland for three and a half years. His return to London at the end of 1707, primarily on a mission for the Irish church, was probably connected with the change in the balance of parties, which in the following year brought the whigs completely into power.

It was now that Swift might hope to gain something from his friendship with whig leaders. But that prospect made it necessary for him to consider carefully his attitude

Reprinted from *Essays in British and Irish History, in Honour of James Eadie Todd*, London, 1949, by permission of the author. Footnotes have been omitted or shortened without notice.

to whig policy. Promotion would come only at the price of political support. Swift wanted to make it clear that the extent of that support must be determined by a stronger duty to the church. To set out the limits within which he was willing to serve a party cause, and perhaps also to warn his whig friends of the danger of arousing church opposition, he published, in 1708, *The Sentiments of a Church of England Man, with Respect to Religion and Government.* In this we have the basic expression of Swift's views on the relations of church and state, but it must be read in relation to its context and it must be supplemented from his other writings. Its main purpose, like that of all Swift's works, was an immediate one. As Herbert Read says: "All that Swift wrote is empirical, experimental, *actuel.* It is impossible to detach it from circumstances; we must consider each book or pamphlet in relation to its political intention." [1] Swift contended that though there were two political parties there was only one church, which was not tied to either of them.[2] She had certain political principles of her own, by which to test competing policies, and on one of the most urgent questions of the day—the treatment of protestant dissenters—*The Sentiments of a Church of England Man* gives a clear and consistent opinion. In doing this it was impossible to avoid raising the fundamental question of the relations of church and state; and though it is pretty clear that Swift disliked arguing about abstract principles, he did not hesitate to answer the question as far as the occasion required. It is because this answer was not the main purpose of the pamphlet, and because, in giving it, Swift had in mind that he was

writing an eirenicon and not a challenge, that we must expand and supplement the scheme of church-state relationship here expressed.

Such an investigation is the more necessary because some of the statements in *The Sentiments of a Church of England Man,* taken in isolation, can be easily misunderstood. Thus, Professor Looten writes, "Sa volonté de conjuguer les deux pouvoirs est si arêtée que jamais pour légitimer l'existence et la mission de l'église il n'invoque son droit divin ou son origine surnaturelle. On dirait qu'il ne la concoit qu'en marge et en fonction de l'état." [3] Not only is the general trend of this contrary to explicit statements in the *Remarks upon Tindal's "Rights of the Christian Church,"* but the last sentence attributes to Swift a conception of the church and state directly contrary to that which he laboured to establish. For Swift held clearly, though carefully, the doctrine that the church's power was derived directly from Christ and his apostles.[4] But he made no attempt to consider this in its wider applications. He barely mentions the possible state of affairs under a heathen government. He thinks it necessary to enter some defence of the conception of the church as a world-wide corporation.[5] He is satisfied to deal with the particular case immediately present—that of the church of England.

---

[1] *Collected Essays in Literary Criticism,* London, 1938, p. 196.
[2] "A Church of England man may with prudence and a good conscience, approve the professed principles of one party more than the other, according as he thinks they best promote the good of church and state" (*Sentiments of a Church of England Man, Prose Works,* ed. H. Davis, ii, 24).

[3] C. Looten, *La pensée religieuse de Swift,* p. 121.
[4] "But as the supreme power can certainly do ten thousand things more than it ought, so there are several things which some people may think it can do, although it really cannot . . . because the law of God [i.e., of the Church] hath otherwise decreed; which law, although a nation may refuse to receive it, cannot alter in its own nature. But the Church of England is no creature of the civil power, either as to its polity or its doctrines. The fundamentals of both were deduced from Christ and his apostles . . ." (*Remarks on Tindal's "Rights of the Christian Church," Prose Works,* ii, 75, 79).
[5] "Here we must show the necessity of the Church being a corporation all over the world: to avoid heresies and preserve fundamentals and hinder corrupting of scripture, etc." (*Prose Works,* ii, 105).

The line of argument used is significant. Swift was, and always remained, essentially a whig in politics, tied to the principles of the revolution and opposed to absolute rule, either by one or by many. But the traditional high-church scheme did not fit easily into this pattern. That scheme had developed during the seventeenth century. By the end of Elizabeth's reign the church of England was free from the immediate danger of a papal restoration imposed from without; but papal propaganda in England continued, and the pressure of the puritans, whether avowed dissenters or nominally within the church, grew stronger. Against this double attack it was necessary to build up a moral defence not only of doctrine but also, and more urgently, of jurisdiction. A solid basis had been laid in Hooker's *Laws of Ecclesiastical Polity*, but his arguments required expansion and particular application. The great problem was to show on what authority the jurisdiction of the church rested. The circumstances of the English reformation, the act of supremacy, and the thirty-seventh article of religion all pointed to the crown; but any doctrine of royal supremacy required to be justified, not only against Rome but against Geneva, both ever ready to detect and condemn erastianism. To avoid secularising the church the anglican theologians had to sanctify the monarchy and to claim that the church and the state were but different aspects of the same commonwealth. To maintain such a position after the restoration, when the dissenters formed a considerable section of the population, was difficult. The revolution made it impossible: the church had to choose between the king and the nation. In this dilemma, the non-jurors, who stuck to the letter of their theory, were compelled to experience its logical result in their extrusion from their benefices; for church and nation could not represent the same commonwealth if they had different kings. Not unnaturally, the non-jurors saw in this exercise of state authority that erastianism round which they and their predecessors

had been steering so careful a course for over a century.

The witness of the non-jurors made it necessary for those churchmen who had accepted the revolution to reconsider the basis of the church's authority. It was the need to do this which sharpened the demand that convocation should be allowed to function. Bishop King, of Derry, who wanted the Irish church to enjoy the same privileges as the English, put the matter succinctly: [6]

> The first article in magna carta is that the church of England shall be free, and that freedom can consist in nothing but in choosing the ecclesiastical constitutions by which she is governed in convocations. . . . If the church once come to have her constitutions altered without convocations, which are her legal representatives, she is no more free but an absolute slave, and our religion would in earnest be what the papists call it, a parliamentary religion.

But the meeting of convocation could not settle the question, for it met by royal authority, and could transact business only by royal license. Yet the revolution had shown that if the church possessed any divine right it must be separable from that of hereditary monarchy; or else the non-jurors were, as they claimed to be, the true church of England. Swift's common sense revolted from a conclusion which would have branded the bulk of the nation as schismatics.[7] But he was equally unwilling to accept the opposite extreme, that the church had no divine right at all. His task was to reconcile such a divine right in the church with his own whig principles in politics. As in his political theory he goes back to a social contract by which power passed from the many to the few, so here

[6] Bp King to Southwell, 21 Dec., 1697 (T.C.D., MS N3.1, p. 149).
[7] The attempt to continue the schism by consecrating new non-juring bishops aroused Swift's contempt: ". . . a parcel of obscure zealots in London, who, as we hear, are setting up a new Church of England by themselves" (Swift to Abp King, 13 Nov., 1716, *Correspondence*, ed. Ball, ii, 337).

he goes back to the period at which the state embraced Christianity. Characteristically, he is concerned not with individual conversions but with an official transaction between the rulers of the state and the rulers of the church, by which the former received the doctrines and practices of the church "as a divine law . . . and consequently, what they could not justly alter, any more than the common laws of nature." [8] Clearly, the relations of church and state in England were based on such a contract. The supreme power (which for Swift was the legislature) [9] was morally bound to support the doctrine and discipline of the church; but this doctrine and discipline, being part of the law of God, were, unlike the law of the state, immutable.

Up to this point, Swift's argument seems to make directly for that kind of ecclesiastical independence, that *imperium in imperio*, which has provided one of the recurring problems of political life for many centuries. Of one obvious solution, later epitomised in the phrase "a free church in a free state," he speaks with contempt; the idea of a clergy supported by the alms of the people was repugnant to him. [10] On the other hand, he could not logically quarrel with the existing constitution of the established church in England and Ireland, to the defence of which all his efforts were directed. He finds a way out of the difficulty by distinguishing between the church's power, and liberty to use that power. The former comes directly from God, the latter from the civil authority.

And, therefore, although the supreme power can hinder the clergy or church from making any new canons, or executing the old; from consecrating bishops, or refusing those they do consecrate; or, in short, from performing any ecclesiastical office, as they may from eating, drinking, and sleeping; yet they cannot themselves perform those offices, which are assigned to the

clergy by our saviour and his apostles; or, if they do, it is not according to the divine institution, and consequently null and void. [11]

This theory of church-state relationship was designed to fit existing circumstances, to salve the divine right of the church, without challenging too openly the power of the state or reflecting upon the principles of the revolution. To adapt the phrase which Swift applied to his *Modest Proposal*, it was "calculated" for England and Ireland in the reign of Queen Anne. The expression of it in *The Sentiments of a Church of England Man* is modified by the immediate political problem, but the enlargements in Swift's other writings on the church, in the *Examiner*, and in his correspondence, follow logically from the principles there laid down.

One part of Swift's theorizing on church and state was of immediate practical importance. He agreed with Hobbes that there must be an absolute authority in the state; but unlike Hobbes he placed this absolute authority in the legislature and not in the executive part of the government. [12] The legislature could do no wrong. It was by its authority that the church of England was established [13] and the legislature could at will establish paganism or popery or presbyterianism instead. The safety of the church, therefore, required that her enemies should be excluded from the legislature and from all places of political influence. This was the essential basis of Swift's opposition to the protestant dissenters, both in England and in Ireland. He was ready

[8] *Remarks on Tindal's "Rights of the Christian Church," Prose Works*, ii, 77.
[9] *Sentiments of a Church of England Man, Prose Works*, ii, 23.
[10] *Remarks, Prose Works*, ii. 96.

[11] *Ibid.,* 77. For elaboration of the view that the state legislates in ecclesiastical matters only to give civil force to the decisions of the church, and that no act of parliament can alter ecclesiastical authority, see G. W. O. Addleshaw, *The High Church Tradition*, London, 1941, pp. 36–8.
[12] Hobbes "perpetually confounds the executive with the legislative power" (*Sentiments of a Church of England Man, Prose Works*, ii, 16).
[13] But Swift carefully distinguishes between "established" and "founded": ". . . what is contained in the idea of *established*? Surely not existence. Doth *establishment* give *being* to a thing?" (*Remarks, Prose Works*, ii, 78).

to ridicule their religious peculiarities, but his arguments against them did not arise from a theological horror of schism. He had no objection to toleration, provided the dissenters were not left free to proselytise or to acquire political power. It is significant that he was much less alarmed about possible danger from the Roman catholics, even in Ireland where they formed the vast majority of the population, because their political power was so completely gone that they could not be a danger to the established church.

Swift's determination to exclude protestant dissenters from political influence brought him into opposition with the whigs almost as soon as they had secured control of the government. The great grievance of the dissenters was the sacramental test, and they looked to their political allies to remove it. But the test had stood in England since 1673 and was regarded by the church party as their main security; a direct attack upon it would be unpopular and probably unsuccessful. In the meantime, its full rigour was somewhat modified by the practice of occasional conformity, which the tories had vainly attempted to suppress in 1703. But in Ireland the sacramental test was a new thing, imposed for the first time in 1704 by the action of the English government; and though the church party had welcomed it as a protection against the powerful presbyterian population in Ulster, the latter were naturally hopeful that a whig ministry would remove it. Swift, like many other churchmen, was convinced that the attack upon the sacramental test in Ireland would be merely a preparation for a similar attack in England.

As early as 1707 there had been some sort of move in the Irish commons to repeal the test, a move which had been inspired, or at least encouraged, by the English ministry. It met with strong opposition, and Archbishop King's account shows how readily the government gave in for the sake of securing peace: "You can hardly imagine what a healing measure this has proved, and how far it has prevailed to oblige those that were in great animosities against one another, to comply in all reasonable proposals; whereas, if the repeal of the test had been insisted on, it would have broken all in pieces, and made them form parties on principles which before were founded only on personal quarrels." [14] In the following year the situation was different. The English government was now clearly committed to an effort at repealing the test in Ireland, even before the choice of Lord Wharton as the new lord lieutenant advertised the fact to the world. All this was matter of the greatest importance to Swift. As a whig, he might now hope to secure preferment, but he could not conceal his anxiety about the ministry's ecclesiastical policy; especially since he was a sort of ambassador from the Irish church and so must be drawn into the government's policy for Ireland. In the opening paragraph of *The Sentiments of a Church of England Man* he had expressed his attitude to party loyalty: "A wise and a good man may indeed be sometimes induced to comply with a number, whose opinion he generally approves, although it be perhaps against his own. But this liberty should be made use of upon very few occasions, and those of small importance, and then only with a view of bringing over his own side another time to something of greater and more public moment." But the first occasion on which he had to test the strength of his own influence with the whig leaders provided a disappointment. Swift's journey to England in 1707 had been undertaken with the approval of Archbishop King, of Dublin, for the purpose of soliciting for the Irish church a grant of the first fruits and twentieth parts similar to the grant made by the queen to the English church some years earlier. He was coldly received by the treasurer (Godolphin), put off with vague assurances, puzzled by obscure hints, and finally made to understand that the

---

[14] Abp King to Annesley, 16 Aug., 1707, quoted in Mant, *Church of Ireland*, ii, 186.

government was prepared to make the grant provided the Irish church would accept the removal of the sacramental test.

Once more Swift felt it necessary to make his position clear and to warn his whig friends of the dangers involved in their ecclesiastical policy. The *Letter from a Member of Parliament in Ireland to a Member of Parliament in England, Concerning the Sacramental Test* was published in December 1708, shortly after Wharton's appointment as lord lieutenant. It is a natural corollary to *The Sentiments of a Church of England Man,* for the scheme of church-state relationship described in the latter would be valid only so long as establishment was a reality. The core of the argument in the *Letter Concerning the Sacramental Test* is that the removal of the test would virtually establish presbyterianism in Ireland as a rival church; and there is a clear hint that the government has in mind a similar policy for England. Another pamphlet, the *Letter to a Member of Parliament in Ireland, upon the Choosing a New Speaker There,* also published in 1708, went over much the same ground. But already the whigs were beginning to waver in their determination. When Swift first informed Archbishop King of the appointment of Wharton as lord lieutenant he added a character of the man who was generally expected to go as his secretary: "One, Mr. Shute . . . a young man, but reckoned the shrewdest head in Europe; and the person in whom the presbyterians chiefly confide. . . . As to his principles, he is truly a moderate man, frequenting the church and the meeting indifferently." [15] But before Wharton set out, a change in the government's attitude was reflected in the substitution of Addison for Shute.

Mr Addison, who goes over as first secretary, is a most excellent person; and being my most intimate friend, I shall use all my credit to set him right in his notions of persons and things. I spoke to him with great plainness upon the subject of the test; and he says he is confident my

[15] *Corres.,* i, 127–8.

Lord Wharton will not attempt it, if he finds the bent of the nation against it.[16]

And the archbishop himself soon received similar assurances from the lord lieutenant's friends of his intention to keep the "government of state and church on the same foot as they are." So although Wharton repeatedly urged upon the Irish parliament the need for unity among protestants, he made no open attack upon the sacramental test. By the end of 1710 the tories were once more in power in England and Wharton had been replaced by Ormond. For the next four years the dissenters, both in England and in Ireland, were on the defensive.

Swift had maintained in *The Sentiments of a Church of England Man* that he was in favour of toleration for existing sects, provided that they were excluded from political power and prevented from proselytising; and he seems to have himself acted on this principle. He took no part in the repressive measures against the protestant dissenters which were planned and carried out during the last years of Queen Anne. In Ireland, the great aim of the high church party, the suspension of the *regium donum* of £1,200 a year paid to the Ulster presbyterians, was achieved in 1714. In England, controversy centred round the occasional conformity bill, which eventually became law in 1711. On the *regium donum* question Swift says nothing; and though he mentions the occasional conformity bill from time to time, and must certainly have known what was going on, there is nothing to show that he supported it. He may have been partly influenced by the recollection of his non-committal attitude to the same question in 1703; but it is more reasonable to see here a logical carrying out of the principles laid down in *The Sentiments of a Church of England Man.* His attitude to the dissenters was not an aggressive one, and while their expansion seemed to be effectively checked and their political power

[16] *Corres.,* i, 131.

curbed he was content to leave them in peace.

Swift's transfer of his allegiance from the whigs to the tories in 1710 arose largely from his dissatisfaction with the whigs' ecclesiastical policy. It was not merely their failure to carry through the grant of the first-fruits to the Irish church which had alienated him, but also their attempt to remove the sacramental test, first in Ireland and then in England, and their tolerant attitude towards writers whom Swift regarded as deistical or atheistical. Naturally, he expected preferment from his new allies, the professed patrons of the church; but after many disappointments in England he had to accept the deanery of St. Patrick's, Dublin. Here he retired in 1714, when the whigs returned to power; and such political influence as he retained was confined almost exclusively to Ireland. But his policy in ecclesiastical matters was unchanged. Whether in England or in Ireland, the established church stood in the same relation to the state and had to face the same threat from the protestant dissenters. The changes of 1714 necessarily diminished the political influence of the church, and Swift was not prepared to challenge the new government. The presbyterians naturally rejoiced, the *regium donum* was restored, the occasional conformity act, which was on the point of being extended to Ireland, was repealed, and in 1719 the Irish parliament at last granted a legal toleration to protestant dissenters. To all this Swift said nothing. Even a visit to Ulster in 1722 did not draw from him any public comment on the activities of the presbyterians. But once the question of repealing the sacramental test was raised again, he came forward to defend it.

The new struggle was fought out in the Irish parliament and the Irish council in 1732 and 1733. At one stage Swift regarded the cause as lost. In November 1733, he wrote to Ford: [17]

[17] *Letters of Swift to Ford,* ed. Nichol Smith, 1935, pp. 160–1.

It is reckoned that the test will be repealed. It is said that £30,000 have been returned from England; and £20,000 raised here from servants, labourers, farmers, squires, whigs, etc., to promote the good work. Half the bishops will be on their side. Pamphlets pro and con fly about . . . but we all conclude the affair desperate. For the money is sufficient among us to abolish Christianity itself. All the people in power are determined for the repeal. . . .

But he had over-estimated the danger; the Irish government—directed by Primate Boulter rather than by the lord lieutenant —hesitated to force on a policy so distasteful to the bulk of the house of commons. By the end of the year the repeal project had been shelved. It is hard to estimate the importance of Swift's contribution to this result. His pamphlets simply go over the old ground once again, and the country gentlemen who refused to be cajoled or frightened by Boulter or Dorset did not need to have their opinions and their prejudices expressed for them. Swift was arguing for a cause which would have triumphed without him. But his vigour may have made the government's surrender more speedy and probably helps to account for its completeness. He was on the alert from the beginning. The first signs of danger arose in England and Swift discussed with his printer, Motte, the idea of reprinting his *Letter Concerning the Sacramental Test,* announcing at the same time that "if the same wicked project [of repealing the test] shall be attempted here, I shall so far suspend my laziness as to oppose it to the utmost." [18] Though the pamphlets which this "suspension of laziness" produced show no development of thought on the question of protestant dissenters, one of them does lay stress on an aspect of the matter which Swift was usually content to pass over very lightly. One of the *Queries Wrote by Dr. J. Swift in the Year 1732* is this: "Whether any clergyman . . . if he think his own profession most agreeable to holy scriptures, and this primitive church,

[18] *Corres.,* iv, 362, 367.

can really wish in his heart, that all sectaries should be put on an equal foot with the churchmen, in point of civil power and employments?" The emphasis on theological differences and the direct appeal to the clergy probably arose from the fear that the clergy themselves were no longer solidly against repealing the test. Probably, too, it was this which he had in mind when he complained that "those who by their function, their conscience, their honour, their oaths, and the interest of their community are most bound to obstruct such a ruin to the church, will be the great advocates for it." [19]

Though the project for repealing the sacramental test in Ireland was dropped, and not renewed during Swift's life-time, his fear of the dissenters remained. In 1736 he complained of "the insolence of the dissenters, who, with their pupils the atheists, are now wholly employed in ruining the church and have entered into public associations subscribed and handed about publicly for that purpose." [20] But his alarm for the church during these years did not arise exclusively from the dissenters. The gentlemen of the Irish house of commons, though they had consistently defended the sacramental test, were not inclined to allow their support of the church to interfere with their incomes. They considered tithes a heavy burden, and found a welcome prospect of relief in the argument that no tithe was due from grazing land (tithe of agistment). The question was hotly debated, and in 1735 the commons passed a resolution against the collection of the tithe of agistment. Though this had no legal force it was, in fact, acted upon, and clerical incomes suffered accordingly. Such a move touched Swift on one of his tenderest points. The rights of his order were to him even dearer than his own, or rather, he could not consider them apart; and this attack seemed to him to threaten the ruin of the church: "I have given up all hopes of church or Christianity. A certain author, I forget his name, hath writ a book, I wish I could see it, that the Christian religion will not last above three hundred and odd years. He means there will always be Christians, as there are Jews; but it will no longer be a national religion; and there is enough to justify the scripture, that the gates of hell shall not prevail against it. As to the church, it is equally the aversion of both kingdoms: you for the quakers' tithes, we for grass, or agistment as the term of art is." [21]

Swift's loyalty to his order appears at every stage of his ecclesiastical activity. Of humanity in general he wrote, in a famous passage, that he despised and hated it in the mass, while loving individuals. His attitude to the clergy was almost the reverse: there were few of them with whom he was on consistently friendly terms, but he never lost an opportunity of supporting their cause. In seeking the grant of the first-fruits for the Irish church he was concerned chiefly with the benefit to the poorer clergy,[22] and slackness on the part of the officials who might be expected to forward the affair he interpreted as indifference towards clerical interests. Of one such he wrote, in a letter to Archbishop King, that he "would not give three-pence to save all the established clergy in both kingdoms from the gallows." [23] He was concerned about the material welfare of the clergy both as an end in itself, and because he was convinced that their poverty reduced them to contempt, and deprived them of their proper place in society. [24] It is not

[19] Swift to Motte, 9 Dec., 1732, *Corres.*, iv, 367.
[20] This linking together of "dissenters" and "atheists" or "free-thinkers" was usual with Swift. After he joined the tories he added "whigs." In 1711 he writes of the dissenters and "their comrades, the whigs and freethinkers" (*Examiner*, no. 36, 12 April, 1711, *Prose Works*, iii, 130). The alliance was a natural one, but Swift undoubtedly hoped to damn the dissenters and whigs by their company.

[21] Swift to Ford, 22 June, 1736, *Corres.*, v, 351.
[22] *Corres.*, i, 50, 201.
[23] *Corres.*, i, 104.
[24] In *A Project for the Advancement of Religion*,

unreasonable to see here a close connection between Swift's personal character and his ecclesiastical policy. Few men were quicker to take offence or to detect an insult, and he was inclined to regard himself as open to attack in the person of each individual clergyman or in the clergy as a body. His opinion on the position of the clergy is temperately expressed in *The Sentiments of a Church of England Man:* ". . . he does not see how that mighty passion for the church, which some men pretend, can well consist with those indignities, and that contempt they bestow on the persons of the clergy. . . ." Later, in the *Examiner* (no. 21), he speaks more strongly: "For several years past there hath not, I think, in Europe, been any society of men upon so unhappy a foot as the clergy of England." Swift was thinking of the lower clergy. In spite of his support of episcopacy as a form of church government, his love of independence made it difficult for him to accept episcopal authority. With Bishop Evans of Meath, who was his diocesan as vicar of Laracor, he quarrelled bitterly; and even with Archbishop King his relations were sometimes strained. But in his vigorous support of the lower houses of the English convocations against the upper, he was careful to point out that "a dislike to the proceedings of any of their lordships, even to the number of a majority, will be purely personal, and not turned to the disadvantage of the order." After his retirement to Ireland in 1714 he had stronger grounds of opposition to the bishops, for they were often Englishmen and almost always whigs: "It is happy for me that I know the persons of very few bishops, and it is my constant rule, never to look into a coach; by which I avoid the terror that such a sight would strike me with." [25] When, in 1733, two bills, one for compelling incumbents to reside and build houses on their glebes, the other for the division

of large benefices, passed the Irish house of lords, with the support of almost all the bishops, Swift wrote bitterly of "those two abominable bills, for enslaving and beggaring the clergy, which took their birth from hell"; and asserted that the bishops who supported them had mostly done so "with no other view, bating farther promotion, than a premeditated design, from the spirit of ambition and love of arbitrary power, to make the whole body of the clergy their slaves and vassals, until the day of judgement, under the load of poverty and contempt." [26] This furious sensitiveness touching his order seems to have grown on him in later years, and was probably increased by his feeling of powerlessness.

Swift's work as an ecclesiastical statesman cannot be easily summarised or accurately estimated. His career was made up of broken patches. He entered late upon the political world, and was thrown in with a party which, on grounds both personal and of principle, he could not long stand by. Later he won favour and influence in a party which he could honourably serve but which, in spite of his efforts, was ruined by internal dissension. He was exiled to Ireland, where he could exercise only indirect influence on the course of government, through his powerful friends or through the mob. So Swift's work for the church was neither that of a scholar nor that of an experienced administrator. He was essentially a man of action, but his hopes of taking an effective part in directing the affairs of the church and of the nation were constantly thwarted, and he was forced to find an outlet in the vigorous administration of his little kingdom of the liberties of St. Patrick's and in defending its independence against the archbishop's seneschal. The same love of action appears in his writings on church and state, every one of which is related to some immediate problem. More than this, he wrote for power and place. It would probably be possible

Swift advocated "lay-conversation" of the clergy (*Prose Works*, ii, 54).
[25] *Corres.*, v, 18.
[26] *Corres.*, v, 17.

to find some personal motive behind every pamphlet; and though Swift never allowed such motives to pervert his principle, the bitterness of his attacks upon the whigs for their ill-treatment of the church owed something to political expediency and, in his later life, to disappointed ambition.

This element of partisanship is the ruling factor in Swift's achievement as an ecclesiastical statesman. On the one hand it weakened his influence within the church. Those who already suspected his orthodoxy were not reconciled by the violence and apparent instability of his party attachment. Thus, though the grant of the first-fruits and twentieth parts to the Irish church in 1711 was largely due to Swift's patient negotiation, the bishops felt it wiser to give the credit to the duke of Ormond, or to the queen herself. On the other hand, it was just because he was both a clergyman and an active member of a political party that Swift was compelled to face the problem of an established church in a parliamentary state. It was not in his nature to produce a complete system; he solved problems and answered difficulties as they arose. But in doing so he laid down principles, briefly examined in this paper, which form an important contribution to anglican thought on the relations of church and state, and might have guided the church into a middle way between the fantastic unrealities of the non-jurors and the blank erastianism of the Hanoverian bishops.